OUT OF NOWHERE

OSPREY
PUBLISHING

Kill one man, terrify a thousand

Ancient Chinese proverb

An American study revealed that in the First World War it took about 7,000 rounds of small arms ammunition to kill a single enemy soldier. By the time of the Vietnam War, this had risen to around 25,000 rounds. The average sniper requires 1.3 rounds.[1]

Dieu n'est pas pour les gros bataillons mais pour ceux qui tirent le mieux.

God is not on the side of the biggest battalions, but of the best shots.

Voltaire

OUT OF NOWHERE

A history of the military sniper,
from the sharpshooter to Afghanistan

Dedication

To all of the men and women whose experiences made this book possible, and to snipers everywhere, past and present.

Praise for this book

'The best overall book on snipers I have ever read... If you own one book on snipers, this should be the book.'

Surplus Rifle

'Factual books on military snipers are few and far between ... readers of this excellent, deeply researched book will now be more knowledgeable about a rarely discussed subject.'

Harry Furness, one of Britain's most skilled Second World War snipers

'top quality, well-researched and comprehensive ... this volume presents a marvellous overall coverage on the important aspects of military sniping.'

Guns Australia

'This is the best book of its type to be published so far ... a remarkable, well-illustrated book that is recommended for those interested in military history or military arms.'

Mark A. Keefe IV, Editor-in-Chief, *American Rifleman*

First published in Great Britain in 2004 by Osprey Publishing,
Midland House, West Way, Botley, Oxford, OX2 0PH, UK
44-02 23rd Street, Suite 219, Long Island City, NY 11101, USA
OSPREY PUBLISHING IS PART OF THE OSPREY GROUP

E-mail: info@ospreypublishing.com

This revised paperback edition published in 2011 by Osprey Publishing Ltd.

A CIP catalogue record for this book is available from the British Library

ISBN: 978 1 84908 645 5

Page layout by Myriam Bell Design, France
Index by Alison Worthington
Typeset in Sabon and Conduit
Originated by PDQ Media
Printed in China through Worldprint Ltd.

11 12 13 14 15   10 9 8 7 6 5 4 3 2 1

Osprey Publishing is supporting the Woodland Trust, the UK's leading
woodland conservation charity, by funding the dedication of trees.

www.ospreypublishing.com

Front Cover: US Army
Beck Cover: Author's collection
Unless otherwise stated, the images are from the author's own collection.

CONTENTS

ACKNOWLEDGMENTS

The world of the professional sniper is closed to all but a few men and women who are, or have been, snipers. They seldom talk of their experiences and do not encourage questions. Through my interest in interviewing veterans of the First and Second World Wars, I was very fortunate over the years in meeting a number of snipers who, having satisfied themselves of my motives, answered my questions without reservation. They patiently dealt with a difficult subject matter factually and humanely. What came through in my conversations with them was not an image of cold-blooded killers, but of men who took great pride in their professionalism and skill and their great humanity. I did not ask any of them about body counts, and only rarely was that information offered. Not one of those I spoke to took any pleasure in the killing of their fellow man; all regarded it as a necessary duty of war. A number of past and serving snipers that I have spoken to have wished to remain anonymous, or have used pseudonyms, so to all of them I offer a very big 'thank you'. There are many other people who have helped greatly with information and deserve my thanks, and they are as follows:

Individuals

Andrew Evans-Hendrick and Bob Stone of Riflecraft. 'Aitch'. Majors John Conway and Peter Laidler, of the Army Weapons School, Warminster. Men of the Parachute Regiment and the Royal Marines. The Sniper Training School, Brecon. Gerry Embleton and Martin Windrow for their help with early warfare. Malcolm Johnson and Chris Scott. Bob Maze, Bob Burbage, George Yannaghas, Dr Roger Payne, Roy Jinks and Geoff Sturgess for access to their collections and knowledge. Mark (Humpy) Humphreville, who knows more about rifle construction and ballistics than I'll ever learn. Jerry Decius for much Confederate information. Jim Leatherwood, inventor and engineer. Albrecht Wacker, Franz Kramer and Thomas Meyer for the loan of their German material. Clive Law for his generosity in letting me plunder his research. Bjorn Neilsen for his German translating skills, Karen Watts and Serge Cormerias for their assistance with French material and Paul Tamony for help with all things Soviet. A word of special thanks to Harry Furness, ex-sniper and friend who has proved a bottomless fount of information and encouragement. My chum 'Russ' who gave me an insight into the dark world of the freelance sniper that few others have shared and Simon Deakin for all his help and Tony Barton, whose patient proofreading has been of the greatest help.

Museums, Institutions and Companies
The United States Marine Corps and United States Army photographic archives. The Royal Armouries Museum and National Firearms Centre, Leeds, The Imperial War Museum and National Army Museum of London, Durham Light Infantry Museum and King's Own Royal Regiment Museum, Springfield Armory and Historical Site, the Australian War Memorial, Canadian Military History Museum, Major J. L. Keene and the South African National Museum of Military History. Accuracy International, Portsmouth, Norman and Rocky Chandler of The Iron Brigade Armory, North Carolina. Remington Firearms Inc., NY, Barrett Firearms, Anzio Armory.

Finally, to my lovely wife Katie, my greatest support who over many years has learned more about sniping than she ever wanted to know.

FOREWORD

'Achtung, Scharfschütze!' 'Sniper!' This dreaded warning, often heard too late, was shouted by soldiers of both the First and Second World Wars as yet another of their leaders dropped dead, shot through the head. The warning was sufficient to make all soldiers dive for cover in the vain hope they wouldn't be targeted, for a sniper's bullet seemingly comes out of nowhere, unexpected and from any distance.

I have found that these days the words 'sniper' and 'sniping' are often defined in a demeaning way. Look up those two words in any modern dictionary and you will see definitions informing us that they are aggressive terms expressing ill will towards others, either physically or verbally with spiteful words. The most disturbing definition I found explained sniping as 'someone shooting from a concealed position at unprotected people'. Shooting at the unprotected was the exact reverse of my Second World War experience for those I sniped were heavily armed enemy soldiers, mostly fully protected with excessive firepower available from artillery, tanks and even fighter planes. But as long as the military sniper works in secrecy, then misunderstanding over their role in combat will remain. New developments continue at a fast pace and sniping will remain an important part of all future military deployments as you can be certain that regardless of the ever developing high-tech weaponry held in reserve by the great powers, we will always need to deploy our new age warrior, that highly trained specialist, the military sniper.

Factual books on military snipers are few and far between, so I find it refreshing and timely that this new edition has been published which will provide the reader with the true facts about these unique soldiers; and readers of this excellent, deeply researched book will now be more knowledgeable about a rarely discussed subject. You have to dig deep to bypass the many half-truths in order to reach any conclusion as to why mankind continues to wage wars that kill off the cream of our young society, but it might be said that if it is the fate of a soldier to die in battle, then a sniper's swift killing bullet must be preferable to dying from devastating wounds.

Harry M. Furness, Sniper-Sergeant,
British Army Second World War, February 2004.

1

THE SNIPER IN PERSPECTIVE

Since mankind first invented projectile weapons, he has devoted considerable time, effort and expense attempting to make them deliver their stones, arrows, shot and shell further, faster and more accurately. The singling out of an individual as a target by an archer or bowman is as ancient as the use of the weapons themselves, as the skeleton of an ancient Briton excavated at Maiden Castle showed, for embedded in its spine is the iron bolt from a Roman ballista.[2] Whether he was targeted by accident or design is impossible to say, but there is no doubt in the case of King Richard I during the Crusade of 1199, when a Swiss mercenary crossbowman named Peter de Basle fired a carefully aimed shot that struck the King in the shoulder. Richard subsequently died from infection of the wound. Of course, such events were undoubtedly rare, and even 300 years later, when the *handgonne* or early hand-musket had become more commonplace in warfare, its use for the specific purpose of killing at long range was virtually unheard of. While it is sometimes reported that Leonardo Da Vinci used a rifle to help repel besiegers of Florence during the siege of 1520, there appears to be no actual proof of this. However, it does seem certain that another great artist, Benvenuto Cellini, worked as a sharpshooter whilst a soldier of Pope Clement VII in 1527. Fighting alongside other defenders of the Holy City during the siege of Rome, he used a large bore, heavy matchlock musket. Writing later of his experiences he stated:

> I will give but one particular which will astonish good shots of every degree,
> that is, when I charged my gun with powder weighing one fifth of the ball,

it carried two hundred paces point-blank. My natural temperament was melancholy, and while I was taking these amusements, my heart leaped with joy, and I found I could work better than when I spent my whole time in study.[3]

One of the shots he fired almost certainly killed the Constable of Bourbon, although Cellini admitted that the heavy fog on the day made accurate aiming very difficult and a great element of luck was involved. Such accounts must be kept in proportion of course, for the smoothbore muskets of that time were generally not well suited to accurate long-range shooting. However, this is not to dismiss entirely the early use of firearms for such activities, for organised target shoots were a regular event in Europe, and were certainly well established in Holland and the German States by the 16th century, where smoothbore and rifled muskets were used for competitive shooting matches. The term generally used for these men was *scharfschützen*, or 'sharpshooters'.

By the late 18th century the word 'sniper' was being used in letters sent home by English officers serving in India, some of whom took to referring to a day's rough shooting as 'going out sniping'. The snipe is a small, fast-flying game bird with mottled black and brown plumage and a particularly erratic, twisting flight that make it difficult to see and even more difficult to hit. It took a skilled sportsman with a flintlock gun to bring down a snipe in flight. Such an accomplished shot was regarded as above average and inevitably during the 18th century the term 'snipe shooting' was simplified to 'sniping'. However, in a military context, soldiers who were particularly able shots were referred to as sharpshooters or marksmen, but never snipers, and its use appears to come from the press during the early months of the First World War. From this date onwards the word specifically implied a soldier equipped with a rifle that was generally (but not exclusively) fitted with a telescopic sight, who fired at military targets from a concealed position. Sadly, as Harry Furness mentioned so appositely in his foreword, the term has now become so debased that some dictionaries are using it as a secondary term for 'murderer'. At the time of writing there have been a couple of incidents in the United States where deranged individuals have been randomly shooting people at relatively close range using hunting rifles, an event widely referred to by the American media as 'sniping'. Such inaccurate terminology does disservice to highly trained and dedicated military snipers who were, and are still, fighting for their countries. One sniper training establishment in Virginia was so incensed at the abuse of the word that they invited members of the press to a demonstration. They were asked to find a camouflaged sniper in a field, which, not surprisingly, they were unable to do. At a signal, the invisible rifleman fired at a target 220 yards away, placing the shot straight through the forehead of the image.[4] The astonished press were duly informed that **that** was sniping and they were requested to use the term 'rifleman' in subsequent news reports.

The skills required of the true sniper are manifold and training is intense. On average, over one third of potential candidates fail the rigorous selection to become a fully-fledged sniper. To pass they have to master a complex range of interrelated skills that will enable them to survive, often alone, in the most hostile of combat environments. Camouflage, movement, observation, map reading, communications, intelligence gathering and accurate shooting must all be mastered. It is also a prerequisite to have the ability to remain alert in cramped, uncomfortable surroundings for days on end, as well as having strong personal discipline and unlimited patience. Among those requirements it is of fundamental importance that all become highly competent shots. They will have to master not only range estimation, accurate to within a few feet at 800 or 900 yards, but also those most difficult of skills, wind, temperature and humidity judgement, and target movement. Added to this is the extreme stress of constantly working on the edge of, or inside, enemy territory and the knowledge that they are always surrounded by soldiers to whom the concept of 'surrender' is an alien one where snipers are concerned. It is fact that the fate of a captured sniper is almost inevitably death. As one commented matter-of-factly, if he were caught he would 'become the main source of entertainment for the next day'.[5] There were many accounts of riflemen captured during the American Wars of Independence being summarily executed, although this was strictly against the accepted rules of warfare, and an interesting sentence in *The New York Times* showed the way in which sharpshooters were regarded during the US Civil War, the first conflict in which they were specifically employed. Commenting on the early use of Colonel Berdan's Sharpshooters by the Union Army, the writer stated the primary dangers for the sharpshooter in battle, 'by which they take the risk of being cut off by cavalry, or executed, as they certainly would be if taken'.[6] This comment on their fate is an illuminating one at this early date and gives an insight into the antipathy ordinary soldiers had towards sharpshooters. It has always been the case that infantry under sniper fire will go to extreme lengths to find and kill their assailant, even if this includes calling on artillery fire, direct tank assault or even ground strafing by aircraft. George Mitchell, an Australian infantryman, serving at Gallipoli, wrote in his diary: 'May 7th. The Turk gets very little mercy from us. Whenever a sniper is caught he is put to the bayonet immediately.'[7] Harry Furness, after shooting a high ranking German officer, was subjected to an artillery barrage of such length and ferocity that on several occasions he was blown out of his foxhole and flung to the ground. He escaped stunned, deaf and shaken, only by sheer luck. Nowhere else was the shared hatred of the sniper more openly demonstrated than in the war on the Eastern Front between 1941 and 1945, where snipers invariably carried a pistol, not for personal defence, but to prevent themselves falling alive into the hands of the enemy.

The Effects of Sniping

While it would be an exaggeration to say that the outcome of an entire battle could be shaped as the result of sniping, it often had profound effects on the ability of one side or the other to function effectively. During the American Civil War at the Battle of Gettysburg in 1863, two Confederate sharpshooters working on Little Round Top killed two Union generals, badly wounded a third, then killed a colonel and up to four other senior officers. It caused consternation in the Union camp and artillery were called upon to try and flush them out, with little success, reinforcing two main problems for infantry. The first was in finding the sniper and the second, dealing with him. Never truer was the old adage 'it takes a thief to catch a thief'. 'Counter-sniping', the seeking out and killing of enemy snipers, became the main priority of every army. Once enemy snipers were silenced, the successful snipers could then concentrate on finding specific targets, and the vital tasks of observation and intelligence gathering could be undertaken. These tasks have increasingly become a core part of the sniper's role. So why did the infantry fear the sniper so, and expend so much time and effort in attempting to eradicate him? The answer lies in the complex psychology of war, where an infantryman accepts with a certain fatalism the chances of death or wounding, however it may occur, as the capricious and impersonal fortunes of combat. This is regarded as being outside the control of the individual and most men are mentally protected by their innate belief that 'it won't happen to me'. Of course, comrades do get killed and wounded, which is their bad luck, but few soldiers will ever accept that they could be the next casualty, believing that their chances of survival are reasonably good. The appearance of the sniper changes all of that in an instant. Suddenly, everyone is the target and war has become personal. Frontline soldiers find this very hard to accept as well as being both frightening and debilitating. A bullet that comes apparently from nowhere and kills with clinical accuracy is unnerving in the extreme. The friend a soldier was talking to one second would be lying at his feet the next, and worse, such events often happened away from the heat of battle, where men believed they were comparatively safe. To come under sniper fire was an utterly debilitating experience for most soldiers. A Falklands veteran, Ken Lukowiak, wrote vividly of his first experience of being a target:

We crossed another field and approached a hedgerow. As we met the hedge we turned left and began to follow it to the corner of the field. A bullet shot past my face. It was so close, I felt it physically. All of us automatically dived to the ground and crawled up to the hedge in search of cover. A voice shouted out, 'Can anyone see the enemy?' Slowly, one by one, we began to look over the hedge. There was nothing there. Just an open field and another empty field beyond that. Another shot flew by, Tony screamed and fell to the ground. Fear began to push thoughts into my mind. If he could be hit behind the hedge, then so could I. Where would I be hit? In the head? In the chest? I became aware that I was working myself into a state of panic. I began to try and talk myself into becoming calm. If I were to be hit then I would be hit, that was that and there was nothing I could do about it. Someone called out, 'It's a fucking sniper'.[8]

The shock of becoming a sudden target frightened soldiers more than anything else. It was not only individuals who were demoralised, but as men cowered in foxholes or trenches, reluctant to obey any orders that meant exposing themselves to accurate fire from an invisible enemy, so chains of command became broken and discipline impaired. Small wonder that a captured sniper's life was generally regarded as forfeit. A rare glimpse during the First World War at the reaction of infantrymen upon capturing a sniper is contained in the laconic diary entry by Lieutenant S. F. Shingleton, an Officer in the Royal Field Artillery, who noted that on 16 July 1916, 'Royal Scots catch and hang one sniper. Shelling and great deal of sniping.'[9] A British sniper had a similar experience after flushing a German sniper from a house during the advance through France in 1944. The German had run out of ammunition, thrown his rifle from the window and walked out of the back door with his hands up. A British officer, whose men had suffered grievously from the sniper's accurate shooting, walked past and shot the German dead with his revolver.[10] On occasions even senior officers made it clear that they did not entirely approve of sniping in warfare. In 1944 General Omar Bradley let it be known that he would not disapprove of snipers being treated 'a little more roughly' than was the norm. After all, 'a sniper cannot sit around and shoot and then [expect] capture. That's not the way to play the game.'[11]

Perhaps more curious is the dislike many frontline soldiers showed for their own snipers, for one of the great ironies of a sniper's life was the fact that he was often disliked almost as much by his own men as he was by the enemy. This originated in the trenches of 1914–18 and was simply because of the explosive retribution that was brought down upon the heads of the hapless occupants if a sniper was operating in their sector. This could manifest itself as a hurricane of shells or trench mortars as enraged enemy soldiers attempted to avenge the death of a comrade, often inflicting heavy casualties on the resident infantry, who quite reasonably believed they did not deserve it. Yet there was a deeper and darker side to the open dislike many men had for the sniper and his profession. In civilian life we are all brought up to regard human life as sacred, yet this most fundamental concept of the value of human life must be suspended in wartime. Generally, most soldiers can abandon their peacetime beliefs, when faced with killing to survive or to protect comrades, and such a choice is regarded as morally acceptable. Yet the concept of a soldier deliberately stalking a human quarry as one would an animal was to most infantrymen a repugnant one. One reason for the discomfort of combat soldiers was undoubtedly that among them the sniper was unique in literally having the ability to hold life or death in his hands and, suddenly, death was personal. One German sniper wrote that he had but a single rule when out sniping, and that was once he had a target in his crosshairs he would shoot, regardless of who the individual was or what they were doing.[12] Few other soldiers ever had the questionable luxury of deciding whom to kill or when. To the average soldier war was a matter of obeying orders, so the majority were able to treat fighting as a relatively impersonal job to be done as quickly and at as little risk as possible. Partly because of the secretive nature of their work, as snipers were instructed never to talk about what they did or where they went, they began to acquire a reputation as cold killers. Frederick Sleath, a British sniping officer who served in France during the First World War commented that the line infantrymen did not mix easily with his snipers 'for there was something about them that set them apart from ordinary men and made the soldiers uncomfortable'.[13] This comment is echoed down the years by infantry who understood little of the work a sniper did, seeing them only as unprincipled hunters on the loose and appreciating little of the vital work they did in protecting their own men from opposing snipers. Often the dislike was palpable, with men deliberately moving away from snipers when they were at rest and refusing to mix socially with them. Yet frontline snipers were the only effective method of counter-sniping, and the infantry knew it, for when pinned down by an invisible enemy, the first call was invariably 'Get a sniper up here'. In 1944 a British sniper recalled heading towards German lines early one morning, past foxholes containing a company of his own men. They jeered at him as he walked by, angering him to the extent that he used his fighting knife to open up the stomach of a very dead cow nearby, treating the men, who were unable to move from their foxholes, to the very unpleasant stink that emanated from it.[14] Marine snipers in Vietnam were often greeted with the words 'here comes Murder Incorporated', a comment that they accepted stoically.

Snipers also felt that their actions caused much disquiet among the civilian population, particularly in Allied countries, and an air of secrecy generally cloaked their actions, with few details of their exploits ever being reported. During research, only three newspaper articles could be found relating specifically to snipers, all in provincial papers, and only one actually had an interview and photograph of the sniper, Private Francis Miller of the 5th Battalion East Yorkshire Regiment. Few serving snipers would agree to such public coverage, even to the extent of refusing to have their photographs taken for press use. They disliked publicity and the knowledge that people at home might get to know and disapprove of their trade. This attitude is understandable and had much to do with the traditional ideals of waging 'sporting' warfare. In fact it seems not to have been the case that civilians at home were critical of the work undertaken by snipers, as retaliation of any sort against the enemy was generally regarded as positive by those who had no ability themselves to fight back. The widow of one British sniper who served from 1944 to '45 said that she knew what he did during the war and although he rarely spoke of his experiences, he knew she approved:

> Night after night we had endured their [German] bombing and many people I knew were killed, mothers, kiddies, old folk. The fact that Jack was giving the Jerries some of their own medicine was a tonic to us all. Those what [who] knew he was a sniper would say 'Tell him to get one of the bastards for me'.[15]

Yet there was a curious inconsistency about this, for within their own sections the snipers themselves generally had a fairly dry sense of humour about their role and it has to be said that they did little to improve their standing, enjoying their quiet notoriety. As Sergeant Furness explained, most were strong individualists, often solitary types who had the right temperament for such work. 'All snipers were volunteers, it never happened that soldiers who are known to be good shots are then detailed into joining the sniper section. You would never find the life-and-soul-of-the-party in a sniper section.' He was actually told by his Regimental Sergeant Major that he was the most unsociable NCO that he had ever come across, which amused Harry but perhaps said more about the temperament of the RSM than of the snipers. Most were quiet, cautious men, for it was a profession that did not allow for haste and this was also reflected in their social habits. A minority were smokers as it adversely affected their ability to control their breath for shooting and lowered their levels of fitness, and the majority were only moderate drinkers. These restrained habits put them at odds with their infantry contemporaries who took any opportunity to indulge in revelry. Added to this was the fact that for operational reasons snipers lived together and didn't share normal frontline duties, mostly working in secrecy, so the fact that they were mistrusted by their own infantry was almost an inevitable consequence which they accepted philosophically. At times they could even approve of the nicknames given to them by their comrades. The Hallamshires' snipers accepted with some pride being called his 'Grim Reapers' by one officer of whom they were fond.[16] Some raised their skills in waging psychological warfare to new heights as the Second World War sniper Sergeant John Fulcher wrote. Himself a Sioux Indian, he commented that 'half the boys in the sniper squad were Indians, including two Sioux from the Black Hills. I overheard some of the other GIs referring to us as "savages". They said "the war party's going out scalping". They said it in admiration, and that's the way we took it.'[17] In fact, Fulcher and his Indians did on occasions scalp dead Germans, leaving them prominently placed as a warning to others. Word came back that any sniper or Indian captured would be executed on the spot. Even in the late 1980s one British line infantry battalion's sniper section was universally known as 'The Leper Colony'.[18]

Making the Shot

How did operational snipers reconcile themselves to the fundamental nature of their profession? The answer lies in the personality traits of the men, allied to a mix of effective training, enthusiasm, professionalism and sheer determination. At some point all snipers had to take the decision to pull the trigger, and all reacted to the challenge with different emotions. First World War sniper Charles Burridge of the Queens Royal West Surrey Regiment, told the author that he could still see the look of surprise on the face of the first German he shot, and it haunted him. Others took a far more pragmatic view. Private Francis Miller, whose ebullient attitude to sniping in the Second World War was perhaps untypical of the average sniper, commented that killing Germans to him was 'like going ratting'.[19] Unsurprisingly, those men who had hunted for sport were far less moved by the emotion of the event than by the sheer excitement of making a clean kill. Lieutenant-Colonel John George, an experienced game hunter, recorded the moment he shot his first Japanese soldier in Guadalcanal:

> I nudged his chin with the broad [crosshair] post – a measure calculated to plant the bullet somewhere on his chest at the 350 yards range. Then I gave the last pound or so of the three pound trigger pull a 'gentle snatch'. The scope settled back in time for me to see the bullet strike the Jap and splash sand behind him. I cannot recall the least bit of thinking I had just killed a man for the first time. All I remember is a feeling of intense excitement – the same as that experienced when one downs a hard sought big game trophy.[20]

For most snipers, firing their first combat shot was the culmination of months of study, practice and sheer hard work, and they were simply doing exactly what their training had taught them to do. Even snipers who had considerable combat experience could find the testing of their skills to the limit a daunting experience. US Marine Private Daniel Cass and his observer, Private Carter, were on a ridge in Okinawa trying to work out how to tackle Japanese machine-gun nests some 1,200 yards (1,100 metres) away. Cass had never fired at such ranges before but the Marines were taking heavy casualties and he had little option but to try, using all the skill and training he could muster:

> 'We don't have time for anything else' I muttered, sweat popping from every pore in my body. Deep breath. Let half out. Hold. Crosshair, crosshair, squeeze. Carter grunted 'All right!' as my first round plunged into the enemy's barricade. The machine-gun fire ceased. Several minute figures scurried from the barricades like rats smoked out of a barn. That was when I took a deep wavering breath. I had done my job hadn't I? Below on the valley floor, Marines were starting to clamber cautiously to their feet. One of them turned and waved thanks back at us. I felt good about it. I had done some damn good shooting.[21]

While some snipers regarded their job as a technical exercise in meeting the difficult requirements of shooting, others found that killing never became easy. Harry Furness said that his first shot was quite instinctive as 'a group of Germans ran across a street in front of me. I raised my rifle and took aim at one, giving a little lead to allow for him running. I fired and he dropped instantly.' It was the only time he was to see the result of his handiwork close to, for as his squad advanced, he had to jump over the dead German, whom he recalled as being 'a young corporal, blond and good-looking'.[22] He disliked the experience intensely and never deliberately repeated it. Fulcher recalled that his section's grisly behaviour came back to haunt him in peacetime:

> Later, much later, when times were normal again, all this bothered me. I woke up sometimes sweating from nightmares. But for that time, in that place, killing was an everyday fact of life... Scalping struck fear into the Germans. It made them overcautious and leery about taking chances. It helped save GI lives.[23]

James Gibbore served in Vietnam and wrote candidly of his feelings as he targeted enemy sentries:

> You begin to shake, your knees begin to get weak and you find it more and more difficult to breathe ... you try to hold steady but your crosshairs shake all over the place, you're so excited. In your mind you're thinking, how far is he? Where do I hold? A little higher, a little lower? I knew if I only wounded one of those VC [Vietcong] and not killed him instantly he would have screamed out in pain, shaking the entire camp awake.[24]

Gibbore's training, and his fierce determination to succeed, ensured that he did exactly what he was trained to do, but it raised spectres in his mind that time would not erase:

> Could you, would you have squeezed that trigger? Could I, would I, have taken a man's life, just because he was the enemy? Would I stay cool enough to do all the things I just talked about? Could you do that? Think about it.

Now try to think about how it would feel to carry that picture in your mind all the days of your life. That's the time I knew I had de-evolved back from a man to some sort of animal … a thing. I never missed one shot. Fourteen men lay dead … I counted down each one as I pulled down on them. This is only one of the pictures my mind carries around, and will carry around all the days of my life.

Some simply didn't perform effectively and were sent back to resume normal infantry duties, while others were unable to adjust mentally and became medical cases. Joe Ward remembered seeing a fellow sniper in Vietnam, who sat glassy-eyed and staring, oblivious to the world around him, unable to cope any longer with his chosen profession. Still, the vast majority were able to reconcile their duty with their consciences and the highly effective 'sniper shield', while invisible and anonymous, was undoubtedly effective for there are hundreds, if not thousands, of ex-servicemen alive today who would now occupy a few feet of soil in a distant war grave, were it not for the skill of their battalion snipers. As one Second World War veteran said, 'every enemy sniper I killed saved the lives of some of my mates, not that many of the buggers ever knew it'.[25]

During the conflicts of the later 20th century the expectations of the sniper's abilities had gradually risen along with the advance of technology that enables him to see more and to shoot further and more accurately than ever before. Not all modern wars are fought along organised rules of combat, however, and many now involve complex internal factions, very fluid combat lines and great distances. Operationally these conflicts are very difficult and actually telling friend from foe is at times almost impossible. During the Angolan Civil War (1975–89) one American irregular employed as a sniper watched in bewilderment as opposing Angolan soldiers fraternised, whilst their respective European 'advisers', Soviet, Cuban, and French, sat down to share a meal. 'I wondered what the hell was going on, and who in fact I was working for. I began to get very uneasy about where this was leading me.'[26] American snipers in Somalia were at times unsure as to which side was firing at them, or whether to open fire for fear of killing soldiers from the wrong factions. While open warfare has still occurred in places such as the Falklands or the Gulf, 'limited wars', as they have become known, have become more frequent and hotspots such as Vietnam, Somalia, Bosnia or Chechnya became fertile territory for the sniper. In these so-called 'dirty wars' many snipers were used for covert operations, where they were dropped by helicopter in remote locations, equipped with food, ammunition and communications, and ordered to create as much mayhem as they could. These missions were often cloaked in secrecy and the snipers knew that if plans went awry, they could expect little or nothing in the way of help. Suitably equipped, and with pre-arranged supply drops, they were expected to survive for days or weeks, reporting information back to headquarters and wreaking havoc whenever possible. Such covert work, with little or no official recognition, simply reinforced to the sniper the fact that, however highly trained he might be, he was expendable. James Gibbore was ordered to take part in a clandestine mission and was understandably alarmed at his briefing:

> This mission is important. We have to show the VC he isn't safe even in a place we're not supposed to be. US forces are not allowed to be anywhere inside the countries of Laos or Cambodia. We want to hit the Viet Cong where he will never expect us to be. You must not be spotted. Most of all don't get captured! No help will be sent to you. Your mission is to quietly take out as many VC as you can, using the special forces team as back up.[27]

Despite orders such as these, few snipers ever wavered from the task, regardless of how heavily the odds were stacked against them. In Somalia, two US Army snipers, Master Sergeant Gary Gordon and Sergeant Randall Shughart went to the aid of a downed US helicopter, in the full knowledge that they had insufficient rifle ammunition to keep the insurgents away for very long, and both had resorted to using their pistols by the time they were overwhelmed and killed. Nevertheless their actions saved the crew and both were posthumously awarded America's highest decoration, the Medal of Honor.

How the rifleman became the sniper, and the means by which he was able to do it, are the subject of the rest of this book.

2

THE RIFLEMAN EMERGES, 1500–1854

Despite Benvenuto Cellini's aforementioned claims, smoothbore military muskets used during the 16th century were not generally capable of accurate shooting, having an aimed range of perhaps 100 yards (90 metres). However, the use of the musket for sport shooting was an entirely different matter. The earliest known date for the creation of a shooting club formed specifically for the use of firearms comes from Lucerne in Switzerland, where one club has a charter dating from 1466. Shooting of both crossbows and muskets was hugely popular, as evidenced by the *Schützenfeste* which took place throughout the year in Munich. Small companies of shooters (*Schützenfähnlein*), formed in the 15th century in the southern German states and German and Swiss cantons, proudly carried flags that depicted a crossbow on one side and a target rifle on the other. The *Kränzel* was held in the New Year, *Schmalz* at Easter, and at Whitsun there were the *Jakobi*, *Kichweiß* and *Gans* shoots. The shooters used smoothbore matchlock muskets, each man being required to fire 24 shots at three hanging targets, and it was specifically stated that longarms with rifled barrels were *not* permitted, as they were considered to hold an unfair advantage. Ranges varied from 200 to 300 paces (about 175–200 yards, 157–180 metres) and target sizes were between 28 and 40 inches (70–100 cm). Some idea of the standard of shooting that was achieved can be gauged from the fact that in 1584 it was recorded that, out of 133 shooters, each firing 24 shots, some 40 scored between 20 and 24 hits. With smoothbore muskets this was indeed an impressive feat. In war, many of these companies acted as scouts, occasionally forming skirmish lines that pre-dated Napoleonic tactics by 150 years.

In Britain, sport shooting was not widely practised, although there are several accounts of men armed with sporting guns being used during the English Civil War (1642–48) to pick off officers and NCOs. The death of the charismatic Lord Brooke during the siege of Lichfield in March 1643 is one of the better documented. Two royalist soldiers were watching from their vantage point on the roof of Lichfield Cathedral. One of them, John Dyott, was armed with an early, long-barrelled matchlock. Parliamentarian commander Lord Brooke, emerging from the shelter of a house porch, paused and leaned forward to observe the situation. Dyott took careful aim and fired, the ball striking Brooke in the left eye, killing him instantly. The distance, of about 300 yards (270 metres), is not excessive but it should be remembered that Dyott was shooting a large calibre smoothbore musket, firing a homemade bullet cast from lead torn from the cathedral roof. By the standards of his day, it was an extraordinarily fine shot.[28] Of course, at this period individuals such as Dyott did not in any sense compose an organised sniping force and such feats of marksmanship were rare indeed, which was doubtless of little consolation to Brooke. However, the firearm was becoming increasingly important in warfare and great strides were being made to improve its effectiveness.

Early European Use of the Rifle

Although the rifle is regarded today as primarily a late 18th century development, there is evidence of its use far earlier. In an inventory of the King of Dresden's armoury dated 1606 were listed: 'Danish hunting rifles, large Danish shot-rifles, Bavarian grooved hunting rifles, long Bavarian shot rifles, rifles from Dessau, French rifles, old Brunswick guns ... and rifles from Salzburg, Silesia, Holstein, Augsberg and Brandenburg'.[29] The benefits of the rifle were obvious enough, for it enabled greater range and accuracy to be achieved, as the lead bullet gripped the grooves in the bore, which in turn imparted spin to it. This created gyroscopic stability that greatly enhanced accuracy, giving the rifle an aimed range of about 300 yards (270 metres), roughly treble that of a smoothbore musket.

However, the issue of rifles on any scale to military units was still not deemed either practical or necessary, but there were some riflemen appearing in small numbers on the early battlefields of Europe. The Swiss raised companies using rifles based on the very accurate weapons they used for competitive target shooting and the King of Sweden, Peter the Great, employed rifle companies in his armies, whose job was specifically to pick off enemy officers. However, their numbers were comparatively tiny and their tactical use, such as it was, had no overall effect on the general conduct of wars. The contemporary English firearms writer Hans Busk had noted that as early as 1680, each troop of the British Household Cavalry was equipped with eight 'rifled carbines'. The very forward-thinking King Gustavus Adolphus II of Sweden had introduced a lightweight musket in 1624 and armed two thirds of his army with firearms, the normal ratio at the time being one half pikemen to one half musketeers. The musketeers were placed in three lines with pikes providing a protective screen and this form of linear warfare was to be common on the battlefields of Europe for well over 200 years. Adolphus' faith in the future of the musket as the primary weapon of war never wavered, partly because of his experience fighting in the German states during the Thirty Years War (1618–35). The Germans had used sharpshooters armed with rifles as well as employing similarly armed mercenaries. To what extent their expertise influenced Adolphus is not known, but at least one Polish sharpshooter left his mark at the Battle of Dirschen in 1627. A bullet, possibly aimed at Gustavus Adolphus' head, struck slightly low, hitting him in the neck and causing a wound that was to trouble him for the rest of his life.

The increasing prominence of the musketeers meant that they were even being portrayed in art of the period. The Dutch, like the Germans, had a long tradition of shooting for sport and by the 16th century they had formed numerous *Schutters* guilds, a mixture of gentlemen militia and shooting associations. The Dutch had a well-respected gunmaking heritage and exported their firearms all over Europe; there are dozens of paintings depicting these groups with their longarms and accessories prominently displayed for the world to see. It was becoming clear to everyone, Dutch, Swedes and Germans, that firearms were no longer a novelty, that the countries that led in their manufacture and development would profit both materially and militarily, and that the rifle was the way forward. That many individuals recognised the early worth of the rifle over the musket is indisputable. In 1742 Benjamin Robins wrote with conviction that:

> Whatever State shall thoroughly comprehend the nature and advantage of rifled-barrel pieces and ... shall introduce into their armies their general use ... will by this means acquire a superiority which will almost equal anything that has been done at any time by the particular excellence of any one kind of arms and will perhaps fall but little short of the wonderful effect which histories relate to have been formerly produced by the first inventors of firearms.[30]

Despite claims by some historians that the use of the rifle in battle was first and foremost an American idea, it should be remembered that it was the German states, embroiled in the Seven Years War (1756–63), who began to make the first serious use of sharpshooters on the battlefield. With faint pre-echoes of 1914, the long tradition of the *Jäger* or hunter in German society had provided Frederick the Great with a reserve of skilled marksmen who were used as riflemen and skirmishers, reporting on enemy movements and harassing them with accurate fire. These men carried and used their personal rifles, distinctive heavy stocked guns with short octagonal barrels, normally no longer than 32 inches (814 mm) and of large calibre up to .75 inch. The stocks were straighter than those of the musket, to absorb recoil and had sliding wooden patchboxes set into the butt. Crucially, they had iron rather than wooden ramrods, as the force required to ram home a ball down a fouled rifle barrel would have quickly reduced a wooden ramrod to matchwood.

In 1740, the first Prussian Jägers had begun life as a small force of sixty *guiden* whose purpose was to protect reconnaissance parties and guide regular troops. Within four years these green-coated riflemen had been elevated to company status with two companies, each comprising 100 men. By 1760 they had been formed as an entire battalion of over 800 men. In rough country the Jägers excelled, as their short, heavy rifles were capable of outshooting anything else on the battlefield. However, their slowness in loading was to prove a serious drawback if they were caught in the open, a situation that was to occur frequently during subsequent wars. Colonel von Heereingen, who had himself commanded a company of Hessian riflemen, commented that often riflemen 'were mostly spitted to trees by bayonets ... it takes them a quarter of an hour to load and meanwhile they feel our bullets and bayonets'.[31] In October 1760, a battalion of Jäger caught in the open by Cossacks near Spandau were wiped out almost to a man. Clearly the military application of tactics that were suitable for use by these riflemen had some way to progress.

Although often overlooked, the Swiss also provided a surprising number of trained riflemen, who fought on the battlefields of 18th century Europe. Although modern Switzerland as we understand it did not exist in the 17th and 18th centuries, the various cantons had a long and honourable tradition of providing a hard core of skilled men who served as mercenaries or regular soldiers in almost every war in Europe. Swiss mercenaries had a reputation as tough swordsmen, but as the requirement for these skills faded, the rifleman gradually began to take their place.

It was a formative period in Europe during which the advance of weapons technology led to a broader understanding of the tactical possibilities of the rifle, and exactly what a rifleman was capable of doing. The main problem with the rifle was that it was expensive and the military authorities could conceive of no widespread use for it on the battlefield, when linear warfare was the primary method of fighting. Generally the purpose of an infantry musketeer rifleman in the late 18th century was not to target individuals but to fire *en masse* at the advancing enemy. This was how wars were conducted and few could see any reason why the rules should be changed.

The American Rifleman

Ironically, many German and Swiss Jäger were to reappear within a short space of time on another continent, America. The simmering discontent between Britain and France over the colonisation of the country had led to a number of clashes, in which both American and European mercenaries were employed, many of them armed with rifles. There is even some evidence of the early official issue of rifles in the Americas during this period, during the battle for Fort Ticonderoga in 1758. The orderly book of Captain Alexander Moneypenny, a senior staff officer on General Abercrombie's staff tantalisingly noted that 'each regiment to receive ten rifled pieces from the store and to return the like number of firelocks to them'.[32] As this order covered no fewer than six regiments of foot as well as the 60th Light Infantry, it would appear to have been a reasonably large issue of rifles. That the Americans understood the value of the rifle, and its tactical use in the wooded terrain that covered much of that country, is evidenced by the experiences of the British Army during the Revolutionary Wars (1775–1815).

As children, many Americans learned to shoot accurately, hunting for small game and birds to help feed their families. Aimed shots at ranges of over 300 yards were well within their capabilities. In many respects these riflemen were to set the standard for much of what was to be learned about sharpshooting in future warfare, although it took many decades for the lessons to be fully understood and put into practice. In the heavily forested Eastern states of America, the old Jäger rifles brought over by early German immigrants proved to be largely unsuitable. They were too heavy and their calibre unnecessarily large for hunting at short ranges, so the Pennsylvania and Kentucky gunsmiths began to experiment. They realised that a large calibre bullet of perhaps .65 or .75 inch was too big and that smaller calibres of between .40 and .54 inch proved to have the same accuracy and greater range for the same amount of powder. A typical .70 inch ball weighed 730 grains, whereas a .54 inch was a mere 370 grains so an additional benefit was that a rifleman could carry more bullets per pound weight. The form of these rifles gradually changed as well, to reflect the needs of the riflemen and the nature of the terrain. The stock developed a distinctive droop and invariably a brass patchbox was inset in the right side of the buttstock while the buttplate had a deep curve that allowed it to sit tightly in the shooter's shoulder without slipping. The barrel was usually fully stocked to the muzzle and both front and rear sights were fitted. Barrel lengths varied from around 42 to 44 inches and bullets were carefully patched to prevent windage, the loss of burning gas past the ball. Patching was the practice of using a small piece of greased cloth or thin leather to wrap around the ball as it was rammed down the barrel, creating a gas seal and assisting in removing fouling. If these early rifles appear to be lacking in sophistication, it is worth recalling that in tests undertaken by the National Rifle Association of America in the 1950s it was found that a .45 calibre ball could attain an initial muzzle velocity of 2,400 feet per second, which compares well with that of a 20th century cartridge rifle.[33] While the slow burn rate of the powder and poor aerodynamic efficiency of the lead ball meant that velocity dropped at an alarming rate, it was still a very deadly tool in the hands of a skilled shot as many English soldiers and officers could testify. Major George Hanger was serving in America, and was himself a very experienced sporting shot. He recounted in a later book how he and General Tarleton became the targets of an American sharpshooter:

> A rifleman passed over the mill dam, evidently observing two officers and laid himself down on his belly; for in such positions they always lie, to take a good shot at long distance. He took a deliberate and cool shot at my friend, at me and at our bugle-horn man ... Colonel Tarleton's horse and mine ... were not anything like two feet apart ... a rifle bullet passed between him and me; looking directly at the mill I observed the flash of powder ... the bugle-man jumped off his horse and said, 'Sir, my horse is shot'. I have passed several times over this ground and ... I can positively assert that the distance he fired at was full 400 yards.[34]

It is unsurprising, therefore, that young British officers were advised by pundits in the British press to 'settle their affairs' before they went to America, for life expectancy was short. It is indicative of the attitude that British soldiers had towards ordinary musket fire at this period, that it did not actually occur to Hanger to move, even when he realised that they were the potential targets of a rifleman. In an age of rigid military conformity, American riflemen were not instantly recognisable as regimental soldiers, for most wore the ordinary clothing that served them well in their civilian lives, and they carried commercially manufactured long rifles. Their clothes were homemade and eminently practical, as described by a contemporary writer:

> On the frontiers ... the dress of the men was partly Indian and partly that of civilised nations. The hunting shirt was universally worn. This was a kind of loose frock reaching halfway down the thighs with large sleeves ... and so wide as to lap a foot or more when belted ... the hunting shirt was generally made of linsey, sometimes of coarse linen and a few of dressed deerskins.

These last were very cold and uncomfortable in wet weather. The shirt and jacket were of common fashion. A pair of drawers or breeches and leggings, were the dress of the thighs and legs, a pair of moccasins answered for the feet much better than shoes ... the cape was large and handsomely fringed. The belt which was always tied behind answered several purposes, besides that of holding the dress together. In cold weather the mittens and sometimes the bullet bag occupied the front part of it. To the right side were suspended the tomahawk and to the left the scalping knife in its leather sheath.[35]

The colours of their clothes were sober, practical blues, browns and greens and they blended well with the landscape, unlike the startling scarlet tunics of the British redcoats who had the dubious benefit of white cross-belts that met over their chests, providing the riflemen with a perfect aiming mark. The American frontiersmen were used to travelling quickly and lightly, and were totally self-contained, carrying a full complement of shooting requirements in a small bag slung from the shoulder, providing them with all they needed to survive off the land. Aside from their rifles, their shooting bag was the last item they would part with, for as long as they had powder, ball and flint, they could survive.

The use of riflemen in the American forces was materially helped by George Washington's belief in their effectiveness. He had had direct experience of this while serving under the English General Edward Braddock when fighting the French in Pennsylvania. Braddock's force was virtually annihilated by Indians serving under French command, who would target and shoot a man before silently melting back into the woods, leaving the other soldiers powerless to retaliate. Washington was never to forget this lesson and it was under his authority that in June 1775 Congress authorised the State of Pennsylvania to raise 'six companies of long riflemen' later expanding this to nine companies. The unit was to come under the command of an expert rifleman, Colonel Daniel Morgan, and was subsequently to be known as 'Morgan's Sharpshooters'. Morgan constantly encouraged his men to practise their shooting and backwoods skills, and always advised them, when targeting British soldiers, to 'shoot for the epaulettes'. This was sound advice, for it was an item of uniform worn only by officers. This deeply unsporting concept was not embraced by the British who believed that the specific targeting of officers should not be normal practice for the common soldier in battle, being against the principles of common etiquette required to conduct gentlemanly warfare. Indeed, remnants of this attitude remained very much in the British military mind until well into the 20th century.

One of the men mustered in was Timothy Murphy, who was to fire one of the most renowned shots of the war. Murphy took Morgan's words to heart and during the Battle for Freeman's Farm on 19 September 1777, he climbed a small tree and took aim at a mounted British officer, General Simon Frazer. His first shot grazed the horse's mane, the second lodged in the saddle, but the third struck Frazer a mortal blow. The result was to cause the British to fall back, retreating to Saratoga, where they were subsequently forced to surrender. While it would be overstating the case to say this changed the course of the war, it could certainly be argued that it was an example of a marksman's bullet altering the immediate outcome of a battle. An insight into the shooting abilities of these riflemen survives in the form of a contemporary newspaper account:

On Friday evening last arrived here, on their way to the American Camp, Captain Cresap's company of riflemen, consisting of 130 active, brave young fellows. These men have been bred in the woods to danger and hardship from infancy. With their rifles in their hands they assume a kind of omnipotence over their enemies. You will not much wonder at this when I mention a fact … attested by several … who were eyewitnesses of it. Two brothers in the company took a piece of board, five inches broad, and seven inches long, with a piece of white paper, about the size of a dollar, nailed in the centre, and while one of them supported the board perpendicularly between his knees, the other at a distance of upwards of sixty yards, and without any kind of rest, shot eight bullets successively through the board and spared his brother's thighs! Another … held a barrel stave perpendicularly in his hand, with one edge close to his side, while one of his comrades, at the same distance, shot several bullets through it. The spectators, appearing to be amazed at these feats were told that there were upwards of fifty riflemen in the company who could do the same thing; that there was not one that could not plug 19 bullets out of 20 within an inch of a ten-penny nail. Some of them proposed to stand with an apple on their heads, while others at the same distance shot them off; but the people who saw the other experiments, declined to witness this.[36]

The riflemen's use was still very much limited by terrain and tactics, for their slow rate of loading and firing (about one shot every 30 seconds, half the rate of a musket) made them very vulnerable to infantry assault, particularly when caught in the open with no support. George Hanger was a witness to this:

> When Morgan's riflemen came down from Pennsylvania ... they marched to attack our light infantry under Colonel Abercrombie. The moment they appeared before him he ordered his troops to charge them with the bayonet; not one in four [rifle]man had time to fire and those that did had no time to reload again; the light infantry not only dispersed them, but drove them for miles over the country.[37]

On one occasion, George Washington appeared within shooting range of a young officer named Patrick Ferguson, of the 70th Regiment of Foot. Although Ferguson did not know the identity of the officer in his sights he declined to shoot, commenting 'it is not pleasant to fire at the back of an unoffending individual who was acquitting himself very coolly of his duty, so I let him alone'.[38] It is interesting to speculate what may have happened to the course of world history if he had fired. It was actually the same Patrick Ferguson who would single-handedly succeed in bringing the military rifle to the notice of the British Army and briefly advance the cause of military marksmanship beyond all recognition. Ferguson was a mechanical genius, and had long been fascinated with the workings of firearms, and the rifle in particular. He had examined and tested an earlier design, patented by a Frenchman named La Chaumette, which used a screw-pillar breech loading mechanism, and he believed he could improve upon it. Having had two improved rifles made at his own expense he subsequently demonstrated one to the Board of Ordnance where, in appalling weather conditions, he fired at a rate of up to six shots a minute at a target 200 yards away, repeatedly hitting the bull. In addition he filled the barrel and pan of the rifle with water, unloaded then reloaded it and hit the bull in under a minute. Even the deeply conservative Board could not ignore the possibilities of such a weapon and, grudgingly, the British government agreed that Ferguson could raise and train a rifle unit of 100 men, who adopted practical green uniforms and the skirmishing tactics of the Americans. There is also some interesting contemporary evidence that the riflemen did, even at this early stage, conduct their own counter-sniping campaign. An American veteran of the Kings Mountain Battle in October 1778 commented that many of the dead had been shot through the head by other riflemen, and that they lay with one eye open and one closed 'in the manner of marksmen when levelling at their subjects'.[39] Unfortunately their impact on the war was to prove minimal, for in the wake of Ferguson's death during the Battle of Kings Mountain, they and their rifles quietly faded from sight.

If the British regarded the American way of fighting as unfair, it could not be denied that in the wooded country of the eastern states, it was very effective. There is little doubt that the American riflemen proved their worth during the conflict, and in a probable military first, during the battle for Lake Erie in September 1813, Commander Perry employed over 100 Kentucky riflemen to keep the ships' decks clear of British Marines, thus ensuring victory. Even worse for Britain was its disastrous defeat at the Battle of New Orleans, in January of 1815. A numerically superior force of 8,000 British infantry attacked the Americans, among whom were 2,000 riflemen. The British lost 1,500 men, mostly killed before they could advance to within musket range, for the loss of 60 Americans, mostly through artillery fire. Sadly, the war had already ended by the time the battle was fought, the Treaty of Ghent having been signed on Christmas Eve 1814, but there was no way of letting the combatants know. Clearly, the value of riflemen lay not in their employment as infantry but in utilising their unique skills properly as scouts, skirmishers and marksmen, although it would be a long time before the lessons were generally understood.

The Napoleonic Threat

Although Lord Howe was to subsequently complain long and loud in the British Parliament about 'the terrible guns of the rebels', in reality, the tactical use of the rifle in the American wars had been limited, many American officers actually preferring to replace their men's rifles with muskets and fight in a traditional manner. Besides, a new threat from France was exercising the minds of the British establishment, in the shape of Napoleon Bonaparte, and Britain needed to arm a new and larger army quickly. The military musket had basically remained unchanged since the English Civil War of the 1640s and while flintlocks had slowly replaced matchlocks, the infantry soldiers' firearm had changed little compared to those in use a century earlier. Tactics also had not altered a great deal. Massed ranks still faced each other over open fields and blazed away at short range with well-orchestrated volley fire until one side or the other gave way. The new threat from France presented the more forward thinking British officers with some grave concerns about the state of the Army's muskets and in 1798 the Board of Ordnance went so far as to order some 5,000 Prussian Jäger rifles for issue to light infantry and rifle regiments. This proved a costly mistake, for the majority turned out to be of poor quality and only a small number found their way into the hands of the 60th Rifle Regiment. Clearly a rifle was needed that was capable of shooting out to ranges well beyond that of the common musket, but the Board of Ordnance could not agree on either the type or calibre of rifle required. Almost inevitably they settled on what they knew, a tried and tested design based on the venerable Prussian Jäger rifle. A contract was given to Ezekiel Baker in 1799 to produce a suitable pattern and the following year the first 'musket bore' .70 inch Baker rifles were produced. Subsequent trials showed a reduced calibre was just as effective and somewhat easier to shoot, so the majority of Bakers were produced in .62 'carbine' bore, the first batch of 800 being issued to the newly formed 95th [Rifle] Regiment. The short barrels had seven groove rifling, a straight stock to help deal with the recoil, cheek pad to give a comfortable sighting position, front blade sight and a two position flip-up rear sight. A distinctive scrolled brass triggerguard was fitted to aid grip. Two rifle regiments took part in the campaign, the 5th Battalion, 60th Rifles, mostly comprising German mercenaries, and three battalions of the 95th Rifles. Possibly of more interest from the point of view of subsequent sniping history, was the fact that the men recruited for the 95th were of a better quality than the common soldiery. Most were literate, a substantial percentage had a profession and all were expected to become expert shots. Rifleman William Surtees commented on how his comrades would take part in casual target shooting competitions, for example one holding a playing card out at arm's length for another to shoot at, at ranges of 150 yards (130 metres).[40] Although few accounts of their long-range shooting exist, the shot made by Rifleman Tom Plunkett of the 95th during the Battle of Villafranca, when he killed General Colbert at a range of about 300 yards, is well documented. As this was towards the extreme limit of accuracy for a Baker, it was no mean feat. Bakers were also issued to picked sharpshooters of some of the light infantry companies, seeing service in Portugal, South America and India. The 95th used their Bakers at Waterloo, and it is recorded that some 200 had to be sent out to replace those lost in the battle. These riflemen were predominantly used as scouts and skirmishers, and combat was often fast, deadly and at close range, similar to fighting almost 140 years later through the *bocage* country after D-Day. Accounts of riflemen facing each other in combat are very scarce, but Rifleman Harris gives a rare insight:

> I was startled by the sharp report of a firelock, and at the same moment, a bullet whistled close to my head. Instantly starting up I turned and looked in the direction whence the shot had come ... but nothing could I see. I looked to the priming of my rifle ... when another shot took place, and a second ball whistled past me. This time I was ready, and turning quickly I saw my man; he was just about to squat down behind a small mound, about twenty paces from me. I took a haphazard shot at him, and instantly knocked him over.[41]

There is little doubt that riflemen were very effective on the battlefield, as the comments of an unnamed French officer show:

> I was sent out to skirmish against some of those in green – grasshoppers I call them, you call them Rifle Men. They were behind every bush and stone, and soon made sad havoc amongst my men, killing all the officers in my company, and wounding myself, without [our] being able to do them any injury.

At a higher level, even Field Marshal Nicolas Soult was impressed at the effectiveness of the riflemen. In a letter written to the French Minister of War in 1813, he commented that 'this mode of making war ... is very detrimental to us; our casualties in officers is so great that after a couple of actions the whole number are usually disabled. I saw battalions which were reduced to two, or three officers'.[42] The rifle regiments certainly earned their reputations during the war and they maintained their proud shooting status afterwards. In reality, the gradual abandonment of the musket in favour of the rifle came about not so much as a result of combat experience, but because of manufacturing improvements during the late 18th century, due largely to the Industrial Revolution, which gave gunsmiths easier access to steam and water powered machinery. New and more efficient barrel boring machines meant that rifled barrels could be made faster and more cheaply and by the mid-19th century most European armies were equipped with accurate rifled muskets. However, equipping men was a far cry from training them to be good shots. For decades very few countries actually taught their soldiers how to estimate range or wind speed, and they were instructed to shoot only at the targets indicated to them using volley fire. Such a policy was to have profound repercussions when the high velocity centrefire rifle was adopted for military use in the late 19th century, as few nations had men equipped with the skills to utilise the new firearms technology available to them.

The Percussion System

As was so often the case, continued advances in firearms design, which had continued apace in the civilian commercial world, had largely by-passed the military traditionalists who could still see no reason for issuing anything other than the smooth bore musket. This situation may well have remained unchanged had not two separate inventions at roughly similar times started a chain reaction in firearms development that no military power could afford to ignore. The first was the invention of the metallic percussion cap around 1814, most probably by an English artist named Joshua Shaw who had adopted and improved the earlier Forsyth priming system. A small copper cap, placed on a hollow nipple, could instantly ignite a musket charge. What's more, it could remain safely in place almost indefinitely, and was impervious to bad weather. At a stroke the problems of unreliable flints, reluctant priming powder, rain in the pan and the tell-tale flash and smoke of ignition became redundant. Within a decade, the percussion lock had gained a firm foothold in the ranks of sporting shooters. This in itself may not have been sufficient to interest the military, but the invention of a piece of hollow lead by a French officer, Claude-Étienne Minié, was set to revolutionise the use of the rifled musket in warfare. The problem with using rifles was one of fouling. Gunpowder, the only propellant available, was arguably the worst chemical combination one could choose to fire from a gun. It produced 300 times its own volume in thick white smoke and for a concealed rifleman was the equivalent to having a neon sign flashing overhead. In addition, it left behind a thick, acidic residue that choked barrels and touch holes and made reloading a steadily more difficult process. With a rifle that required a tight-fitting bullet to provide accuracy it was a serious problem as after half a dozen shots it became almost impossible to reload. As a result, most rifle balls were made slightly undersized, requiring the use of a patch. What Minié was to do was both simple and effective. He devised a conical lead bullet that was slightly smaller than the bore but had a hollow base into which a steel cup was inserted. When fired, the propellant gases pushed the cup hard up into the bullet, expanding its lead skirt and enabling it to grip the rifling, and from the early 1840s one European nation after another began to re-equip its army with new percussion rifled muskets.

Parsimonious as ever, the British government attempted to convert stocks of existing flintlocks into percussion muskets, but the lack of accuracy of these old smoothbores and the obvious need for rifled barrels left them little choice but to provide the Army with a new rifle. This was done in the shape of the Enfield manufactured Pattern 1851 Minié Rifled Musket. Initially, the issue of this rifle caused some confusion in the British Army, for never before had soldiers been given the simple order 'aim and fire'. Aiming never came into the equation, soldiers traditionally having been instructed to 'level their muskets' then fire, there being little point in actually aiming them. The Minié rifle changed this, for it had a range in excess of 1,000 yards and a trained soldier could certainly hit a man-sized target at 400 yards. The first issue of improved model P51 rifled muskets, six per company, went to the Army during the Cape Border Wars in South Africa (1846–52). The rifles were given to the best shots, one of whom, Private Wickens, wrote of his delight in the new rifle, commenting that 'when the enemy began to show themselves ... we opened fire on them ... we made them move at a distance of 1,200 yards'.[43] The problem for the Army was in training. For the first time men had to be taught how to judge distance:

At fifty yards, buttons and facial features can be seen clearly, at one hundred the facial features are blurred and the buttons seem to form a continuous line. At 150 the face is a white disc and no uniform detail is visible. At 200 arms body and legs are visible and the head is a dark blob.[44]

It was a difficult skill to learn properly, and most soldiers continued to be instructed in the simple art of volley fire, with an NCO calling out the range, and the soldiers firing on instruction. This enabled NCOs to retain control and certainly prevented the men from having to think for themselves, but it was a short sighted policy that was to have serious shortcomings during the wars in South Africa half a century later.

It was during the Crimean War (1854–56) that advances in communications meant that for the first time media attention could be focussed on how warfare was conducted, and the methods by which it was waged. The war was to provide the British and Russian armies with their first glimpse of the potential of using accurate rifles at long range. The issue of some 17,000 Minié rifles to the British troops serving in the Crimea gave its army an enormous, albeit unrecognised, tactical advantage. War was still being fought along classic Napoleonic linear lines; the vital difference was that now the defending British troops had a firepower capability that was beyond all Russian comprehension, as W. H. Russell of *The Times* reported:

As the Russians came within six hundred yards, down goes that line of steel in front, and out rings a volley of Mini [sic] musketry. The distance is too great; the Russians are not checked, but still sweep onward through the smoke … but 'ere they come within one hundred and fifty yards, another deadly volley flashes from the levelled rifles, and carries death and terror into the Russians. They wheel about … and fly back faster than they came.[45]

The most telling comment in this passage is Russell's mention of the inability of soldiers to hit their targets at 600 yards. This was in part due to the new rifle whose huge .70 calibre bullet was ballistically unstable at long range. In tests it was able to consistently hit a six foot by three foot target at 500 yards but could only manage to place two out of five shots on the target between 500 and 800 yards (450–720 metres). In addition, the men had not been instructed in the finer points of rifle shooting and their ability to shoot at long range was limited. Some indication of what could be achieved can be seen from the words of a Russian officer, Naum Gorbunov, whose regiment came under fire from British riflemen at ranges hitherto believed impossible for aimed small arms fire:

> We dismounted from our horses and watched with curiosity these strange things ... even the artillerymen could not name them, suggesting that these bullets ... were aimed at our artillery's cartridge boxes but were in no way meant for us ... we looked death right in the eyes. But after a few seconds we learned from experience the significance of these 'thimbles'.[46]

The British did have officers who were experienced riflemen though, and Lieutenant-Colonel D. Davidson of the 1st City of Edinburgh Rifle Volunteers, was an interesting example. A keen hunter and target shooter who served throughout the Crimean campaign, he subsequently wrote several articles dealing with his experiences and his belief in the requirement for proper rifle training as well as optical sights to be fitted to Army rifles. He commented on a novel and early use for the new Minié rifle in the trenches of Sebastopol:

> We have a striking example in an incident which occurred in the rifle pits before Sebastopol. One soldier was observed lying with his rifle carefully pointed at a distant embrasure, and with his finger on the trigger ready to pull, while by his side lay another with a telescope directed at the same object. He, with the telescope, was anxiously watching the movement when the [Russian] gunner should show himself, in order that he may give the signal to the other to fire.[47]

The two soldiers had inadvertently stumbled upon the ideal combination for effective sharpshooting and one that would subsequently become the standard for snipers across the world, that of pairing an observer and marksman and using a powerful optical device to spot for targets. Although tacitly this was condoned at a local level, there was no attempt by the Army to develop such skills.

In fact there were already some rifles in existence capable of out-ranging the new Miniés, a very few examples of which saw action during the campaign. John Jacob, a brilliant if rather unconventional officer serving in India, had been designing his own rifle since 1845. It was a double-barrelled weapon capable of shooting a conical lead or explosive bullet out to the extraordinary range of 2,000 yards. Lieutenant Malcolm Green, who was travelling home to England on leave in 1855, stopped en route in the Crimea to see his brother, then fighting in the siege of Sebastopol. Green had with him a Jacob's rifle and explosive ammunition, and decided to make use of it to counter some Russian artillery fire:

> He went to the trenches occupied by the French which faced Green Hill, a
> position held by the Russians, and at a distance of about 800 yards he opened
> fire with his rifle on a gun in the battery which had been giving much trouble
> to the French. In a very short time his fire caused the gun to be withdrawn
> from the embrasure.[48]

Others could also see the potential of such a rifle, and a remarkably prophetic pamphlet published in Bombay in 1855 by Sir Henry Bartle Frere, outlined what he believed could be achieved by trained riflemen:

> Their [the rifle] use implies skilful workmen in our ranks, instead of pipe-clayed
> automatons. It also implies a further change in our tactics, so as to give full
> scope ... to the high moral and intellectual powers of our men. With open files
> and ranks, each man a skilful combatant, but all still acting in concert, they
> would sweep their enemies from the earth, themselves almost unseen while a
> single discharge from a company at 1000 yards distance would annihilate the
> best field battery ... and cavalry would be of little value against them.[49]

Of course, no one took him seriously, for while the technology for accurate shooting existed, so too did the deeply ingrained prejudice of many in the British Army against the likes of Jacob and the intelligent use of soldiers to develop their own skills. If these could have been overcome by logical thought and practical application, then Britain would have led the world in rifle and sharpshooter use half a century before anyone else. Alas, it was not to be.

3

THE AMERICAN CIVIL WAR & EUROPEAN WARS, 1854–1914

After the end of the Crimean War with Russia, the British Army returned to policing the nation's vast colonies around the world, leaving little time for reflection on the musketry requirements of the Army in the event of another European war. There were still important changes occurring, however, although they were inevitably in the area of civilian target shooting. The introduction of the new Pattern 1853 Enfield rifled musket heralded a new era in the manufacture of massed produced, high quality firearms. Made to exacting standards and with parts that were fully interchangeable, it was a quantum leap forwards in manufacturing technology. The idea for mass production had not originated in England, however, but in the eastern factories of American gunmakers such as Eli Whitney, Samuel Colt and the Springfield Armory. Producing firearms using machine, rather than hand-manufactured, parts was cheaper, more efficient and faster. Unskilled or semi-skilled labour could be used without the expensive and time-consuming process of apprenticeship and careful hand-fitting that had traditionally made the high quality of English firearms so renowned, and so expensive. It had long been argued, particularly by the gun trade, that hand crafted firearms were so superior in quality and performance as to bear no comparison with inferior 'manufactured' guns. This was probably true until the 1840s, but advances in machine manufacturing had narrowed the gap until it was almost invisible. An engineer writing in *Scientific American* magazine stated:

> The American guns are made almost entirely by machinery, which enables them to be sold much cheaper and in much larger quantities. The idea so long prevalent that close-fitting joints cannot be made by machinery was demonstrated to be an error by many ... to show how finely fitted the joints of the working parts were, a pencil mark was made on some of the parts and so close was the fit that a single movement ... completely removed it; this was on a gun taken from regular stock and not one specially prepared.[50]

As a result, good quality rifles could now be purchased commercially at modest prices and the introduction of rifles such as the P53 inspired a resurgence of interest in target shooting in Britain. Of course, the sport had for generations been popular through Europe in the form of the *Schützenfeste* and in America at turkey shoots and casual, but highly competitive, open air shooting fairs. In the 1850s, however, the popularity of the volunteer militia movement in Britain, raised to combat the perceived threat from France, allied to the availability of the new rifles, gave the sport a quite unexpected boost. Target shooting became a new passion for the men who made up the ranks of the volunteers. Pride in their units and a strong competitive spirit allied to the often considerable wealth of the commanding colonel meant that the men were often armed with the very best commercially made rifles and they took great pride in knowing how to shoot them. This culminated with the competition for the coveted Queen's Prize held annually at Wimbledon ranges, south of London, until the venue was changed in 1890 to the more practical and less populated open spaces of Bisley in Surrey. The influence of these volunteer shooters should not be underestimated, for they formed a hard core of experienced marksmen who did much to increase awareness among the Army of the capabilities of the rifle, even if the generals who actually commanded the Army chose to ignore the fact. More importantly perhaps, these shooters were prepared to embrace any new technology that might improve their sport. For the first time at a reasonable price, a rifle was available to the shooter whose performance limit could not actually be reached, for never had the old shooting expression 'if you can't see it, you can't hit it' been more true. The rifles being produced in the mid-19th century were quite capable of hitting a man-sized target at 1,000 yards, providing the shooter could actually see his target. Therein lay the problem, for at such distances a human being is a tiny target for the naked eye, and is totally obscured by the width of the foresight blade once an attempt is made to take aim. Some form of magnifying device was needed to enhance the view of the target, and the most obvious was the telescope.

Advances in Optical Science

Some explanation of the basic properties of these early sights might be useful for, like the rifles that were to utilise them, the sights themselves gradually became both more complex and more sophisticated as the 19th century progressed. These early sights belong to the class of optical instruments known as telescopic, whose function is the observation of distant objects. While we tend to regard optics as a relatively modern science, the use of lenses for magnification was well known in the ancient world. A piece of convex polished rock crystal was found in 1853 by Sir Henry Austen in an excavation at Nimrud in the ancient kingdom of Assyria. Tests showed that its properties would have made it perfect for use as a magnifying glass, probably to aid scribes with inscribing the minute texts carved into clay tablets.[51] There are also accounts by Seneca, tutor to the Emperor Nero (54–68 AD) of the Emperor watching Roman games through a device called a *smaragdus*. The implication is that this was a device for enhancing long-distance vision and it may have been a very simple form of telescope, although academics are in some dispute over the exact meaning of the term Seneca uses. It may possibly be the type of optical devices now referred to as a Galilean sight, and these comprise a large diameter convex objective (front) lens and much smaller concave eyepiece, with no intermediate lenses. This provides the viewer with magnifying power and a limited field of view. The concept of the modern telescope has its roots in the simple magnifying lenses first believed to have been used by Galileo Galilei (1564–1642) although there is now a body of opinion that believes they were perfected some years earlier by a Dutchman named Jan Lippershey. The Galilean types have a power of about 2×, which in practical terms means that an object will look the same size through the lens at 400 yards as it would be to the naked eye at 200 yards. Obviously, the greater the power of the lens, the larger this image will appear for any given distance. This brings into force an important secondary factor, the field of view, which is the area visible on either side of the target when viewed through the telescopic sight. With Galilean lenses it is somewhere between 1° and 2°, which is particularly narrow, for at 100 yards a human head will fill the lens and if the target were moving, then following it would prove very difficult indeed. By the 19th century, rifle telescopes were to become far more complex instruments using a multiple lens system that relied on refraction, the bending of light rays as they pass through a lens, to create an image. This is known as an erecting system and it requires a number of lenses, four or more, to produce an image that is neither back to front nor upside down. There were naturally some drawbacks with the available technology of this period. Focussing was difficult, although some makers used a sliding eyepiece with some success, but many early scopes were fixed, and would work only for the eye of a specific shooter. The field of view was usually poor, commonly 3–4°, and would vary with the magnifying power of the scope as well as eye relief, the distance from the shooter's eye to the ocular lens – the general rule is that the greater the magnification, the smaller the field of view. For the early scope makers, the problems did not end there, however, for parallax effect also had to be countered. This was the placing of a graticule (or crosshairs) within the lens to give a point of aim reference that could be adjusted to coincide with the impact of the bullet. The main problem was that there were only two points at which this could be done: at the focal plane of the objective lens or at the focal plane of the erector lens system. For shooting at a fixed distance, such as 1,000 yards, the graticule can be placed exactly at the focal plane that is correct for that specific lens and distance combination, but few live targets are thoughtful enough to appear at a fixed distance, so what tends to occur is that the focussed image falls either in front of or behind the fixed reticle. The practical effect of this for the shooter is that when he moves his eye, the graticule appears to move around the target and at certain ranges the crosshairs will also appear out of focus. To solve this, an eyepiece with screw adjustment began to be provided, which enabled parallax error to be corrected. These early scopes were fixed tubes, matched to the bore of the rifle and zeroed for a very specific distance. This was an impractical method for shooting accurately at varying ranges and soon other means of enabling the shooter to adjust his scope for distance were devised. For scopes mounted above the barrel of the rifle, sliding dovetails or a simple threaded screw system mounted to the receiver and muzzle worked tolerably well. Offset scopes, that sat to the left of the bore, used a variation of front mounted sliding plate and clamping screw, with a ball and socket mount to enable the tube to be moved up and down. Few optical sights had any method of adjusting for windage (side winds), the shooter simply working using a mix of trial and error and experience. By the standards of the day, these scopes were a huge improvement over the naked eye and were to pioneer an entirely new form of military shooting. By the mid-19th century the telescopic sight had been greatly refined and makers in Britain, such as Watson, Gibbs and Fraser, were producing well-made optical sights that were practical for mounting on a rifle.

The early telescopes available in the 19th century were actually little different to those used in Galileo's time, although some improvements had been made in glass quality and casing materials. The standard type was a three or four draw item that gave at best only a reasonable image and the large ones were neither portable nor cheap. One of the great problems with the manufacture of any optical instrument was in the availability of high quality optical glass. Ordinary glass could not be used, for apart from being too full of physical imperfections its chemical constituents gave it at best a generally blurred image or one with a tiny sharp centre and fuzzy edges. Early glass was manufactured from silicon dioxide (quartz) with calcium and some alkali. When cooled it had to be allowed to solidify without crystallising. It could then be formed into lenses and prisms that transmitted light as well as bending and focussing it. The bulk of early optical glass was manufactured in Germany though some also came from Switzerland and a small quantity from France and England, where there was only one company manufacturing optical glass, Chance Brothers of Birmingham.

The trouble with the manufacture of optical glass was that it was such a slow process and the lens grinding was so exacting that makers could not keep up with demand. An early crusader for the use of the telescopic sight and a man often unappreciated for his contribution to the science of accurate shooting was Colonel D. Davidson, who on his return to England from the Crimea undertook much of the pioneering work in mounting and developing optical sights for rifles. He was certainly one of the earliest European shooters to establish that a telescopic sight, properly fitted to a rifle, could be both practical and accurate. He wrote in a paper for the *Army and Navy Journal* in 1864, 'there are gentlemen now at home and in India, who have used the same rifles to which I fitted telescopes, for more than fifteen years without their getting out of order'.[52]

The idea of using a telescope to sight a rifle had long appealed to Davidson and he mentions in his article that he had 'introduced it [the scope] to India some thirty years ago',[53] indicating that the general concept was certainly known and probably already in use in the 1830s, although he does not specify what form this took. He comments in some detail of the benefits of using an optical sight when hunting, noting that 'it not only gives increased precision at long ranges, but enables the sportsmen to aim at deer and bustards which … could not be seen with the naked eye'.[54]

These early scopes were fixed, with no adjustment for range or elevation, and were limited in their use for as he commented, 'the telescopes, pulled on to dovetails run into the barrel … could not be depressed … suitable only for the comparatively short ranges required in deer-stalking'.[55] He continued his development work, and succeeded in producing a scope with range-adjustable front mount, that could be fitted to the side of the P53 rifle. It was, like all offset scopes, awkward to use, but the ability of the scope to be adjusted for elevation up to 12° gave it a theoretical working range of up to 2,000 yards (1,830 metres), although there was no provision for windage adjustment. Davidson also tackled the problem of focussing, for his sights had an adjustable sliding eyepiece that worked in the same manner as an ordinary telescope, the rear part of the sight being pulled backwards until correct focus was achieved:

> Rifles fitted with [these] telescopes would be of great value in rifle-pits, in dislodging bushfighters, and in keeping down the fire of artillery. A heavy, large-bore telescope-rifle, taking a large charge and throwing an exploding projectile, would be serviceable against field batteries at the longest ranges.[56]

With these prophetic comments, Davidson had foreseen what would take the armies of the developed world another century and a half to appreciate – the value of very long-range anti-material shooting.

The American Optical Industry

It was the United States that was to lead the way in telescopic sight manufacture, in part because there was not as much demand for sights in England as there was in the States. The Americans weren't hidebound by convention either and this showed in their willingness to embrace new ideas and technology. They were materially assisted in this because among the many and talented emigrants who had left Europe were skilled men with experience of working in the German and Swiss optical industry. As a result, several gunmakers in the late 1830s began experimenting with the manufacture of very modest optical sights fitted to the new percussion target rifles that were appearing. Prior to this date, the use of the flintlock mechanism precluded any use of an optical sight, but with percussion ignition came a new type of highly accurate target rifle. These were different from the traditional slim barrelled hunting rifles, having very heavy octagonal barrels that could weigh up to 20 lbs, and comparatively large bores of between .40 and .56 inches. They were often supplied with double or single set triggers, and micro-adjustable target sights. Exactly who was the first person to attach an optical sight to a rifle will never be known, for while Davidson claimed to have used scoped rifles in India in the 1830s, there exists no surviving proof of this but it is recorded by several writers that scoped rifles were known on the Eastern coast of America by 1835, although these were doubtless of the fixed type and how effective these were is open to debate. In 1840 an eminent British engineer, John Ratcliffe Chapman, then residing in New York, wrote a unique account of his experiments with telescopic sights:

> I am aware that telescopes have been in use for some time, but to the best of my knowledge they never perform so well as the globe sight, until made and used as described. I shall now proceed to describe such improvements in sighting which I have lately been able to effect by the introduction of a telescopic sight … the tube in which the lenses are fixed is three feet one inch

long, 5/8th of an inch diameter … weighing 10ozs. It can be made very good and true out of sheet iron. To the front end a saddle of steel is firmly fitted and brazed … the object to be attained being stiffness for when fixed on the rifle, a discharge has the tendency to pitch it forward and break out the dovetail. A carriage is made to slide through the bead sight dovetail … through which two screws pass into the saddle, serving as axis or pivots of elevation and depression. The back movement for elevating and depressing without taking out the telescope is designed to adapt itself for all ranges … a property the globe sight does not possess.[57]

In practice, the design worked very well, and while Chapman only manufactured scopes for about 15 years, an almost identical form of mounting system was still in use on telescopic sights still being made by Lyman, Unertl and Stevens until well after the Second World War. The usual problem was in finding a suitable supply of glass and America was particularly fortunate in having a number of glassmakers as well as several highly competent gunmakers who were very interested in the development of optical sights. Foremost among them was Morgan James, a rifle maker based in Utica, New York who had for some time been interested in the possibilities of fitting telescopic sights to target rifles. James understood well the destructive power of recoil on the delicate scope mounts and had done much work on solving the problem of ensuring the optical glass remained secure in the scope tube during shooting. He had a number of embarrassing scope disintegrations before he found a method of fixing the lenses firmly in the body of the scope tube. He also holds the distinction of having manufactured the first internally adjustable telescopic sight in the United States.

What particularly impressed James was the fitting method invented by Chapman, so with Chapman's agreement he began to manufacture Chapman-James scopes from around 1845 to 1865, and they proved to be the best that money could buy, retailing at a hefty $20 each, at a time when a top-quality Hawken percussion rifle was selling at $25. Unfortunately Chapman had neglected to patent his invention, and it was not long before others copied his idea, although few had the optical expertise to match the quality of the James scopes. A contemporary of Chapman and James was

George H. Ferris also of Utica, and he assisted James with manufacturing sights until 1859 when he began to sell his own scopes.

Another name that was to become legendary in the field of optical manufacture was Alvan Clark, the son of an instrument maker, born in Massachusetts in 1832. He began his working life grinding optical mirrors and lenses for what were generally regarded as the best large observation telescopes made in the 19th century. In fact, while testing one of his telescopes Clark was the first person to see and identify a new star, Sirius B. His interest in optical sights for shooting was really a sideline but with his knowledge of manufacturing he was able to make superb, and very expensive, scopes that provided unparalleled clarity, although these were never produced on anything more than a very small scale. In view of the limits of lens and manufacturing technology at the time, there were certain constraints in the production and use of these early optical sights. Although advertised as of high power of 10× to 20×, they were actually quite low powered, using our modern measuring standards, and their field of vision was also narrow, commonly of 3–4°. In addition, all had fixed lenses so there was no focus adjustment for range. The lenses were ground to suit the specific eyesight of the purchaser and were retained in the tube by grubscrews that could not be adjusted in any way, which in practical terms meant that a scope-equipped rifle could only be shot by the individual for whom the scope was made. This was fine for target shooting in good light out to a given range, but they were impractical for military use, where rapid target acquisition was necessary as few targets would be standing stock-still. Subsequently, the limitations of these early scopes would be shown up during the American Civil War when many were pressed into military service.

Things were to improve radically in the shape of the telescopic sights manufactured by William Malcolm of Syracuse, New York from around 1855. Malcolm was the son of a Scottish businessman and much against his father's wishes was determined to become a mechanical engineer, and he pioneered production methods that were to set the standard for the next 50 years. His first innovation was the use of a solid drawn steel tube that was not folded and brazed as had previously been the case. It was much stronger and enabled much tighter tolerances to be achieved when mounting the lenses. The tubes were normally some 6 inches longer than the rifle barrel and of about ½ inch internal diameter. Malcolm's lenses were the first to be fully achromatic, being free from chromatic aberration, which gave better target definition, a flatter field of view and sharp edge definition without that irritating fuzzy fringe of colour around the periphery that earlier lenses had. They were ground uniformly, and were mounted in brass cells retained by tiny screws through the scope body, which enabled them to retain their adjustment on firing. More importantly, the ocular and objective lenses were held by screws that were mounted in slots in the main body of the scope. Loosening these and moving the lens forward or backwards gave focal adjustment for any eye. Scopes could be provided in any magnification of up to 20× and while the basic elevation adjusting system was based on Chapman's, Malcolm considerably improved on the method of compensating for windage, abandoning the front sight dovetail. He applied some finesse to the problem and produced a two part mount with a lateral screw enabling windage to be very finely adjusted. That they were readily accepted by the shooting community at large was testament to their efficiency, as one veteran Rocky Mountain hunter commented. He carried:

> a Sharps [percussion] rifle, .52 calibre ... fitted with a Malcolm telescopic sight. The rifle itself as well as the telescope was something of a novelty in the region in those days and much was the discussion on the merits and demerits of the telescopic sight. Within a year from the time I joined the band every one of the little company of hunters and trappers, procured, and had fitted, the best Malcolm telescopic sights.[58]

Malcolm's timing was to prove unintentionally impeccable, for the outbreak of the American Civil War in 1861 signalled an unparalleled need for accurate rifles for use by sharpshooters. The war between North and South was to prove the first truly 'modern' war embracing all that 19th-century technology could provide – railways, observation balloons, artillery bombardments, the use of breech-loading rifles. More importantly, and due in no small part to the impartial efficiency of the rifled musket, it was to lead to a gradual shift away from the linear tactics of the Napoleonic era.

It was crucial, as well, for the history of sniping, for it was a conflict in which for the first time battalions of sharpshooters would be raised for the **specific** purpose of sniping and where they would have completely free rein over the battlefield. Both Union and Confederate forces raised and used such units to deadly effect.

The Union Sharpshooter in the Civil War

On the outbreak of the war both sides were fairly evenly matched in terms of type of longarms issued, as both predominantly used .58 calibre percussion rifled muskets. The North had access to the major manufacturing plants such as Springfield Armory, and as a result had the very good Springfield rifled musket. The Union Army was the first to accept the potential for having a force of sharpshooters free to roam at will over the battlefield, mainly due to persistent lobbying by the wealthy inventor and skilled shot, Hiram Berdan. The rationale behind the formation of such an elite unit was outlined in an 1861 newspaper article, doubtless prompted by Berdan himself, the correspondent pointing out that:

> the American riflemen prove superior, especially in the hunters of New England and the West. It is the design of the Colonel to have the regiment detached in squads on the field of battle to do duty picking off officers and gunners on the European plan.[59]

Berdan's 1st Regiment, joined shortly after by a second, was approved by the Secretary of War on 15 June 1861 and was unusual in that it attracted volunteers from all over the North and was not State organised. Men from Michigan, Minnesota, New Hampshire, New York, Pennsylvania, Vermont, Wisconsin and other states all served under one command. They were selected for their shooting abilities and had to pass a stringent shooting test. This comprised shooting freehand, placing ten consecutive shots in a target at 200 yards, with a group size that should not exceed five inches. It is a measure of the ability of many men that this was regularly improved on. Every man who was accepted believed himself to be part of an elite unit and all were strong individualists, a trait that is not uncommonly found in modern snipers. Berdan's Sharpshooters were by no means the only ones in the Union Army however. Sharpshooting companies served with the 15th, 19th and 22nd Massachusetts, 16th Michigan and 14th Missouri Regiments and with the 66th Illinois, the 1st to 10th Ohio, the 1st New York Battalion, and the 1st Maine Battalion. These regiments were actually formed to provide skirmishers and scouts to be used along the same lines as the British 60th and 95th Regiments during the Napoleonic campaign, and they were drilled in the normal open-order form of fighting, skirmishing, bayonet fighting and defending against cavalry attack, as well as accurate shooting, judging of distances, signalling and observation. For many sharpshooters, much of their combat experience throughout the Civil War would be in the role of regular infantry, albeit with a greater propensity for hitting their target than the average soldier.

While the other regiments were dressed in standard US blue uniform, in keeping with their elite status, the 1st and 2nd Sharpshooters were clothed in a manner very similar to that of the British rifle regiments. Their clothes were specially selected for practicality in the field, with green jacket and trousers, non-reflective black buttons, a black plumed grey slouch hat, grey overcoat and a distinctive leather tanned 'Prussian' knapsack, Berdan reasonably stating that his decision to select this combination was that the men comprising the regiment will not consent to wear 'the common US uniform' and as they would be skirmishers, they should not be conspicuously dressed. 'The green will harmonise with the leaves of summer while the grey ... will accord with surrounding objects in fall and winter.'[60] While some army units were dressed in a manner that could be charitably described as Victorian Music Hall, the Berdan units from the start were issued with the most practical of clothing. This uniform was not universal though, for at least one example of a Berdan sergeant's blue tunic and trousers exists, with a green cap, arm chevrons and leg stripes.[61] The romantic but dangerously noticeable black plumes soon vanished from the hats and many men preferred to wear their own brand of slouch hat, practical if rather unmilitary, in a wide variety of dark colours. These hats served sharpshooters well, the brims keeping the face in shadow and the crown of the hat blurring the distinctive outline of the head. The uniform was comfortable and above all practical and most sharpshooter units adopted some form of special insignia, Berdan's men having embroidered crossed rifles with 'USSS' on their headgear. In the field the men frequently eschewed military uniform entirely and when Major Charles Mattocks took command of the Berdan Sharpshooters in early 1864 he commented dryly that 'the men are clothed in every shape and present anything but a martial appearance'.

Although there are no existing accounts relating to use of pre-constructed camouflage hides during the war, there are stories of sharpshooters of both sides using leaves and grass in their hats as camouflage and it appears reasonable to assume that natural vegetation was used where required. This could be taken to extremes, however, for many sharpshooters had a propensity for sitting in trees to take their shots, and while this undoubtedly gave an excellent field of view, it frequently sealed the shooter's death warrant, for the cloud of white smoke from the shot was impossible to disguise and unless he was firing at very long range, or very nimble in descending, every rifle in the vicinity would be turned on the offender within seconds. This was a lesson well learned by the end of the war, and trees were seldom used in later conflicts, except by the Japanese in the Second World War who seemed to have a deep and abiding affinity for treetop lairs.

Union Sharpshooter Rifles

If there was some laxity with regard to uniform, there was certainly none concerning the rifles the men wanted. The original plan was to issue the standard Model 1861 Springfield rifle musket, but this was not deemed a good enough sharpshooter's weapon. Like any muzzle-loader the best and quickest method of reloading was while standing up and, while it was possible to reload prone by rolling onto one's back this was awkward and broke eye contact with the target, making target reacquisition difficult. Berdan had tested, and approved of, the M1859 .52 calibre Sharps breech loading rifle but in a scenario that was to become depressingly commonplace where the issue of specialist rifles was concerned, his attempts to order them were blocked by the ultra-conservative head of the Ordnance Department, Brigadier-General James Ripley. He did not like, or see, any requirement for breechloaders, and he was concerned that a Sharps, at $45, was over three times the cost of the Springfield. As a result the 1st and 2nd Sharpshooters were initially issued with the deeply unpopular Model 1855 Colt revolving rifle. Aside from being nowhere near as accurate as a proper rifle, as well as lacking in range and being mechanically troublesome, its penchant for simultaneously igniting all of the chambers in its cylinder when fired left it pretty much free of admirers.

Berdan attempted to obtain the breech-loading rimfire Spencer rifle, but the factory was struggling to meet its existing delivery commitments. So dire was the situation that the Sharpshooters threatened mutiny if the Colts were not replaced and in early 1862, after intervention from President Lincoln, the first half of an order for 2,000 Sharp rifles and accoutrements was issued. These rifles differed from the standard in that they had factory-fitted double set triggers, which could be adjusted for the weight of pull, and they were equipped with a ladder-type rear sight graduated to 800 yards, which was actually well under the achievable range for a good shot. One Berdan rifleman forced Confederate artillery signalmen to leave their observation tower at a range of 1,500 yards, having first fabricated extra graduations for his rear sight out of card. It was a rifle that was capable of great accuracy in the right hands, and with the possible exception of the rare and coveted Whitworth, was generally believed to be the best sharpshooter's rifle then available. There were other rifles in use though, for so many men had brought their own target rifles when they enlisted into the Sharpshooters that two companies of them were formed. These were predominantly heavy-barrelled, single-shot, muzzle-loading percussion target weapons, weighing anything between 15 and 25 lbs and of smaller calibre than the service .58 inch. Many had some form of optical sights fitted and while these were very accurate they were punishing to carry on a long march and their scopes did not stand up well to the rigours of service life. In time most were sent home, but some remained in service being issued when required for long-range shooting.

The Confederate Sharpshooter in the Civil War

The situation for the Confederacy was slightly different, for initially there was little interest in the formation of specialised sharpshooter companies. After facing the US Sharpshooters in combat, the Confederate commanders began to understand the value of such troops and in spring 1862 the southern Congress authorised the formation of their own units. As a result 16 sharpshooter Battalions were established, the 17th and 23rd Alabama, the 1st and 12th Arkansas, the 1st, 2nd, 3rd and 4th Georgia, the 14th Louisiana, the 1st, 9th and 15th Mississippi, the 1st North Carolina, the 2nd South Carolina, the 1st Texas and the 24th Tennessee. A major difference in organisation was that, whereas the Union accepted men from any state specifically to serve with their sharpshooting regiments, Confederate units remained state-raised and not mixed. Usually the best three or four shots from each company would be transferred from their infantry regiments into a sharpshooting battalion for the duration of a specific campaign. The 1st North Carolina, for example, was raised from men transferred from the 21st North Carolina Regiment of Infantry. Neither were they as large as those of the Federal Army, many battalions, such as the 17th Alabama, actually comprising only two companies of sharpshooters. Once on the battlefield there was no pre-determined tactical use for them so they were employed how and where they were most effectively required, which was in many ways a more efficient system than that used by the Union. While most of the men were combat veterans, they still had to be taught the skills required of a sharpshooter – skirmishing, observation, use of cover and estimating distances. Many of the men were already experienced shots, but were unused to owning rifles capable of 1,000 yard shooting. A Confederate officer, Major W. S. Dunlop wrote of an exercise devised to help the men judge distances. Sharpshooters had to judge the distance of a man or object in front of them and publicly announce their estimate. The distances were then:

> increased from time to time, from one hundred, to two, three, five, and nine hundred yards and an accurate account kept of each man's judgement. The practice was continued ... from day to day until every man could tell, almost to a mathematical certainty, the distance to any given point within the compass.[62]

Not for the southern sharpshooters the smart green uniforms of the Berdan regiments, and this lack of a distinctive uniform actually caused some problems for them. As sharpshooters could be required to travel over a wide area of the battle lines, there was always a danger of being apprehended as a deserter, so the Confederacy adopted a broad range of insignia to identify sharpshooters. These were normally made of felt or cloth and sewn on the arm, and they identified the men as specialists in much the same way that the carrying of a scoped rifle did in later wars. The Confederacy suffered from an acute shortage of almost everything, and while there existed, in theory, a standard grey uniform comprising blouse and trousers, short boots or shoes and a kepi or slouch hat, in practice, the difficulties of supply meant that after a short period of campaigning, most southern soldiers were deficient in much uniform and equipment, and used what they could beg, borrow or otherwise liberate. This could mean plundered Union items of uniform and even civilian clothing. One Federal soldier described recently captured Confederate prisoners as 'scarce recognisable as soldiers, in a variety of common clothing fit only for scarecrows'.

Confederate Sharpshooter Rifles

Aside from its own limited production facilities at places such as Fayetteville or Palmetto, the South purchased vast numbers of surplus European rifles and muskets as well as some 117,000 P53 Enfields and tens of thousands of Belgian-made copies.

Every weapon bought from Europe had to be imported by sea, the ships having to run the Union naval blockade. This naturally forced up prices and because the supply of rifles was so uncertain, and accurate rifles were very expensive, Confederate sharpshooters tended to be armed with a broader range of rifles than their Northern counterparts. Captured Federal Sharps, Spencers and Springfields were popular, as were European rifles, but whenever possible, the southern sharpshooter units picked the Enfield P53 as their chosen weapon. Major Dunlop commented of them that while most issue rifles were good at shorter ranges:

> The superiority of the Enfield at long ranges, from 600 to 900 yards, was clearly demonstrated, both as to force and accuracy of fire. The ulterior range of the Enfield's proved reliable and effective to a surprising degree, to a distance of 900 yards, while the other rifles could only be relied on at a distance of 500 yards.[63]

There has been much speculation about the use during the war of Whitworth rifles in the hands of Confederate sharpshooters and perhaps this should be put into context. These rifles, manufactured at Sir Joseph Whitworth's factory in Manchester, England, had a hexagonal bore and target sights which, together with their exquisite workmanship and quality, made them the best rifle of their type available. The problem was that a basic rifle would cost the Confederate Army $600, at a time when an imported P53 would be $150. For a cased Whitworth with optical sights and 1,000 rounds of ammunition the price rose to a staggering $1,000 (about £10,000 or $18,000 in today's currency). The sum total of Whitworths of any type that saw service during the Civil War was probably no more than 150, but they did sterling work. The division under the command of General Patrick Cleburne, who was to become one of the Confederacy's leading generals, received 30 Whitworth and 16 Kerr rifles. During the Battle of Dalton, Georgia, his 46 sharpshooters repeatedly silenced Union artillery at 800 yards range and from the shelter of the woods they annihilated an advancing Federal skirmish line. One Federal officer later remarked that 'so galling was the fire, every man who attempted to rise was shot dead'.[64]

Sharpshooter Combat

It has been said that the Southern states were able to provide more marksmen than the North, as the bulk of Confederates were from poor rural backgrounds, used to hunting for food and being averse to wasting ammunition by missing. There may be some truth to this but in all probability the North and South were reasonably well matched in terms of the number of good shots they could field and the firearms they were able to use. This was demonstrated at the Battle of Antietam (September 1862) when the Union sharpshooters inflicted terrible casualties on the Confederates, whose 200 dead were piled into a mass grave in front of the Sharpshooters' lines. Twice during the Battle for Gettysburg the 1st and 2nd Sharpshooters, serving together, helped repulse attacks that could have overwhelmed the Union positions. Even at this early stage, the ground rules for military sniping were gradually being established, and certain targets were high on the list of priorities. At last riflemen now had the capability to wreak havoc on artillery units, a hitherto impossible target for muskets. Private George Chase of the 1st Berdan Sharpshooters succeeded in keeping a Confederate field gun out of action for two days by shooting at any crew who dared approach it.[65]

Although the Confederacy preferred their sharpshooters to function as line infantry, the men were still given considerable freedom to seek out their own targets along their regimental fronts. Some idea of the capabilities of these marksmen can be seen from the events at the Battle of Spotsylvania Courthouse in May 1864. Having shot dead one Union staff officer, Colonel Locke, and severely wounded General Morris, a Confederate sharpshooter cast the Union forces into confusion by killing General John Sedgwick, commander of the 6th Corps. While on horseback, and pointing at the distant rebel lines, Sedgwick was struck in the face just below the left eye, falling dead from his horse. A later account by a soldier of the South Carolina Sharpshooters commented that:

> [Sergeant] Ben Powell came in and told us that he had killed or wounded a very high ranking Yankee officer. He said that he had fired at very long range at a group of horsemen he recognised as officers. At his shot one fell from his horse, and the others dismounted and bore him away.[66]

Accounts cite Powell as using a scoped Whitworth rifle, and Powell himself said that the target was 'at very long range' although he did not specify exactly how far. In view of the fact that the general was on horseback, which at the best of times does not provide the most static of targets, it was a very fine shot by any standards. It seems particularly ironic that at the time, Sedgwick was sarcastically commenting on the poor quality of Confederate musketry and the nervousness of the men around him, his last recorded words being 'they couldn't hit an elephant at this distance'.[67]

Initially, opposing marksmen would take to duelling openly, as though attending a turkey shoot, to the delight of their respective onlookers. After one spectacular long-range duel a Federal sharpshooter, Private Ide, was eventually shot through the head by a Confederate marksman. As the rebel soldier stood up to take a bow from his own cheering men, he was then shot dead by Ide's officer who had picked up the fallen man's rifle.

However, as the war progressed such behaviour became less common and sharpshooters adopted more discreet methods of stalking. They also became a very useful source of information for their commanders, reporting on movements of enemy troops and artillery and in some instances they were even able to prevent costly mistakes. Berdan Sharpshooter Private Truman Head, more commonly known as 'California Joe', a sharp-eyed hunter from California, was observing some troops in a nearby wood, when a Union officer decided he would make a cavalry attack on them. Head's report that they were Union not Confederates was ignored, so he went out to bring in one of their Union sentries as proof of his observation skills. His marksmanship gained him a legendary reputation throughout the Army, and it was said of him that 'what he saw, he shot, and what he shot, he hit'. Although they may not have understood the phenomenon in modern psychological terms, Infantry commanders certainly began to appreciate the level of fear that an enemy sharpshooter engendered in troops, and their reluctance to expose themselves as targets in the presence of one. Having one in the vicinity quickly resulted in a call for an experienced rifleman to be brought up to deal with him, and the task of counter-sniping gradually began to emerge as an essential element of combat. When the Berdan regiment were pinned down by a skilfully hidden and efficient Confederate rifleman, one man volunteered to creep out of the Union lines at dusk. He remained in a hide between the lines until dawn, when he spotted the discharge of a rifle from a ruined house, whereupon he killed the Confederate by means of a single shot from his Sharps.[68] Even the Sharpshooting regiments were not immune to the attentions of enemy snipers, for Berdan's First Regiment lost one of their founding officers, the Swiss-born Colonel Caspar Trepp to an enemy sniper, a contemporary account stating that he was shot straight through the red diamond insignia on his forage cap.

The sharpshooter battalions of both sides gained enormous experience through the four years of the conflict, not only in inflicting damage on the enemy, but also in scouting, observation and intelligence gathering and this certainly gained them the grudging respect of the men and officers of both sides. It is impossible to know exactly what toll these sharpshooters took, but Union snipers alone accounted for no fewer than six Confederate

Generals, irreplaceable losses felled by an invisible man hidden somewhere in the landscape firing a lead bullet worth a few pence. What effect these men had on the conduct of the war is interesting to speculate upon, but if the war brought a new respect for the abilities of the sharpshooters and their rifles, with peace came a reaction from the Army that was to become all too familiar through history. Units were quickly disbanded, rifles handed back to stores, and the men, with all their hard won expertise, were demobilised and returned to farms, factories and stores. The US Army made no attempt to retain any sharpshooter regiments on its strength and the skills that had been learned at such cost vanished, along with the men, into the ether.

The Introduction of the Centrefire Rifle

In Europe there had been little requirement for the British Army to improve upon its shooting skills after the Crimean War, nor had any improvements in firearms technology been sought or adopted. Certainly, British observers had been intrigued with the United States' wide-scale adoption of the metallic rimfire cartridge during the Civil War, but the physical weakness of these cartridges meant that they were of comparatively low power and made their adoption for military use in Britain unlikely. Besides, as one of the world's great colonial powers, the British were fully occupied in various parts of the globe, ensuring law and order was maintained in regions where it wasn't always necessarily welcome.

It was, therefore, left to the French and Germans to introduce a radical new form of rifle technology in the late 1860s, when they adopted the bolt-action needlefire rifle. The French Chassepot and German Dreyse systems were essentially similar, using a new form of combustible cartridge, a cardboard tube filled with powder and loaded at one end with an 11 mm bullet. Unlike earlier combustible paper cartridges used with percussion ignition, these cartridges had an internal priming cap fitted into the base of the bullet. To reach this, the firing pin had to penetrate the length of the cartridge and thus was extremely long, hence the nickname of needlefire. The rifles were long barrelled, accurate and quick to load and fire, but crucially the Chassepot was capable of outranging the Dreyse, giving French riflemen a distinct advantage.

When the Franco-Prussian War broke out in 1870, this advantage was not lost on the *tirailleurs* of the French Army, who took to settling themselves in vantage points and shooting Prussians from ranges at which the enemy were powerless to retaliate. In one instance, a Prussian unit was fired on from a cottage in the grounds of a large estate near Paris. Unused to accurate long-range rifle fire, the Prussian soldiers were not unduly bothered and moved around openly, but soon paid dearly for it, as man after man fell from the shots. Eventually a young cavalry officer, Baron Steinfürst-Wallenstein offered to stalk the Frenchman, using his personal Jäger rifle. Although he was a skilled game hunter, his foe was a careful man, shooting from the back of an upstairs room, and never approaching the window. For two days the Baron observed but was unable to see clearly enough to make a shot, and was forced to return to his lines at dusk. In that time the French sniper killed three more Prussians and wounded another. When he returned to his lines at the end of the second day, he was ordered by his commanding officer to cease his activities and return to normal duties. He accepted the order, but suggested to his commander that when dawn rose he use field glasses to observe the cottage. The morning revealed the body of the French tirailleur hanging out of the window. Growing over-confident after his successes, he had made a classic misjudgement, firing and then approaching the window to confirm his shot. He was not expecting any retaliation, and it proved to be a fatal error. It is possible this incident may well be the first recorded sniping duel in European warfare.

It was the invention of two colonels, the American Hiram Berdan and the English Edward Boxer that would, within a decade, revolutionise the science of rifle shooting and sniping. Berdan and Boxer had been working, simultaneously but independently, on the problem of manufacturing a totally self-contained, internally primed metallic cartridge for use in breech loading rifles. In the late 1860s they had both produced functioning examples, albeit using slightly different methods of priming. The brass or copper cartridge had a central recessed anvil inset in its base, onto which a small percussion cap fitted. Filled with black powder propellant, with the lead bullet firmly seated on top, the new ammunition did away with the need for separate powder, ball and percussion caps. Crucially, it also meant that a soldier could now load and fire from the prone position, without having to stand upright to reload. Almost overnight needlefire became obsolete and from around 1868 America, Britain and the rest of Europe embarked on an urgent and exhaustive quest for new rifles to utilise this technology. Many countries took the simplest course of converting existing muzzle-loading rifles, but such compromises were only short term, and in 1871 Britain at last armed itself with the purpose designed breech-loading .450 calibre Martini-Henry single shot rifle. The Germans had adopted the excellent Mauser system and the US Ordnance Department continued with its lengthy struggle for a worthy successor to the Springfield.

For a decade or so, matters rested there until in 1886 a French invention was to provide another springboard for ballistics technology, and capitalise on Boxer's and Berdan's inventions. This appeared in the form of a smokeless propellant based around a chemical combination called nitrated cellulose. It burned faster, hotter and more regularly than gunpowder, and did not create the appalling barrel fouling or distinctive clouds of white smoke from the muzzle. It was the answer to the rifleman's prayers and within a couple of years target shooters had taken to it like a duck to water, followed by most European armies. Even Britain, looking for a replacement for the ageing Martini, had finally been forced to acknowledge the fact that single-shot black powder rifles were outmoded and inefficient and had adopted the .303 calibre Lee-Metford bolt-action magazine rifle in 1888. Other magazine rifles followed. Germany had the 7.92 mm (8 mm) Mauser commission rifle of 1888 and the United States eventually settled on the .30 calibre Model 1892 Krag-Jorgensen. Across Europe, rifles by Mannlicher, Schmidt-Rubin, Mosin-Nagant, Vetterli and a host of others were to set the benchmark for military long arms. Designed to fire the new smokeless small-calibre high-velocity ammunition, these rifles provided a degree of firepower, range and accuracy that had never before been achieved. The Mk. 1 .303 bullet was capable of reaching out to well over 2,000 yards (1,830 metres), far beyond the ability of human eyesight. There now existed a whole generation of fast firing, accurate rifles just waiting to be used in conjunction with the much-improved optical sights which were by then becoming available, thanks mainly to development work in Germany. Unfortunately, while sporting shooters regarded these possibilities with mounting excitement, the military were not concerned with such details.

It was still not regarded as desirable, or even necessary, for soldiers to be trained to shoot out to extreme ranges, and if they had to, then clearly volley fire was the answer, as it always had been. This attitude was soon to have unpleasant consequences for Britain several thousand miles away.

The Boer War

Of particular concern to the British government had been the trouble brewing in South Africa since the 1870s. British interests were gradually being threatened by the encroachment of Boer settlers and a small war had already been fought in 1880–81 which had led to an uneasy stand-off. This did not last long and in late 1899 a large military force, eventually to total nearly 450,000 men, was dispatched to deal with the growing problem. The men of the Queen Victoria's regular Army were tough, well trained and believed themselves, with some justification, to be the equal of any professional army in the world. The problem was, the Boers were not a professional army, and no one had informed them that they should agree to be beaten by the British. In fact, they were barely an army at all, being more a loose and flexible alliance of farmers, all of whom were experienced horsemen, equipped with the very latest bolt-action rifles, and all excellent shots. The British had no concept of the type of war they were to wage in Africa, and if they expected a short, sharp decisive battle, they were soon disappointed. Despite marching hundreds of miles in pursuit of their enemy, the soldiers almost never saw a Boer, yet frequently came under devastatingly accurate rifle fire, from positions so distant their attackers could not be identified. F. M. Crum was serving as a lieutenant in the 1st Battalion, 60th Rifles. Himself a keen rifleman, he made early comments on the abilities of the Boers that are worth repeating:

> It was a new kind of war. The invisible, galloping crack-shot Boer, with the modern quick-firing long range rifle, was thoroughly at home ... while we, to make up for our slowness of movement, often had to make long and exhausting night marches over difficult ground.[69]

So effective was the Boers' shooting that night marches became the normal practice, as the lines of soldiers and straggling baggage trains made pitifully easy targets for the Boer marksmen in the daylight. The British Army had no means of dealing with this problem, for while they certainly had a number of fine shots within the various infantry regiments, the men had no training in long-range shooting or fighting guerrilla warfare. In an open battle they could, and did, give good account of themselves; Crum reported a hussar armed with a rifle (not the usual carbine), who shot three distant Boers in quick succession. However, generally the British were outmanoeuvred and outshot, and the infantry were still being instructed by NCOs at what range to shoot. This was extremely difficult to judge when there were few reference points as Crum recounted:

> The Boers were above us… Peeping over the crest, I counted some 500 ponies and many Boers. What was the range? Major Greville thought it was 1,200 yards. I put it at more. We called for a rangefinder, but it had been left behind.[70]

Aside from their shooting ability, another reason for the Boers' success was in their use of natural cover and their personal dress. They understood the benefit of using the terrain to its best advantage, and were used to the difficulties of shooting up or down hill, where the bullet trajectory has to be compensated for, as well as being able to judge the deceptive distances of the open veldt very accurately. Boer clothing was also practical, green or brown coloured jackets and trousers, with wide brimmed slouch hats to protect them from the burning sun. Moreover, they did not waste water by daily shaving, and most had thick beards as well as being tanned from years living in the open. As a result, they did not have that tell-tale pale facial disc, which normally provides such a good target for a rifleman. When hidden in scrub or dug into a ridge, they were practically invisible. Militarily, it was proving almost impossible to defeat them so the British took drastic action against their families, destroying farms, burning crops and herding survivors into 'concentration' camps. Still the fighting continued, with the British taking unpalatably heavy casualties from accurate Boer rifle fire at battles such as Spion Kop, where the photographic image of huddled British dead piled in inadequate trenches shocked the nation. Crum himself became a victim of a Boer bullet, an event that he never forgot and one which spurred him into demanding specialised training for British snipers in the early months of the First World War:

> I took two men ... and with them, crept round the flank of the only two Boers that I could see. I took a rifle from one of my men, and crawling up, took a good aim at a Boer, when from another antheap another man fired and got me in the right shoulder. The rifle dropped with a thud. I thought my arm had been shot clean off, and was only hanging by a few khaki threads. The fingers were twitching and dancing and seemed far away. I caught them and said goodbye to them affectionately.[71]

Fortunately for the history of British sniping, Crum eventually made a full recovery but many were not so lucky. British battle casualties in the Boer war were some 7,582,[72] of whom 10% were officers. Fortunately, other officers besides Crum were to remember the effects of the Boer's fire when war broke out in 1914, and they were to provide a vocal hard core of professional soldiers dedicated to persuading a reluctant high command to begin training schemes to turn out skilled marksmen. Until then, however, the British Army were apparently content to forget the entire unpleasant South African experience for, after all, the chances of such a war happening again were unlikely.

4
THE FIRST WORLD WAR: THE WATERSHED, 1914–16

The seeds of war had been sown in Europe when the 39 separate German states had united in 1871. This wealthy, powerful and heavily industrialised new Germany embarked on a course of international expansion that would bring it into direct conflict with Britain. These two major European industrial powers thus embarked on an arms race that could have only one eventual outcome. Britain, confident of its military and naval might, expected there would be a short, sharp conflict with the inevitable British victory. However, the Germans were equally confident, and with good reason, for behind the United States it was not Britain but Germany that was the second greatest industrial power in the world, with a manufacturing capability that outstripped every other nation in Europe. Few politicians on either side were too surprised when war finally broke out in August 1914 but what was to concern the British was the course of the war that followed. After the initial fighting across France and Flanders had slowed with the onset of winter in 1914, both sides had been forced to halt and dig in, in scenes uncomfortably reminiscent of the Crimea. While the British high command had no intention of allowing their army to get comfortable, the Germans were more pragmatic and had carefully chosen positions that were tactically superior. Wherever possible, they constructed trenches on high ground, partly for the obvious reason of observation and partly because of the necessity for drainage, particularly in Belgium, where at the best of times the water table was never more than a couple of feet below the surface of the fields.

From the very earliest days of the war, the British soldiers had been troubled by particularly accurate rifle fire from the German lines although in the ebb and flow of the heavy fighting in 1914, few took any real account of it. In late summer 1914, Private John Lucy, of the Royal Irish Rifles, was occupying some shallow trenches in Flanders and saw first hand the first effects of deliberate sniping when a popular sergeant stood up to help a wounded German lying out in front of the trench:

> In spite of our warnings, the Sergeant stooped out over the trench ... there was a loud crack, someone said 'My God', and Benson slipped back into the trench on to his feet, staggered a pace or two, and sagged down dead, with a bullet through his pitying mouth. Benson spouted blood and made no sound. The bullet had come out of the back of his head.[73]

It was a classic sniper's shot, the bullet entering the mouth and exiting at the neck, severing the spinal cord and causing instantaneous death, although few would have understood the significance at the time. The casualties suffered by the British due to German rifle fire were merely accepted as the inevitable fortunes of war, and it must be said that the British Regular Army, with their aimed 15 rounds a minute rifle fire, had themselves made a serious dent in the German advance on several occasions. For the most part, comments by soldiers about deaths from single shots invariably employed the term 'stray bullets' as it was believed that random shots were responsible for a great number of these casualties. However, as the war became more static, the British soldiers began to notice that even in quiet parts of the line, the number of men dropping from bullet wounds to the head was beyond the simple explanation of being hit by a 'stray'. On average a line battalion could expect between 12 and 18 casualties a day, most from rifle fire. From the earliest days of 1914, the German snipers dominated the front lines and their prowess was soon legendary. In a vain attempt to combat the growing menace, the British used whatever they could lay their hands on to provide makeshift sniping positions, but the men had no training and were often frighteningly naive:

We had a snipers post, which was just a sheet of metal two inches high and a foot wide – just a hole big enough to put the end of a rifle through. We had two boys, they were orphans, they'd been brought up together. They were standing in the trenches and one said 'What's this George, have a look through here,' and no sooner had he approached it than down he went with a bullet through his forehead. Now, his friend was so flabbergasted he too had a look, and less than two minutes later he was down in the trench with his friend.[74]

'Sniper's light', dusk or dawn, was particularly dangerous for the unwary, as few soldiers appreciated the ability of a sniper with telescopic sight to make use of low light levels and most believed themselves to be safe in poor light as the cloak of darkness hid from the naked eye what could be clearly seen through a telescopic sight. Crum mentions one such event in 1915, as he was with a working party at dusk:

Alas, we lost a fine young officer, shot through the head by a sniper. He had asked me to help put in loopholes in a rotten parapet he was rebuilding that night … he jumped up and without my noticing peeped over just on my left. There was a crash and a smack and I realised he had been hit. The bullet passed through a rotten sandbag in the top layer and got him low down in the head. He died as he fell, without a groan or a word. The bullet had come from a well-concealed loophole 250 yards to our left.[75]

As the war progressed, the British became increasingly wary about any form of exposure that could lead to a sniper's bullet and vulnerable trenches were often posted with a board on which was painted a skull and crossbones with the word 'SNIPER' underneath. Some idea of the reason behind this wariness can be gleaned from the entry in the diary of a young artillery officer, Lieutenant S. Shingleton, made on the night of 5 February 1915:

I was sent in charge of a working party at night time to build dummy redoubts behind the front line … we crept along, taking advantage of the hedges etc. There were not many hours during the period between nightfall and moonrise so we had to get to work sharp … for to be seen standing in the open meant instant death from a sniper's bullet. It was even dangerous to wear a luminous wrist watch for the light from the same could be seen a long way off in the pitch darkness; a few snipers bullets whistled past us, and the R.E. officer in charge suggested that my luminous watch was the cause, whereupon I put it in my pocket.[76]

That the Germans were so successful was due to their ability to put the right equipment into the hands of properly trained men.

German Training and Tactics

From the outset of the conflict, the Germans had taken the decision that sniping would be a vital requirement in waging war and their approach to it was extremely practical. Sniping rifles were issued to each infantry company and it was the responsibility of the company commander to determine which of his soldiers would become snipers. At the start of the war there was no shortage of men from which to choose; hunters, gamekeepers, and men in the Jäger Regiments provided a deep pool from which company officers could fish. How was Germany able to take such a dramatic lead in this new form of warfare, and why was Britain so woefully deficient? The answer lay not so much in the equipment available, but in the differences of culture and geography. Germany and Austria abounded with thick forest and for generations hunting had been not merely a sport, but a rite of passage for young men, who would learn to shoot from an early age in one of the many rifle clubs, then go out with their relatives and friends to learn the skills of the hunt. Fieldcraft, observation, stalking and accurate snapshooting were thus second nature to a large number of young men who were already in the pre-1914 reserve, or who had joined the German Army on the outbreak of war. Exactly how many were already skilled enough to qualify as snipers is impossible to know. However, the number of men with hunting experience potentially gave the German Army a substantial reserve who could be quickly trained as snipers, as they already possessed the basic skills.

In Britain the culture and available technology were very different to that on the continent. Hunting, aside from rabbits and the occasional deer poached from local landowners, was the exclusive preserve of the upper class, for whom the hunt was not so much a sport as a necessary social function. Stalking deer in the Scottish highlands, or taking grouse or pheasant, was expensive and exclusive and the nearest the working man came to it was by being employed as a beater or gun carrier. Moreover, with that curious disdain that the British had for technology, rifles with optical sights were not generally regarded as acceptable for deer shooting.

Within the German Army, soldiers with above average shooting scores, hunting experience, or who had simply proved steady under fire were selected and issued with rifles and cased telescopic sights complete with tools and instruction manuals. Then in theory, at any rate, they would be given a short instructional course by their most experienced regimental snipers. Depending on the level of aggression in their particular stretch of line, this instruction could last anywhere between a few days and two or three weeks. The neophyte sniper would accompany his mentor into hides or on patrol along the trenches and would learn the tricks of the trade without exposing himself to unnecessary risk. In practice of course, this did not always work out, some regiments who did not regard sniping as important merely issued rifles to aspiring snipers and sent them straight into combat. One Saxon private commented that his training was an hour reading the instruction manual supplied with his telescopic sight before being called upon to practise his skills. This haphazard selection procedure was prone to errors as well, as men were chosen who were temperamentally unsuitable or who were not as good shots as perhaps they believed. The fact was that, despite the myth of the German Army having limitless numbers of experienced snipers, in truth, although many were good shots, they were often inadequately trained at the start of the war. Generally though, the system worked quite well, with some regiments developing fearsome reputations for the quality and skill of their snipers, and forming their own unofficial sniping schools. Gradually the German Army introduced a more organised approach to training, and sniper schools were set up behind the lines that were run somewhat on the basis of target shooting clubs. These were well equipped but with a somewhat regimented approach to teaching sniping which prompted Hesketh-Prichard to comment that:

Of the Germans as a whole one would say that with certain brilliant
exceptions they were quite sound but unenterprising ... the Bavarians were
better than the Prussians while some Saxon units were really first rate.[77]

The syllabus covered the normal regime of shooting, fieldcraft, map-
reading, observation and camouflage. The requirement was that the sniping
rifles be issued on the basis of six per infantry company and a German
battalion sniper section usually comprised 24 men who were free to use
whatever methods they chose to carry out their tasks. Working from
sniping posts in the line invariably meant two men should be employed,
although in practice a majority of snipers seemed to prefer to work alone,
a possible legacy of solitary stalking in the forests. Mannfreid Gossen
served as a sniper in a Bavarian regiment and commented that:

I preferred to work alone, for I was more comfortable in that way. It was
tiring because it was not possible to look through a sight for a long time, but
I chose my position well and only ever fired when I was certain, one or
perhaps two shots and I rested [my eyes] as much as I could.[78]

These *scharfschützen* were free agents in the line and they could shoot from
wherever they determined would be most effective: hides in No man's land,
buildings or woods behind the lines, or from the trenches themselves. Some
were given roving commissions and could travel along their Regimental
front at will, working from anywhere that the soldiers who occupied the
trenches deemed useful. All snipers were encouraged to get to know the
ground in front of them intimately, and they worked out ranges by studying
maps, crawling into No-Man's Land at night and marking out pre-
determined reference points, which were then plotted onto range cards kept
in each sniping post, along with notes of relevant landmarks and any
comments that might prove useful to fellow snipers. It was an excellent
system later adopted by the British.

Problems with Plates
From the outset, the Germans had the use of sniper plates, large magnesium
steel shields with loopholes that could be closed by means of a small

swivelling plate. At first these would merely be set on top of the parapet, packed into place with sandbags or simply supported by an angled metal bar that bolted to the rear face of the plate. Frederick Sleath described a typical arrangement in 1915:

> The early German shields were huge cumbrous steel plates, defying any attempt to hide them. They used to stand up brazenly on the German parapet, sometimes right against the skyline, so that the loophole was plainly visible whenever the protecting panel was swung open.[79]

In 1914 and early 1915 the British were so short of artillery ammunition that such strongpoints could be used with impunity. The loopholes proved to be a real problem for the British, who had no means of defeating them. Moreover, as the Germans gained experience, the plates so casually piled up around a trench gradually disappeared to be replaced by carefully inset shields, set well back in the parapet wall and often covered with sacking or other camouflage. They were placed in enfilade, at an acute angle to the line of trenches, facing both left and right, giving an interlocking field of fire. Spaced out at roughly 100 yard intervals, the loopholes enabled the German snipers to cover each other's frontage if required and made retaliation very difficult indeed as any observer looking from the front would be totally unable to spot the loophole. As Major Hesketh-Prichard commented:

> In 1915 there were very few loopholes in the British trenches, whereas the Germans had a magnificent system. In the early days when I used to be told … that there was a German sniper at such-and-such a map reference … I very rarely found a loophole from which I could reconnoitre, and as every German sniper seemed to be supported on either flank by other German snipers, looking for him with one's head over the top of the parapet was simply a form of suicide.[80]

This was a stumbling block to be overcome by the British, for no ordinary .303 inch ball ammunition could penetrate the steel of the German sniper's shields, and while a good rifleman could put a bullet through an open loophole he had to be both quick and lucky. In a desperate attempt to deal with the German snipers, the British War Office purchased some 62 large bore sporting rifles for issue to marksmen: 47 of .450 calibre, four of .470 calibre, one of .475 calibre, four of .500 calibre, two of .577 calibre and four of .600 inch. Each rifle was inspected at Enfield prior to issue then marked with the War Department broad arrow. Some British officers supplied their own, Crum using a .333 calibre Jeffery about which he gleefully wrote:

> I got it in London when at home. The German sniper has iron loopholes; you watch and watch and at last you see the slot slowly opening... Now that's the time for the elephant gun – a steady aim and bang, goes the great steel bullet through the steel plate, and Mr Fritz does not bother you again that day.[81]

Crum's sniper section also had use of a big .416 Rigby. Stuart Cloete, the sniping officer for the King's Own Yorkshire Light Infantry, went one better, opting for the biggest calibre then available:

> We used a heavy sporting rifle – a 600 Express. These heavy rifles had been donated to the army by big-game hunters and when we hit a [steel] plate we stove it right in. But it had to be fired standing or from a kneeling position to take up the recoil. The first man who fired it in the prone position had his collar bone broken.[82]

All of these calibres had sufficient velocity and bullet weight to punch through the toughened steel, but it took the Germans very little time to realise that their loophole plates were vulnerable to these massive rifles, and they countered the threat by simply placing one plate behind another, and filling the gap with earth. This effectively rendered them proof against any rifle calibre bullet, and put the British snipers back to square one. Not all officers were adept with their rifles though. Major Penberthy related the story of officers in a line regiment early in 1915, who purchased between themselves a sporting rifle equipped with a telescopic sight, which none knew how to zero. This didn't dent their enthusiasm, however, and after some weeks of use and abuse, another officer, experienced with telescopic sights, spotted it and asked to examine it. He checked its zero and found at 200 yards it was shooting 2 feet right and 3 feet high from the point of aim. 'Oh', replied one of the owners, 'that explains what happened yesterday. I was aiming at that loophole plate over there and a Hun sniper fell out of the tree to the right of it'.[83]

The Germans also benefited from having front lines that were a chaos of textures, colours and shapes; a mess of wire, multi-coloured sandbags, rubble and odd lengths of corrugated iron. The British obsession with orderliness meant that by late 1914 their own trenches were laid out with neat precision, well-packed sandbags forming flat parapets that were more or less uniform in colour and size. Hesketh-Prichard described the difference very eloquently, commenting that the British lines were as unvarying as a breakwater, while the German parapet:

> looked like the course of a gigantic mole which had flung up uneven heaps of earth. Here and there a huge piece of corrugated iron would be flung upon the parapet … there stood one of those steel boxes, more or less well concealed under a heap of earth. Here and there lay great piles of sandbags, black red green, striped, blue dazzling our eyes. The Germans had a splendid parapet behind which a man could move and over which he could look with comparative impunity.[84]

With the British becoming increasingly wary of the sniper menace, many Germans found they had little to do and one German sniper on the Aubers Ridge amused himself over a period of days by shooting a large cross into the wall of a cottage behind the British lines. Gossen commented that 'at times things were very quiet in the line, and we snipers had little to do but observe or sit in the trenches and smoke our pipes'.[85]

German Rifles

The armies of all of the major powers were using the same basic mechanical design and shot ammunition of broadly similar ballistic capabilities. The actions of these rifles utilised a locking, rotating bolt system with a central firing pin, and loading was through the top of the receiver, using a clip of cartridges that were inserted into a box magazine.

The Mauser was a tried and tested design that had seen hard use in the Boer War and had proved to be both accurate and durable. It had only a five round magazine capacity, which could be a disadvantage in combat, but this was seldom a problem when used for sniping, and its long barrel gave it an edge over the Enfield for longer-range shooting. One drawback was the all-encompassing woodwork around the barrel, which was a problem by no means unique to the Mauser. The most accurate target rifles had long been known to be those with thick-walled free-floating barrels. In other words, no part of the barrel touched the wood from the breech forwards. The reason for this is barrel harmonics, for when a shot is fired the barrel will vibrate at a certain pitch, somewhat like a tuning fork. As long as this is allowed to happen then each shot will be as accurate as the previous one, but the military insistence on covering barrels with wood to protect them and prevent the soldier from burning himself, while laudable, did little to help accuracy, for any part of the woodwork that touched the barrel interfered with the harmonics. Some shooters believed that by carefully packing the barrel to support it, accuracy could be improved, but this was not the case unless the barrel was so tightly supported as to be utterly rigid and this is well-nigh impossible when using wood as a medium for bedding, for some space has to be left to permit barrel expansion on firing. The problem that arose in the wet conditions found in trench warfare was that the soaked wood expanded, pressing against the barrel, and this was never satisfactorily resolved.

Early war German sniping rifles can be categorised into two basic types, the pre-war commercial and purpose made wartime examples. In 1914 the Army requisitioned a large number of optically-equipped hunting rifles (*Jagdgewehre mit Handelsüblichen Zielfernrohre*) which were gathered up by the Duke of Ratibor, who had been tasked to secure as many as he could find. There are various estimates as to the numbers involved but it is probably in the region of 8,000 to 15,000. While they served as a useful stopgap, most were too fragile to withstand the rigours of warfare and few survived long in service. In the meantime rifle factories such as Mauser Werk, Sauer and Sohn and Carl Walther were instructed that rifles which proved of superior accuracy during test firing should be put to one side to be converted to *Scharfschützen-Gewehr 98* (Sharpshooter Gew. 98).

The Mauser's great advantage from the point of view of sniping was in the design of its receiver. This had two very solid mounting points for scope bases, the rear bridge above the bolt, and over the chamber. It is a contentious point as to whether this was a deliberate design feature; the answer is almost certainly not, but it was undoubtedly very convenient. With no official military pattern of mounts or telescopic sight in use, there was no single standard type of fitting, with each maker using the system that they believed to be best, although all were roughly similar in function and most scopes were of similar type. As a result there are an almost limitless number of variations on a theme between scopes, mounts and bases to be found on these rifles but almost all were of the claw-mount type, using hooked lugs and a locking spring catch to retain the scope in its mountings. Both civilian and military personnel were employed in the exacting task of fitting the telescopic sights. To mount the scope, the machined steel bases were loosely screwed into place on the rifle and the scope and mounts fitted. The scope was collimated (mated to the bore) and the bases were then soldered and screwed in place. The rifle was placed into a special cradle and test-fired to ensure the scope was properly zeroed. The body of the telescopic sight, which was not intended to be used on any other weapon, was engraved or stamped with the serial number of the rifle. This meant that even identical makes of scope and mounts would not prove to be easily interchangeable due to fractional tolerance differences.

Elevation was by means of an adjuster drum on the top of the scope body, windage was by means of a worm screw fitted to the rear mount, turned by a small key supplied in the scope carry case. This enabled the rear mount to be moved left or right although the drawback was that the front mount, being fixed, could not move, so any major adjustment could put a strain on the body of the scope and cause damage. In practice this seldom happened as the amount of windage adjustment that needed to be done by the sniper was tiny, enough to zero in a new batch of ammunition, or deal with a consistently strong side wind. To counteract this problem, some rifles were also fitted with a front dovetail mount, based on a pre-war commercial design, that could be finely adjusted to give a precise zero. All original sniping rifles had turned-down bolt handles but only some had a 'U' shaped cut-out in the woodwork to accommodate the handle.

This was simply dependent on the type of mounts used. Low ones gave insufficient clearance for the bolt handle on cocking, and it would foul the scope body. Putting a few degrees of additional bend on it provided clearance, but at the cost of trapping the shooter's fingers between the bolt and woodwork next to the receiver. The cut-out eliminated this problem. Most German scope mounts also permitted the standard iron sights to be used when the scope was in place, for German rifles with offset bases used curved mounts to place the telescopic sights as close above the bore as possible. The benefit of the offset mounts was that the sniper's line of sight for the standard iron sights was unhampered.

Although it is often overlooked, in 1914 the Austro-Hungarian Army was also equipped with a good, issue sniping rifle, the Mannlicher Model 95, a straight-pull weapon that was fitted with German made scopes and mounts, and unusually there was also a scope-equipped carbine version. Aside from having a comparatively limited range their short barrels produced excessive muzzle flash and recoil, which would have been difficult to conceal. It has been suggested that they were made for alpine units, for whom long rifles were cumbersome to carry, but it is difficult to understand what use a carbine sniping rifle could have been put to at the sort of ranges at which mountain fighting took place. The Mannlicher rifles often used Oigee or C. P. Goerz scopes with a distinctive spring release catch underneath the rear body of the scope.

German Optics

If the opposing powers facing each other were fairly well matched in terms of rifles and ammunition, the same could not be said of the situation regarding optics. Arguably the finest quality glass had begun to be produced in 1884 at the Glastechnisches Lab in Jena, Austria, later to become the Schott Glaswerke. They had perfected the science of making superior optical glass, and they continue to supply much of the world's demand for this commodity. This enabled long established companies such as Zeiss and Voigtlander to produce what were possibly the best telescopic sights available in the world and they had a virtual monopoly. By 1914 there were numerous makers in Germany – Fuess, Gerard, Oigee, Voigtlander, Goertz, Bock, Zeiss, Busch, Hensoldt, among many others,

An arquebuser of the Tudor period, with .50 calibre smoothbore matchlock musket. He holds the matchcord in his right hand and carries a sword for close protection. Although outwardly primitive, these muskets were capable of penetrating armour at 55 yards (50 metres).

An irregular American militiaman of the Revolutionary Wars. His long-barrelled rifled musket was capable of 328 yard (300 metre) accuracy and he carried everything he required to survive in the wild. British soldiers found these men a formidable foe.

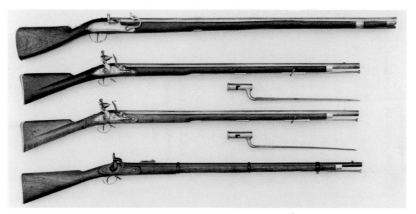

The issue muskets for the British Army from 1670 to 1853. From top: Matchlock, two India Pattern Muskets (or Brown Bess as it was more commonly called) and Pattern 1853 Enfield rifled-musket. The first was barely able to hit a target at 87 yards (80 metres), the last was capable of 1,094 yard (1,000 metre) accuracy. (Courtesy of the Board of the Royal Armouries)

The first sharpshooter of the British Army, a rifleman of the 95th Rifles, *c.*1805. He wears a practical green uniform and carries a .62 calibre Baker rifled musket, the first such weapon issued to British front-line infantry. It could outshoot any musket on the battlefield of the time.

A scoped .40 calibre percussion rifle by W.H.Barnes of Boston, c.1840, with early Malcolm-type telescopic sight. These heavy barrelled target rifles were extremely accurate and hundreds were carried to war by union and confederate soldiers although generally they were too heavy and fragile for military use. This example was carried by a Massachusetts sharpshooter.

A dead Confederate sharpshooter at Gettysburg. He appears to have been using an Enfield rifle, widely regarded as the best long-range rifle then available.

A group of Boer *Kommandos* camped in the veldt. Their rifles are Mauser M.1888s, with which they were deadly shots, particularly at long range.

A German sniper post, *c*.1915. The snipers are using loopholes, but two snipers working this close together was unwise, and would inevitably lead to discovery and retaliation.

A German NCO with a hunting rifle and massive scope. Commercial rifles were commonly used early in the war and provided they were carefully looked-after, were very effective. Lack of 8 mm hunting ammunition proved to be a long-term problem, however.

Vernon Hesketh-Prichard, the man whose determination and enthusiasm led to the eventual formation of British sniper schools and an effective training programme.

A British sniper post, possibly in a forward sap on the front lines. There is minimal cover and the snipers must have been confident that there were no German snipers facing them. The rifle appears to be an SMLE with PP Co. scope.

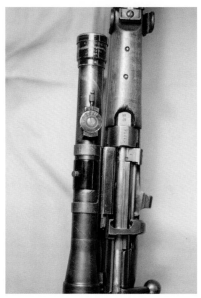

A Galilean sight, in this instance an Ulster or Neill sight. The objective lens which clamped to the muzzle has a black aiming dot visible and the ocular sight, which mounted to the safety-catch screw has a small magnifying lens. Such sights were simple, relatively cheap and, in good weather conditions, surprisingly effective.

An SMLE with PP Company mount and Aldis scope fitted. This was the most commonly used set-up in the British Army, but suffered from the offset of the scope to the left, which made aiming very awkward.

A Gew.98 with an Oigee scope and rare 20 round magazine. The offset claw mounts are visible, as is the dismounting lever on the rear mount. The magazine proved impractical in trench conditions.

An Australian sniper waits for his observer (to the right, out of camera-shot) to signal a target. He would then snap-shoot over the parapet. Kangaroo hunters were particularly adept at this risky past-time. (Courtesy of the Australian War Memorial)

A French sniper in the Artois region waits for a target during the First World War.

An unusual photo of an Austrian sniper with what seems to be a Mauser M.1895 carbine. This would at first seem to be an odd choice for sniping, having very limited range, but would actually be quite practical in areas where long-range shooting was seldom possible.

produced hunting telescopic sights that in 1914 needed no modification to be adopted as military sights.

There had been some significant improvements in the science of telescopic sight manufacture since the 1860s and Germany had led the way. Lenses had become larger, permitting better light transfer with an improved field of view of between 6° and 8°. With the exception of the Zeiss prismatic scope, all of the German makers used the erecting system, usually with five lenses and a graticule that could be either lengths of fine wire or be etched on the glass itself. Etching had its advantages over wire, for although it introduced another glass surface into the body of the scope, it was less prone to damage from shock and temperature and could use any form of graticule pattern desired. There were many different types used in these scopes, although the most common was the vertical post and horizontal bar pattern, and the crosshairs were designed so as to leave a measurable gap that aided the sniper in range judgement. The distance between the cross bar and vertical post on the Oigee scope equated to 6 inches at 100 yards (15 cms at 90 metres), about the width of a human head, and at 300 yards (270 metres) the gap equated to 18 inches (450 mm), the width of a human body. In fact the type of graticule used actually made little difference in shooting terms, although individual snipers each had their own preferences. However, Germany was not alone in making advances, for the Allies were also determined to win the sniping war.

Allied Rifles

Surprisingly, the British Army had broken with tradition and taken quite a radical decision in opting to replace the Boer War period Long Lee Enfield with a more compact rifle, acceptable to both infantry and cavalry, and doing away with the need for manufacturing both a rifle and carbine. The Short, Magazine Lee Enfield (SMLE) was adopted in 1903 and was destined to be Britain's longest serving rifle, not being declared obsolete until replaced by the FN-designed L1A1 SLR in 1954. It was beautifully made but it was not cheap, a pre-war Lee Enfield costing £3 10s ($5) at a time when the average weekly wage for a semi-skilled man was £2 ($3). In the hands of a very experienced shooter it could be reasonably accurate out to 1,000 yards, but as a battle rifle 400 yards was the maximum range for a good shot to guarantee to hit his target. The SMLE proved to be an excellent combat rifle but it was never designed to be a sniping weapon, and it was deficient in a number of areas. It had a comparatively short barrel, at 24½ inches (623 mm) it was shorter than those of most other countries with the exception of the American Springfield, and while this did not radically affect its performance at the normal ranges for trench sniping (between 100 and 300 yards) it did not make the Enfield a particularly good choice for longer range shooting. Some shooters felt that the action was not as smooth as that of the Mauser, and it, too, suffered from being enclosed in wood. Major T. Freemantle, commander of the 2nd Army School of Sniping, calculated that a deviation of just .001 (one thousandth) of an inch caused by pressure on the barrel would result in an alteration in the point of impact of 9 inches at 500 yards, enough to entirely miss a target.[86] Some Canadian sniper units, equipped with the Ross rifle, simply cut all the forward woodwork off their rifles, freeing the barrels from any pressure and improving their accuracy and consistency, but such sacrilegious treatment was not encouraged in the British Army. Of greater concern than long-range accuracy was the fact that the design of breech and receiver made the fitting of any mounts for a telescopic sight on an SMLE an awkward business. There was in fact an alternative rifle already available had the British War Office sought to find a solution, and this was the Pattern 1914 Mk. 1*. Based on the Mauser action, the P14 had originally been devised to chamber a new .276 inch cartridge and while very accurate it was not considered strong enough to be adopted as a battle rifle. At a time when the ability to mass-produce service rifles was of paramount importance, setting up new production facilities to manufacture the P14 was deemed impractical and it was thus sidelined in the early stages of the war, so Britain lost the chance of adopting what was subsequently to prove an excellent sniping weapon.

It is a fallacy, however, that Britain possessed no optically equipped rifles at all in 1914. A very small number of big game rifles used in the trenches were equipped with scopes, mostly of pre-war German patterns and nearly all of these were in the hands of officers, many of whom did sterling service with them, although for the most part their sniping careers were unhappily brief. One unnamed officer in the Staffordshire Regiment used a scoped

Mauser rifle, belonging to a relative, that had been a pre-war gift from the Kaiser, and Second Lieutenant Oliver of the 2nd Battalion Durham Light Infantry used a Ross rifle equipped with a scope, with which he was famously photographed. Possibly the best documented commercial rifle was the Model 1905 .280 Ross used by Lieutenant L. Greener, of the Greener gunmaking family. This was fitted with a Carl Zeiss Prismatic scope, and he achieved 54 confirmed kills with it before being killed while on patrol in No-Man's Land. This is not to say that Britain, or its Commonwealth allies, were totally devoid of any shooting talent in the ranks. Far from it, for target shooting was a hugely popular sport, and the big annual contest at Bisley was hard-fought, attracting competitors from all over the world. E. Penberthy and N. A. Armstrong, (later to become Commandant of the 2nd Army School of Sniping) were both well known and enthusiastic target shooters, and many men who joined the colours in 1914 were able to put their target shooting skills to good use in the flat fields of France and Flanders. There were also some countrymen in the ranks who were adept at knocking over a fast rabbit with a single shot but sadly in the early months of the war many of these potential snipers were killed as they tried single-handedly to take on the better trained and equipped Germans. Sergeant J. K. Forbes, 4th Gordon Highlanders, was typical of many who served in the early months of the war. A very skilled shot, he took it on himself to be his company's unofficial sniper, but with no training or special equipment he recorded the difficulties of locating the Germans in his diary:

I stand on the firestep, head and shoulders above the parapet and peer into the doubtful shadows. Of a sudden something catches my attention there. Surely it is a man ... I grabbed my rifle ... when our patrol went out that night there was no trace of a dead German despite many shots fired.[87]

The well-intentioned, but amateur attempts by British soldiers to take on the Germans at their own game were doomed to failure. As the number of British casualties increased, so grew the demand from frontline officers for some means by which this new menace could be combated. It was now clear that the German sharpshooters were working in a methodical and carefully orchestrated manner and increasingly, letters home from the British trenches mentioned a new terror – the 'sniper'. It is from this period that a hitherto little-used slang term began to be assimilated into everyday language. Why it should have happened at this particular time is a mystery, although the most likely explanation is that it was used by British regular army soldiers who had returned from service in India to fight in France in 1914. Whatever its origin, it caught on quickly and the press were soon reporting on the new menace threatening Tommy at the front. Officers quickly discovered that the psychological effects of having a German sniper in the vicinity often outweighed the actual physical damage that they did. Men became nervous and were reluctant to move from the safety of the trenches. Crum commented that such was the proliferation of sniping that 'a man might be hit standing at his post from what seemed to be behind, and this ... caused that lack of confidence known to the troops as "getting the wind up"'.[88] Such was the nuisance the shooting caused that for want of any means of response, artillery was often called up to deal with the sniper, assuming his position could be identified or shells were available. As a response this was wasteful and frequently ineffectual, but at least it made the soldiers feel better, until the next shot arrived.

The Allies Fight Back

It was evident that Germany held a commanding lead in the field of sniping at the start of the war, and Britain needed both men and equipment to fight the Germans on equal terms. Initially they found an answer in the form of a simple optical sight that had been in existence for some 300 years, the Galilean sight. These magnifying sights had found favour with pre-war target shooters and several makes existed: Lattey, Martin, Neill (also known as the Barnett or Ulster sight) and the Gibbs. Because so little has been written about them, there is a general assumption that they were only rarely used or proved so ineffective as to be regarded as near useless. In fact there is strong evidence that they were purchased and used in considerable numbers. Colonel Freemantle, in his manual on sniping devoted some four pages to their description and use, something he was unlikely to do for an item that had no practical use in the field. War Office figures for late 1915 and early 1916 show 9,000 Lattey, 4,250 Neill, 775

Martin and 100 Gibbs had been supplied to frontline regiments.[89] They were not particularly cheap, with the Gibbs costing £5, the Martin £3, the Barnett £1 10s (£1.50), and the simple mass-produced Lattey, a more modest seven shillings and sixpence (38p).[90] They all took a broadly similar form, with an objective lens of between 1 and 1½ inches diameter and an eyepiece that consisted of either a small concave lens that fitted to the back sight or an aperture type rear sight. Their power was low, around 2×, and aiming was by means of either a centrally painted dot on the objective lens (Martin, Neill), pointer and crosshair (Gibbs) or in the case of the Lattey, using the foresight blade itself to provide the image. Some empirical testing was done with both a Lattey and a Martin on a 1916 production SMLE to gauge how effective they might have been and the results were interesting. Generally, the sights proved surprisingly effective when used in good weather. Target acquisition was good, particularly as movement could be detected easily on either side of the foresight which, unlike a telescopic sight tube, does not block the shooter's peripheral view. They did improve the shooter's ability to pick out targets in poor light, although with nowhere near the efficiency of a telescopic sight. On the down side, vision was impaired by moisture which settled on the foresight and the field of view was poor, although the clear vision on either side of the objective lens did counteract this to a certain extent. They were also prone to working loose due to recoil, but if used within their limitations, they were certainly an improvement on the human eye and in ideal conditions would enable a competent rifleman to make a head shot at around 300 yards (270 metres).

Pre-war aperture target sights, with their micro-adjustable rear sight, could also be easily fitted to a service rifle and gave a sharper definition to the target. Throughout the war there were snipers who proved very competent indeed with these, and they did not suffer from the shortcomings associated with optical sights. They were particularly useful in that when not required, they could be folded flat against the receiver of the rifle. The majority were manufactured by BSA, Parker Hale, Westley-Richards or Alex Martin. There are also surviving records showing Government purchases of commercial telescopic sights in late 1914 and early 1915 and these total some 2,914 items.[91] Among them were German Zeiss, Goerz and Voigtlanders, British Watts, Aldis, Rigby, Evans and Winchester scopes.

These were fitted to SMLEs by all manner of mounts and bases, designed and produced by almost every gunmaker who had the facility for doing so. Some, such as the Rigby, Purdey, Holland and Holland and Evans, were well designed and extremely solidly constructed, others rather less so. The Army also made use of captured German scopes, and there is at least one example of a German claw mount fitted to an SMLE held in the MOD Pattern Room collection.[92] If the list of scopes and mounts available at this time appears somewhat haphazard, so was their issue. Some rifles went to soldiers who had achieved marksman status in training, others were issued to men who simply professed an interest in shooting or had target shooting experience. Their efficiency in the hands of this largely untrained soldiery was at best questionable, and at worst a downright liability. In most instances, the British Army had no real idea of the true nature of sniping or the capabilities of sniping rifles, and frequently issued orders for their use that were wholly inappropriate. Canadian sniper Herbert McBride, who admired the enthusiasm of the British snipers but was largely unimpressed at their standard of shooting early on in the war, commented on this waste after observing a pair of British snipers equipped with scoped rifles, shooting at distant German targets:

> The nearest enemy targets were at least eleven or twelve hundred yards away … my personal experience has been that the firing of single shots at individual targets, at ranges of more than a thousand yards is just a waste of time and ammunition. I just had to admire their spirit even if their judgement was bad. I ventured to ask the officer if he thought it was worth while to shoot at targets located a mile or more off, and he replied they were acting under orders.[93]

The situation was improving though, for by the spring of 1915 Britain was becoming better organised and developing the means of producing weapons to wage war on a truly monumental scale. There were now no fewer than 19 firms occupied in the supply and setting up of scoped SMLEs, and a long overdue specification for a sniping rifle was finally sanctioned on 4 May 1915. The contract, No. S.A.390,[94] was offered out to tender by the War Office for the production and supply of a telescopic sight and mount capable of meeting stringent requirements and being easily fitted to the service Mk. III Lee Enfield. Two firms, the Periscopic Prism Company of London, and Aldis Bros. of Hall Green, Birmingham, initially offered to meet these requirements. The system of supply was convoluted, for the scopes and mounts were to be properly mounted but their range drums had to remain unmarked. The rifles were then sent in batches to Bisley ranges where they were carefully test-fired. Each rifle was expected to group at 2 minutes of angle (2 inches) at 100 yards. The drums were then scribed with the relevant elevation marks and on their return all rifles had to be submitted to the Chief Inspector of Small-Arms at Enfield Lock. Each rifle then had the appropriate scales engraved on the range drum, and the serial number of the rifle marked on the body of the scope. The regulations laid down strict procedures for the selection and testing of these rifles, stating 'if one fourth of any delivery was found to be inferior in any way to the contractor's sample, or contrary to the terms of this specification, the whole consignment will be liable to rejection'.[95]

Rifles were then supplied with a leather carrying-case for the scope, cleaning kit, lens cloth and packed in a wooden carry-case, and only then deemed suitable for issue. Typical of Government penny-pinching, the cost of transport for this work and moving the rifles to and from the ranges had to be met by the contractors. This contract was in fact eventually met by three main suppliers, The Periscopic Prism Company, (PP Co.) supplied some 4,830 units by the end of the war. Aldis which came a close second with 3,196 units and the commercially procured American Winchester A5 made up a further 907 rifles. In common with all telescopic sights at the time, the new instruments were prone to fogging up in wet or humid weather, particularly if carried in a damp carry-case, and it frequently proved impossible to dry them out. Presumably these minor problems were of little concern to the War Office, for some indication as to the value they placed on sniping rifles in general was evidenced in a communication received by XI Corps in July 1916 from GHQ. They requested advice as to 'whether the issue of sniping rifle cease in view of the urgent requirement for economy'.[96] Doubtless the various Corps sniping officers made their opinions known, as nothing further was heard of the matter.

It seems rather ironic in view of the care put into the manufacture of the Enfield rifle that the basic design of mounting should have been so impractical, for unlike the majority of telescopic-equipped Mausers, the Enfields were fitted with a design of scope that was mounted offset to the left. Why this happened is difficult to comprehend, the most widely accepted explanation being that the Ministry had little comprehension of the nature of sniping, and insisted that the SMLE retain its provision for charger loading, presumably so lone snipers could single-handedly beat off massed frontal attacks by waves of German infantry. This design presented the snipers with a number of problems. The first and most obvious was the inability to maintain the crucial 'cheek-weld' necessary to achieve consistent shooting. This is the contact between the cheek and the top of the stock, which enables the sniper to obtain correct eye-relief, rapid target acquisition and to maintain a relaxed posture, all of which are attainable with an over-bore mounted scope. The PP, Aldis and A5 were all offset, forcing the shooter to either aim with the left eye or raise his head from the stock to use his right eye. Many men wrapped field dressing packs round the stock to create a cheek pad, and some risked punishment by screwing a shaped wooden block to the stock. The other problem was the cause of much complaint, as Hesketh-Prichard noted:

> With the Government pattern of telescopic sight, which was set on the side of the rifle, it was impossible to see through the loopholes in the steel plates … as these loopholes were naturally narrow; and looking into the telescopic sight … one got nothing but a fine view of the inside of the steel plate and the side of the loophole. I believe this decision was taken in the War Office … who ever was responsible can have no knowledge whatever of the use of telescopic sights.[97]

This decision meant that under certain circumstances the Enfield rifle could not be brought to bear on a target that was at an extreme angle to the sniper, a problem the Germans did not have to contend with. Hesketh-Prichard's comments are very pertinent regarding the use of offset scopes and loopholes and there is little doubt that a number of German soldiers survived the war because of this design foible.

Ammunition Development

Regardless of his skill, a sniper and his rifle were of little use without high-quality ammunition, the importance of which had long been recognised by peacetime target shooters. Until 1900 most service ammunition was round nosed, for generally it was believed that a round nose gave a bullet greater 'knock-down' power, but experiments in Germany in 1905 had shown that greater range and stability could be achieved by the use of pointed bullets, without sacrificing any impact power. The pointed shape of the nose bent back the pressure wave in front of it and reduced drag. These new pointed bullets were called *spitzer* in German and, as a result of testing, America adopted the new bullet type in 1906, with Britain following suit in 1911. The construction of these bullets comprised a lead core with metal jacket although uniquely in the war the French continued to manufacture their bullets from a solid copper alloy.

Ballistic science was in its infancy but research clearly showed that the overall shape of a bullet had a considerable effect on its performance. It was further discovered that while the new pointed, flat-based German spitzer bullet was good at ranges where it was supersonic, at long range it proved to be a different story, for as its velocity became sub-sonic, the compression wave in front of the nose rapidly diminished and drag then became the primary factor affecting both stability and accuracy. To counteract this, streamlining was enhanced by tapering the rear of the bullet, to reduce the drag effect as air flowed over it, and these were referred to as 'boat-tail' bullets. This design gave remarkable benefits, increasing the absolute range of a standard service bullet by up to 1,500 yards. The Gew. 98 rifle was chambered for the standard 7.92 mm S-Patrone (*Spitzgeschoss Patrone*) cartridge for which there was no special sniping ammunition issued, but in terms of ballistic performance over the previous generation of black powder ammunition even the standard ammunition was a huge step forwards. For the early-war German snipers using pre-war commercial rifles this posed a problem for many were chambered for the old round-nosed Patrone-88 ammunition. When used with the new spitzer ammunition (particularly the heavy S.m.K armour-piercing round) the barrels could fail. Commercial rifles were often inlet with a small engraved plate with an outline of the Pat.88 bullet and the words 'NÜR FUR PATRONE-88, KEINE S-MUNITION VERWENDEN' denoting that the rifle was to be used only with the old Pat.88 ammunition. There was also a downside to the spitzer ammunition, in that the new shape caused heavy erosion in the barrel and it was initially issued for machine-gun use only, snipers being warned against it because of the rapid wear it caused in barrels, advice which most of them cheerfully ignored.

What this actually meant in terms of practical performance was not immediately appreciated by the majority of soldiers, but these improvements had many implications for accurate shooting, for they not only affected bullet velocities, trajectory and drift but the more efficient bullets also created a change in the type and severity of wounds inflicted, and gave rise to the Great War myth of the 'explosive' or 'tampered' bullet. Major T. Freemantle made the point simply in his instructional guide to British sniping techniques that 'the MkVII [.303] bullet travels about twice as fast as the [.450 inch] Martini-Henry, and 20% faster than the MkVI that was in use until four years ago'.[98] Many soldiers who served during the war believed with total conviction that the Germans (and their snipers in particular) routinely used explosive or 'tampered' bullets, often referred to as 'dum-dums'.[99] Such comments were engendered by the average soldier's lack of understanding of the power of a service rifle cartridge, and the severity of wounds caused by its high velocity bullet. A .303 inch bullet travelling at 2,700 feet/sec moves up the rifle bore with pressure of 18 tons per square inch behind it, spinning at a rate of 2,900 revolutions per second. The energy generated is impressive when translated into practical terms. At 100 yards it is capable of penetrating 9 inches (228 mm) of solid brickwork, 14 inches (355 mm) of the lime mortar used to bind bricks together, 18 inches (457 mm) of hard-packed earth or sand-filled sandbags or 4½ feet (1.37 metres) of loose piled earth.[100] It comes as little surprise then, that the human body, with the density of a bar of soap, topped by a skull equivalent in strength to a jelly-filled teapot, was especially vulnerable to such projectiles, and would suffer accordingly. Head shots invariably totally emptied the brain cavity and limb bones would be shattered into fragments. Yet myths are nothing if not enduring, and even 70 years after the war, veterans interviewed by the author insisted friends had been killed by the use of these tampered or dum-dum bullets. Frederick Sleath referred to a typical incident in a trench in 1915:

Just after evening stand-to, he was standing on the fire-step with the sergeant and another sniper, gazing over No-Man's Land. It seemed impossible for them to be seen by the Germans. A bullet sang between officer and sergeant. Their companion slid down into the bottom of the trench with a hole in his head into which a man could have put his fist. 'Tampered bullet' the sergeant said curtly.[101]

In fact, no sniper who wanted to stand any chance of making an accurate shot would have dreamed of tampering with his ammunition. Altering the physical properties of a bullet, by cutting or filing the tip down, would lighten it, radically altering its ballistic properties and changing its point of impact as well as possibly destabilising it. Nevertheless it was widely believed throughout the war that this was a common practice used by the Germans. Sleath made clear his own attitude on the matter when, having captured a German sniper, he ordered him to hand over his equipment:

'Let me see your ammunition.' The German unloosed his cartridge belt and handed it over to him. The bullets were regulation pattern. Had they been tampered with, the Sniper would have been inclined to shoot the man at once.[102]

However, there was truth in the stories of the Germans' use of reversed bullets, but for entirely practical reasons. Early in the war, experimenting on steel plates they had discovered an odd phenomenon. If a bullet was extracted from its cartridge case, then reversed and reinserted, firing it base-first at a steel plate would enable the projectile to penetrate it. It was a very early use of what was to become, in artillery terms, the armour-piercing hollow charge and it seems certain that some snipers carried these rounds for dealing with hard targets prior to the issue of proper armour-piercing ammunition. Hesketh-Prichard noted that 'the occasional snipers on the Hun side reversed their bullets … because we were continually capturing clips of such bullets'.[103] The Germans were of course a step ahead of the Allies in supply of armour-piercing ammunition and from late 1915 onwards, there was a supply of S.m.K AP ammunition available on a limited basis to snipers.

The manufacture of all service ammunition was rigidly controlled and throughout the war quality generally remained high. Despite this, a major problem faced by all snipers was in finding a brand or 'lot' of ammunition that was of consistent quality, for the accuracy of any shot depended upon the consistency of the ammunition, the bullets of which must be totally uniform in size and weight, matched to precisely measured powder charges, with high quality primers and uniform case sizes. Once a rifle and scope had been zeroed for a given lot of ammunition, use of any other, even the same make but with a different batch or lot number, would almost certainly shift the point of zero. Britain, America and Canada all manufactured .303 inch ammunition and as none could supply special ammunition for use by snipers, it was left to the men themselves to determine what worked best. Herbert McBride, one of the most experienced shooters wrote:

> there were several brands made by the old, established companies and Government arsenals that were really up to standard and could be depended on to function properly at all times and when we came upon any of these particular brands, we made a point to hide all we could.[104]

Generally, cartridges made by Kynoch, Royal Laboratories and Greenwood and Batley were among the more favoured British makes. Winchester was seen as good but other American ammunition was regarded with suspicion, particularly by Canadians armed with the fastidious Ross. Many had had bad experiences with US-manufactured ammunition that had poorly annealed brass, which expanded in the chamber and prevented extraction or enabled the rim to be torn off by the extractor.

Sniping on Gallipoli

The landings at Gallipoli on 25 April 1915 had raised the possibility of opening an Allied second front, that would not only enable the Allies to supply Russia with equipment but also destroy Turkish resistance and bring about a speedy end to the war. It was a fine theory but no one expected the largely conscripted Turkish Army to display the level of bravery and soldierly qualities that equalled anything the British and Canadians faced in France. Neither had the Allied commanders expected the Turks to have shooting skills that in many instances matched or exceeded those of the ANZAC forces. The trenches that were soon established were the perfect arena for sniping, and a war within a war began in earnest. The Turkish infantryman was armed with a 7.65 mm Mauser rifle basically similar to the German Gew. 98 and many Turks, like their Australian and New Zealander counterparts, had grown up using rifles to hunt. From the first day of arrival, Allied casualties from head shots were alarmingly high and the soldiers quickly became adept at keeping low. Those who didn't paid the price:

> We lost twelve men each day ... as they stood up from their cooking at the brazier ... or carelessly raised their heads to look back at ships in the bay, and in the night there were sudden screams where a sentry had moved his head too often against the moon.[105]

The Turks had no access to optically-equipped rifles, and their shots were made using ordinary iron sights. Like the Germans, the Turkish Army certainly had some tactical advantages, for they were holding most of the high ground, enabling them to fire down into the Allied lines. However, within the ranks of the ANZAC forces were many fine shots, in particular the kangaroo hunters of the Australian outback and the New Zealand deer hunters. Their skills were almost tailor–made for sniping for they had learned how to observe silently and use cover, and they had rapid reflexes and the ability to make an accurate snap-shot at ranges of up to 300 yards. Probably the greatest exponent of this, and a man who was to become legendary during the campaign, was Billy Sing of the 5th Light Horse. Of mixed Indian and English parentage, Billy was of unprepossessing appearance, described by his spotter, Ion Idriess as 'a little chap, very dark, with a jet black moustache and goatee beard'. Sing used a standard Mk. III Lee Enfield, that was possibly fitted with an aperture sight, and his methods were simple but effective. His spotter would wait until a careless Turk showed himself, but Sing would not shoot until the victim had grown confident enough to guarantee that his snap-shot would hit its mark. He would ready his rifle and at his spotter's command would rise and shoot. His best confirmed tally for one day was nine. So feared was he that in a scene reminiscent of a Hollywood film, two Turkish counter-snipers were sent to deal with him. One almost succeeded, smashing the scout telescope being held by his observer, Tom Sheehan, the spent bullet smacking Sing on the shoulder. By the end of the campaign, Sing's tally was over 200, and afterwards he continued to serve on the Western Front, eventually gaining a DCM and MM.

No ANZAC soldiers were employed specifically as snipers, but the requirement for men to combat the Turkish menace gave many the chance to achieve high scores. Others were simply enthusiastic shots but unskilled in the finer points of sniping. Nevertheless they took on the Turks at their own game, with mixed success. Initially, sniping took the simple but dangerous form of using a mirror to spot for targets, then taking a quick shot over the parapet. It wasn't always successful, many shooters themselves falling victim to Turkish sniping, as Private Frank Brent later wrote:

> The bloke next to me was Robbie Robinson, a corporal in my Battalion. I can just see him now grinning all over his face and the next thing his head fell on my shoulder. A sniper had got him through the jugular vein. I really think that was my baptism as Robbie's blood spent all over my tunic.[106]

So desperate were the troops to find some method of fighting back that the Royal Navy were asked to supply boilerplate that could be used to make loophole plates. Some snipers such as an Australian Sergeant named Brennan, a cook with the 7th Light Horse, were only able to work part-time. After his duties were finished for the morning he would work his way down the line, looking for Turkish sniper posts reported to him by the men, then he would settle down to wait for a chance to even the score. As they became more adept at camouflage and fieldcraft, the ANZAC snipers established specific sniping posts on any usable high ground and began to adopt the paired system of observation as it was quickly appreciated that fatigue and eye strain could be alleviated by having one man resting while the other watched. Even so, the snipers were often themselves sniped:

> My best mate and I used to go on the firing step together in Lone Pine. One morning moving into Lone Pine trenches one soldier just ahead of me turned

to his mate and said 'Come on, Dick you and I will go on together this time.'
One used a periscope to see what Johnnie Turk was doing. The other was
ready for any quick sniping at anything that moved. The next minute 'bang'
Dick got a bullet right though the head, and he fell at our feet. He made no
sound at all. He was still alive when the stretcher bearers took him down …
but he died there. We think an enemy sniper must have been just out in front
using slight ground cover waiting for our relief guard to come in. I made sure
I got that sniper later on.[107]

While the ANZAC armies all possessed extremely capable men their
sniping abilities were hampered by the lack of suitably equipped rifles and
their successes were achieved using open-sighted rifles sometimes equipped
with target aperture rear sights. While many British-made sights had,
pre-war, found their way to Australia and New Zealand, the most
commonly found make was the BSA-Martin, by virtue of the fact that it
was manufactured under licence in Australia. These had been in
widespread use for competition target shooting since about 1907 and many
of the ANZACs who flocked to the recruiting offices in 1914 carried their
sights with them. They proved particularly useful for sniping on Gallipoli,
as did a number of Galilean pattern sights, such as the Lattey and Neill,
where no other forms of optical equipment were available. On Gallipoli
most sniping activity had been informal local counter-sniping and it was
not until early 1916, when ANZAC troops began to arrive in France, that
any formal sniper training was given to them. All colonial units by then
were using the same SMLE rifles as their British counterparts, but in
general their snipers were not overly impressed with it, and after the war
the Australian Army went on develop its own rifle, based on a much
improved version of the faithful SMLE.

5

THE FIRST WORLD WAR: THE FIGHT BACK, 1916–18

Not for nothing were the early British snipers jocularly referred to as 'The Suicide Squad', but the situation was gradually improving. By the latter months of 1915 a steady trickle of optically equipped rifles became available and were finding their way to the front line. Not that their arrival necessarily heralded effective use in skilled hands as Hesketh-Prichard noted:

> I had gone down on duty … and there found a puzzled looking private with a beautiful new rifle fitted with an Evans telescopic sight. I examined the elevating drum and saw that it was set for 100 yards. 'Look here,' I said, 'You have got this sight set for a hundred. The Hun trenches are four hundred yards away.' The private looked puzzled.
> 'Have you ever shot with this rifle?' I asked.
> 'No Sir.'
> 'Do you understand it?'
> 'No Sir.'
> 'How did you get it?'
> 'It was issued to me as trench stores sir.'
> 'Who by?'
> 'The Quartermaster, Sir.'[108]

If Britain were still somewhat deficient in its shooting equipment in 1915, then the same cannot be said of the efforts made to train snipers. Some officers of the calibre of Crum, Penberthy, Freemantle, Richardson and Hesketh-Prichard had managed, through a mixture of enthusiasm, astute lobbying and practical demonstration, to form their own quasi-official sniping training schools in early 1915. As Crum said:

> We were full of ideas ... the scandal of hundreds of men getting bowled over simply from want of teaching and imagination, stirred us to great efforts so that in addition to building a range in a chalk quarry close by, and greatly improving our marksmanship we were able to give demonstrations to troops resting out of the line.[109]

However, official acceptance for the formation of organised training schools was to come in early 1916, when the first Scouting, Observation and Sniping (SOS) training schools were set up, one for the 1st Army at Linghem, a second for the 2nd Army at Acq and a third for the 4th Army at Bouchon. Immediately, improvised courses started, staffed for the most part by enthusiastic officers and NCOs. These men were prepared to put any amount of effort into ensuring they turned out the best possibly trained snipers. Initially it was believed that instructing officers who could then return to their regiments and teach their men would be the best method, but in practice it proved to be an inefficient means of producing snipers. The comments of the commander of the 3rd Army SOS, Major Penberthy, on the difficulties of setting up the schools are illuminating:

> The intensive character of the training is obvious when such a range of subjects was covered in ten days by students who in most cases had never seen a military map, a prismatic compass ... in their lives before. We were supposed to teach in the days what I would not undertake to teach in peace-time to do in under six months.[110]

It was determined that the British sniper sections should comprise 16 men, plus one corporal and one sergeant under the command of a Sniping Officer. In practice, because of training, leave and wounds, an actual battalion sniping establishment varied, but was frequently no more than eight or ten men at any given time. The content of the training courses was based on practical experience, for most of the instructors had considerable peacetime shooting experience as well as having learned the basic art of sniping in the front lines. Some, such as the 1st Army's Lieutenant Gray, of the Scottish Rifles, was not only a regimental sniping officer but also a highly skilled target shooter whose knowledge of all forms of accurate shooting was of incalculable value to the sniping schools.[111] These schools gradually began to work towards a common syllabus, which naturally included shooting, but which also placed strong emphasis on other disciplines. Patience, good reflexes and consistency were more valuable traits than extreme accuracy and it was soon realised that many men put forward for sniper training were unsuitable. However, many times the most unpromising turned out to be most adept, as Major N. Armstrong, commander of the 2nd SOS commented, the best were 'game hunters, trappers, prospectors, surveyors lumberjacks and poachers'. Bisley standard accuracy wasn't required, as Major Penberthy pointed out:

> It is interesting to note that experience showed us that a good 'competition' shot of say, a high Bisley meeting standard did not necessarily make a good sniper. There is the width of the world between the leisurely peace-time business of firing at a distinct target at a known or easily calculated range ... and getting one quick and accurate shot at such almost invisible and momentary targets as the Bosches presented.[112]

Some men, despite their best efforts, turned out to be poor shots but excellent observers, and they would be attached to sniper units purely in that capacity. Many men who applied for sniper training suffered from what would now be seen as a psychological inability to deal with the particular form of warfare that was required, but most were determined to fight the Germans at their own game and as one commented:

> Being a sniper wasn't like being in close combat. I never took any pleasure in sniping, and I don't want to think that I'd killed anyone, although you'd never really know if you had or not. My job was to prevent them from killing us, but not to kill them unless they were a real danger to us, then we had to deal with them of course.[113]

The courses varied slightly between the different corps but all normally lasted fourteen days and covered a multitude of practical skills. The course at Acq, always slightly theatrical and occasionally controversial, covered:

> Mind body and spirit. Sniping: Shooting, quick eye; Loopholes and Sniper's Posts; What to look for and how to look; Visibility and cunning; Observation: Observation Posts and What to Observe; Information for Artillery, Trench Mortars and Rifle Grenades and catapults; Reporting Results of observation; sketching and map reading; Other duties requiring picked men; Messengers and guides, Scouts, Fixed rifles.[114]

Of all of the skills that needed to be taught to the neophyte snipers, the most difficult, as Hesketh-Prichard recalled, were the continual problems of learning to judge distance and estimate wind speed. Distance was generally easier to teach, as man-made features such as houses, telegraph poles and even window apertures gave a good indication of the range when compared to the height of a man. An average man is 24 inches (610 mm) from forehead to navel and at 300 yards (270 metres) this is a comparatively small target. While a head shot was the ideal, over or underestimating the range by even two feet would result in the bullet going over the target's head or landing around his knees. To optimise the chances of a kill, the snipers were therefore taught what the Germans had appreciated for some time, that with rifles zeroed at 300 yards (270 metres) the aiming point should be the teeth. While this seems macabre, it was entirely practical. A perfectly placed shot would not be deflected by the brittle teeth, and would result in instant death. If the range were incorrectly estimated, the chances are that a head or chest hit would still result, with generally fatal consequences. It was possible to survive such shots however. Lieutenant Siegfried Sassoon was the target of a German sniper on the Somme, whose range estimation was perhaps a little faulty, and whose shot struck low:

> No sooner had I popped my head out of the sap than I received what seemed like a tremendous blow in the back – between the shoulders. My first notion was that I had been hit by a bomb [grenade] from behind. What had really

happened was that I had been sniped from in front. Anyway, my attitude towards life and the war had been completely altered for the worse.[115]

Incredibly the bullet punched through Sassoon's chest and exited between his shoulders, without hitting anything vital. Unlike many of the German scopes, the pattern of graticules used on British scopes did not give the shooter any means of judging range through target measurement, so accurate estimation was vital. Neither could there be any leeway when it came to judging the wind, which as any shooter knows, usually blows in brief gusts. The SOS staff therefore taught by example – that there were six basic wind patterns, gentle, moderate, fresh, strong, very strong and gale and the men were shown how to use grass or trees to estimate the wind speed. A stalk of grass nodding gently would indicate a light breeze of perhaps 1–2 mph, whereas stalks being blown almost horizontal would show very strong winds of perhaps 12–15 mph. Most men became very adept at judging the wind, but anyone could get caught out by the unexpected. Private James Hills was instructed to deal with two German observers in front of new British positions and described how he crawled slowly through thick grass into No-Man's Land to reach his quarry:

I … carefully parted the grass with my .303 and the only thing that stopped me firing straight away were the bits of grass and poppies that blew in front of my rifle. I drew a bead on the first [German] … but just as I was going to fire a poppy blew in front of my eyes and I hit the second one instead. It was a beautiful shot and I was tickled pink by that. I put my head back down in the grass and lay there without moving for half an hour. I wasn't going to stick my head out for some retaliation. Eventually I moved my position back another fifty yards, which took about two hours because I had to work backwards on my elbows and toes. I couldn't move straight backwards, because when the sun shone it would show up a trail of flattened grass that could easily be seen, so I had to move sort of zig-zag … and I thought to myself, 'cor, what I wouldn't do for a cup of tea'.[116]

There were calculation charts available, giving degrees of adjustment for given ranges and wind speeds but many less educated soldiers had difficulty with the figures, besides, while range was easy to adjust, windage adjustment was often a difficult process and the men soon learned that the tried and tested method of 'aiming off' was quick and effective. To do this, the shooter needed to practise continually with his rifle and scope until he was absolutely sure where the point of impact would be, and Hesketh-Prichard devised a simple means of teaching whereby one instructor fired at the butt-stop in varying wind conditions, and the men observed through their telescopes where the bullets impacted:

> The puff of dust gave away the exact point at which the bullet struck. This system had the further advantage of teaching the snipers what a distance of two feet [windage] looks like at three hundred yards. But individual practice was the only way to learn wind-judging.[117]

To ensure consistency, a sniper had to learn how to support his rifle properly, breathe correctly and maintain the all-important 'cheek-weld' between his cheek and the butt of the rifle. He must maintain correct eye-relief for the telescopic sight as well as keeping steady his aim. Trigger pull had to be smooth and not snatched and the rifle had to be kept tight into the shoulder for the follow-through of the shot. Most riflemen had a tendency to lower the rifle immediately the shot was fired, which could not only affect their aim but made the chance of a follow-up shot impossible. One skill that was nearly impossible to teach, but was vital to survival, was that of patience and men either had it or did not. Hotheads rarely made good snipers and men who were anxious to 'get even' or possessed quick tempers seldom completed their training, or survived long afterwards if they did.

The schools went to a great deal of effort to replicate the trenches and teach sniper tactics. Not only did men have to know how to construct hides, but also how to use them correctly. Many men had died simply as a result of opening the curtained entrance to a sniper's post while the observation loophole was still open. The sudden flash of light would inevitably result in a retaliatory sniper's bullet. From summer 1915 the SOS schools had formulated a syllabus based on the broad mix of experience that the instructors had gained. At the start, much of the training was undertaken in makeshift camps, with the barest minimum of equipment. Men were asked to bring whatever their battalions could spare. With no standardisation, a wide assortment of rifles and optical devices appeared. One of the most basic needs of the snipers was for trench periscopes and spotting telescopes to enable them to observe the German lines. There had been many proprietary devices rushed on to the market in the first months of the war, some more useful than others. Crum noted in late 1915 that men turned up with:

> Ross periscope monocle glass and metal tube, Negretti and Zambra monocle glass and tubes, Sinclair's Una periscope and, a prism telescopic periscope … Zeiss and other good glasses converted to single glasses for use with periscopes.[118]

The men brought their own rifles, the majority of which were ordinary service weapons and virtually none were fitted with telescopic sights. Even the rare few rifles that were so equipped were often well past their first flush of youth, with damaged scopes or shot-out barrels, but hard-pressed quartermasters, short of good rifles, could hardly be blamed for sending men with less than perfect weapons. Many men sent on these courses were already battalion snipers with virtually no formal training, but the schools gave them an opportunity to be taught by professionals, and many needed it. Hesketh-Prichard commented dryly on one man whose sniping style, despite being equipped with a telescopic rifle, was to stick his head over the parapet, take a snapshot and duck back down again, and whose service career was likely to be measured in days rather than weeks. Courses behind the front lines were of necessity shorter duration, of around ten days, as men were required to return to their units as quickly as possible. The home-based schools established later in 1916 such as the one run by Northern Command at Rugeley in Staffordshire, lasted a more leisurely 17 days.

There were some differences in approach. Initially, the 1st Army at Linghem believed that it was best served in teaching instructors, who could then go out and pass on their skills at battalion level, although this opinion changed in the wake of experience, whereas the 2nd Army at Acq placed greater emphasis on training front-line snipers. In addition to normal shooting skills, men had to learn one mode of shooting that was alien to almost all of them, and this was shooting at night. Crum purchased welding goggles for the men to wear to enable them to become used to night vision, while other schools taught night shooting by the simple means of taking men onto the ranges in the dark. It was difficult to judge distance at night, so it was important that ranges were known. Generally this was not a problem as all snipers' posts had simple hand-drawn maps in them, giving detailed ranges for all of the visible landmarks within range.

During their daylight observation, the men were taught that anything out of the ordinary should be noted and reported, however insignificant, and these snipers' reports were to become a vital part of frontline intelligence gathering. In a case reported by Hesketh-Prichard, the daily appearance of a large tortoiseshell cat on the parapet of the German lines resulted in some debate among the snipers as to whether, being German, it was a legitimate target or not. In the end, it was left alone and its presence duly reported. The battalion intelligence officer, his curiosity roused, ordered some aerial photographs to be taken, which showed that very heavy construction work had been undertaken in the vicinity. An artillery bombardment was requested with the result that an enemy HQ and its inhabitants were destroyed. Alas, the fate of the cat went unrecorded. By spring of 1916 the course of the sniping war was no longer in the hands of the Germans. More scoped rifles were now arriving at the front – 'raining telescopic rifles' as Crum put it, and the men were at last being taught using the proper equipment. Not that every sniper was enthralled to be sent on a course. Cloete mentioned a Canadian sniping officer who accompanied him on a two week refresher course who promptly took to his bed:

He ... said he knew more about scouting, tracking tactics and shooting than anyone there ... as he was a trapper and guide by profession, and that ... he had his pistol by his bed and would shoot anyone who disturbed him. So there he lay, resting and sleeping for fourteen days.[119]

The Lovat Effect

In the training of snipers and scouts, Britain had one great advantage not possessed by any other country, and that was the use of the Lovat Scouts. Formed in 1900, this organisation comprised around 200 Highland *ghillies*,[120] whose powers of observation, camouflage and stalking skills were unsurpassed. The Lovats provided a cadre of highly skilled men whose only parallel elsewhere was to be found in some of the German hunting guides from the Black Forest. They also possessed an item of clothing that was subsequently to become the universal garb for the sniper, the ghillie suit. Devised to replicate the natural cover in the Scottish highlands, each man made his own according to his preference. In general terms it would consist of a very loose hooded sacking or burlap jacket and trousers. The fabric had randomly attached strips of green brown and black cloth sewn onto it to disguise its outline and natural vegetation such as grass and bracken was often added. Hesketh-Prichard was of the opinion that no man, unless very skilled in observation, could spot a hidden Lovat scout wearing one from a distance of 10 yards. While some snipers had the facilities to make such suits, many when in the line opted for a simpler 'sniper's robe' which might take the form of a long poncho style garment, or even a khaki boiler suit, muddied up and camouflaged with foliage. The issue service tunic and trousers were normally adequate for use when in a hide, but the useless puttees were invariably left off as they could restrict circulation when a man was lying in a cramped position for any length of time. The flat service cap was a disaster for sniping purposes and was usually replaced with a soft knitted cap comforter, which could be pulled down over the face, and eye slits cut in it. Crum mentions that his men often wore face-masks painted to look like foliage, bricks or stone so that 'the outline of the head was destroyed'.[121] Some men began to adopt mesh camouflage scrim, borrowed from artillery dumps, as their head and body cover and scrim increasingly became used for camouflage, as it was light, cool and did not hinder movement. By early 1917 the provision of specialist clothing had become more widespread and included the Symien sniper suit, a loose, hooded jacket and trousers covered in painted strips of material, which would not look out of place on a modern battlefield. Painted groundsheets were also effective and the outline of the rifle was blurred with torn strips of sandbag or scrim wrapped around the barrel.

It was not solely camouflage that the Lovats were able to teach the snipers, but also basic fieldcraft using the natural cover of the ground, and observation. One of their special tricks on courses, while under observation from their students, was to leave a trench unseen then crawl round behind the watchers before standing up to reveal themselves. When students could emulate this feat, they were well on their way to being proficient scouts. It seems odd that, in view of the power of the Scout telescope that the Army had, it should have been largely ignored as the sniper's 'second weapon' by almost all of the other combatant powers, whose use of the binoculars for spotting was universal. Of 20×, the four-draw brass scopes were identical to those used for deer hunting and target spotting on civilian ranges and they were widely available. There were many advantages in their use, for the telescope had a very small frontal area, presenting a tiny target and its sliding sunshade protected against reflection that could give away the observer. Its power was also considerably greater than any but the largest naval binoculars. In clear weather experienced observers could spot enemy troop movements 10 miles distant, and their ability to pick out fine detail at closer ranges was unparalleled. Hesketh-Prichard said of the Lovats' powers of observation that 'if they reported a thing, that thing was exactly as they had reported'. Some indication of the importance attached to the scout telescopes can be seen from the fact that Major Freemantle's *Notes of Lectures and Practices in Sniping*[122] devotes no fewer than five pages to the use and care of the telescope, ending the chapter with the advice that 'it is an indispensable friend to the sniper'. It also took skill to master, and care had to be exercised when using one from a hide, as one newly apprenticed sniper wrote:

> I was gaining experience in using the telescope when one day I became suspicious of a small dark triangular patch in the earth almost 300 yards in front. Staring at it for some time I couldn't make out what was a light circular patch in the middle of it, when to my utter amazement I saw very clearly the side of the face of a German, with light brown hair. I kept watching as I speculated, then suddenly I saw a wisp of smoke and instinctively ducked as his bullet zipped viciously through the sandbags over my head.[123]

The scout telescope was, however, tiring to use, so the two-man system adopted by Britain was a positive advantage, as one observed while the other rested. It was known that the best method of resting the eyes was to look, without focussing, at some greenery in the middle distance as this helped to relax the eye muscles.

There were other things taught on sniper courses besides the official syllabus, priceless lessons from experienced snipers, who by skill and some good fortune, were still alive and could pass on the tricks they had learned. 'Shape, shine, silhouette, shadow and movement' were vital signs to look for. Covering the lens of a telescopic sight with fine netting to prevent reflection, ensuring the boot-heels were camouflaged (they could lay above the line of the sniper's head when prone), placing wet sandbags under the muzzle in dry weather to stop dust being kicked up, never shooting through foliage, as it could easily deflect a bullet, even watching the behaviour of birds or animals could all save a sniper's life for it was the cautious and the observant who survived. Ion Idriess made this point well, in his account of hunting a Turkish sniper in Mesopotamia. Horses fell wounded and men scattered as the sniper opened fire from a well concealed hide in a field of green barley. Knowing distant observation would achieve little, Idriess ran to a dry gully and began a long, infinitely slow crawl into the crop to search for his man:

> Somewhere in that field lay the waiting sniper. Where I knew not. He would not move, but his eyes would be seeing and his ears would be hearing. And he would shoot. He would simply wait, every instinct, every nerve every sense tuned to the uttermost with the thrill of longing to put a bullet in my brain. Without lifting my chin from the ground, my eyes ... would alight on the caroling lark, as it hovered ... singing shrilly – and it seemed as I wormed farther and farther into the field to hover constantly over one particular spot. Then something moved. It was only the turn of his cheekbone ... the perfectly shaped tiny black dot of his rifle muzzle I could see and below the telescopic sight, the bony brown finger knuckles. Many barley stalks were in the way ... such a tiny thing might deflect a bullet, and a man would be allowed only one shot. Then the indrawing of a deep breath, the raising of the rifle ... the 'first pull' ... 'Crack!' Within a foot of the Bedouin's body ... was a little nest, and in it one solitary fledgeling, its eyes still shut but its mouth wide open. Such an insignificant thing to cause the death of a man![124]

The British snipers were gradually becoming more proficient and learning how to be inventive in dealing with their German adversaries. Private Jack

Rogers, a sniper with the 2/7th Sherwood Foresters was asked to eliminate a particularly troublesome German sniper who was shooting into a communication trench and hitting men. Unable to pinpoint the sniper's post, the sniper section set up three posts along the line occupied by scout snipers and took compass bearings on where they thought the shots were coming from:

> We all took bearings which we compared when we met at HQ that evening and checked them on a map. We drew lines along each bearing and where they met we marked the position. Next morning we could see a large bucket, that didn't seem to have a bottom to it. We three snipers set our sights on the bucket, and when there was a shot from it we all fired simultaneously, rapid fire.[125]

Sniping from that particular German position ceased.

All snipers kept their own logs, to record relevant information: shots taken, ranges, scope setting, weather conditions and any other comments that they felt to be pertinent. These also existed to keep a tally of hits, or scalps as some snipers wryly referred to them. This was not done for personal glory, as few snipers ever mentioned, even to their closest comrades, the number of kills they had made, but to ensure that all claims were verified. No shot made without an independent witness could be logged as a kill, and many were simply entered as 'probable'. This system prevented wild claims being made and gave the Intelligence Officers a reasonable idea of the effectiveness, or otherwise, of sniper units as well as useful intelligence data. It is a system that is still in use today among snipers. As the long and bloody summer of 1916 passed, while there was little reason for Allied celebration as the costly Somme campaign dragged to a close, British and Commonwealth snipers were gradually gaining the upper hand where trench sniping was concerned.

The Commonwealth Snipers

When they first entered the trenches in 1915, the Canadians suffered badly from the German snipers. Private George Hancox, of the Princess Patricia's Light Infantry commented that:

our main casualties ... were caused by enemy snipers, and it was soon realised that something was going to have to be done about it. So a sniping section was formed in our regiment. These were almost entirely men who'd been big game hunters and were crack shots with rifles. They were used to stalking and if they had any kind of a target at all, they were sure to hit it. They'd pick out spots where they could get good observation on the enemy lines. As soon as a German went by, they would let him have it. It's very hard to say how many they got, but I think they paid the Germans quite well for any of our men they shot.[126]

The Canadian troops had one great advantage in that they entered the war with a remarkably efficient sniping rifle, the Ross Model 1910. Designed by Sir Charles Ross in 1896, it used a straight-pull bolt-action with interrupted-thread bolt locking system, similar to that on the breech of an artillery piece, and had a double-pressure trigger. It was originally designed to shoot the very potent .280 Ross cartridge, but all military rifles were chambered for the British .303 inch round. Its inherent accuracy and immediate availability as a sniping rifle when equipped with the bulky Warner and Swasey Model 1908 (later Model 1913) prismatic scope meant that the Canadians were able to respond quickly. They were soon suffering far fewer casualties from sniping, a fact not entirely lost on the adjoining British regiments.

The Warner was extremely expensive at $58 each (£11 10s), but in many respects it was ahead of most of its rivals, being fitted with large and simple elevation and windage drums. However, it had a number of faults. The drums could on occasion conspire to cause a loss of zero, as pointed out in a report by Lieutenant W. B. Curtis. He was sniping officer of the 31st Battalion CEF and in a report to HQ 6th Canadian Infantry Brigade he expressed what many Canadian snipers thought about the Warner:

The lens's [sic] are good and give a good field and clear vision. The method of elevating the sights allows for a certain amount of play, and when a shot is fired the sight moves and does not come back to its proper place; this makes it practically impossible for two shots to be fired at exactly the same point. For reasons which no-one knows, the lateral adjustment is hard to depend upon as, when the sight is taken off the rifle, it is necessary, even under exactly similar conditions … to re-adjust the sight laterally. Rubber bands have been used to help hold down the sight to its true position, but even with this it is not to be depended upon … we have in use one Aldis sight which gives good results. Men returning from a sniping course, however, are convinced that the Winchester [A5] sight is the best for practical work.[127]

In addition, the scope was notorious for having a short eye-relief of only one inch, so they came fitted with a heavy rubber eyecup to help protect the eye when firing. It took considerable training to prevent men from flinching as they fired and not for nothing did McBride comment that the Ross/Warner combination could 'make a flincher out of a cigar-store Indian'. The mounting could also cause trouble, for its dovetail was not always a perfect fit, and despite each scope being hand fitted, it could loosen in use, allowing the scope to wobble. McBride had a simple solution for this:

By using a wedge – made of a piece of safety razor blade – and salt water, [I] got her on so tight that I came near to being court-martialled when I finally turned it in as the armourer could not get it off.[128]

Despite these shortcomings, the Canadian snipers were arguably the best-equipped Allied soldiers in the early years of the war, and they had some 500 Ross/Warner rifles by February 1916. Though often criticised, the Ross/Warner combination was, by the standard of the time, a fairly competent pairing. Herbert McBride was with the 21st Battalion Canadian Expeditionary Force (CEF) and in his book he commented of the Ross that:

[they] were exceptionally accurate and dependable with Mk.VII ammunition. Now, I have had a lot of unfavourable comments against the Warner and Swasey sight … however it is my opinion, that when compared to the others we had at that date and time, it was a pretty good sight.[129]

Nevertheless, still more telescopes were required, and the Canadians turned to the popular Winchester A5, purchasing between 75 and 100 units as well as a number of PP Co. scopes and mounts, all of which were fitted to the Ross. Subsequently, many Canadian snipers were also issued with the SMLE, equipped with either A5 or PP Co. scopes. There was great enthusiasm in the Canadian ranks for sniping and those selected were sent to one of the sniping schools, predominantly at Bernes-en-Artois, where they were tested for proficiency. The Canadian sniper instructors were ruthless in their selection – of 39 applicants on one course, 11 were swiftly returned to their units. Those who already had sniper experience or knowledge of the use of telescopic sights had a ready advantage, although not always. One private, W. Rogers, arrived for sniper training with a Ross rifle equipped with mounts for a Winchester scope, but no actual scope was fitted. In addition the iron sights had been removed, rendering the rifle utterly useless for any form of shooting.[130]

Many of the finest Canadian snipers proved to be Natives, whose backwoods skills, patience and acute eyesight made them ideally suited to the task and Canadian soldiers provided some of the best snipers of the war. Their kill rate was extraordinary: with his Ross, Corporal Francis Pegahmagabow, arguably the finest sniper Canada fielded, was officially accredited with 376 kills, obtaining a Military Medal and two bars in the process. Despite the Ross infantry rifles being replaced by the more reliable SMLE in 1916, a large number of Ross sniping rifles continued in service throughout the war. Interestingly, the Canadians had found that in certain conditions, the Ross's iron sights could prove superior to a telescopic sight. Indeed, Herbert McBride had quite strong opinions on the subject of iron sights:

> If the light was right, I would use the 'scope sight; if not, the iron ones. The service sights on the Ross rifle were so good that, by using the large aperture, one could see plenty of the territory in the vicinity of the target. The telescopic sight is not always better than the iron ones ... never as good in fog, and sometimes even on bright days when there is a heavy mirage. The scope exaggerates everything, including ground haze and the distortion of the target by the mirage. I cannot for the life of me, understand why ... in a country that has developed some of the finest types of aperture sights ... we could not have an equally good one on a military rifle.[131]

He did however concede that 'in the average light and especially early on some mornings and late in the evening the scope is all to the good'. In fact, the new iron sights proved so good that tests at some sniping schools showed that they could at times out-perform the telescopic sights, and for shooting training most of the schools used the naked P14 rifle fitted with open or aperture sights.

South Africa too had many fine shots serving in its ranks, and some regiments formed their own *ad hoc* sniper units, but the South African Army was unique in raising its own dedicated sniper regiment at the suggestion of Sir Abe Bailey, a millionaire philanthropist. The Union Government gave its approval for a unit of 100 snipers, the cost of which would be borne by Bailey himself. Bailey's South African Sharpshooters (the BSAS) had to meet stringent shooting requirements to join. These included five prone shots from cover, five shots fired after running 30 paces at 200 yards and five shots snapshooting at 200, 300 and 500 yards, the target's exposure being only 5 seconds duration. Recruitment was actually quite slow, simply because so many men had already joined the Army. Eventually some 24 men were sent to France in mid-1916, under their officer, Second Lieutenant Neville Methven, himself a highly skilled target shooter and big game hunter. However, small though it was, the unit was soon heavily employed at Arras, Passchendaele, and in the later battles of the Somme, being attached to various British regiments, notably the 2nd King's Royal Rifle Corps, then the 1st Northants Regiment.

The records of the BSAS are of particular interest to posterity as they give a rare clue into the combat effectiveness of snipers, a question often debated by historians and frequently by their own military commanders. Methven commented in an interview long after the war that, in their 2½ years service, the unit tally was 'over 3,000 Germans' and that his personal score was well in excess of 100.[132] These figures do not seem to be unreasonable, given the standard of marksmanship within the unit. Indeed, Methven was personally awarded the Military Cross by Major-General Stickland, for his contribution to the war effort, and the unit itself suffered a 35% casualty rate, compared to 5% overall for other South African forces. Interestingly, the BSAS were not armed with standard PP mounted SMLEs but with the much rarer Purdey-built offset mount, probably fitted with Aldis Mk. 3 scopes. These were of excellent quality and the most expensive of all of the commercially supplied rifles, at £13 13s 6d (£13.67) each, the cost being underwritten by Sir Abe Bailey.

America Enters the War

The United States' entry into the war in 1917 posed their army with something of a dilemma. The Americans were enthusiastic but inexperienced and their induction into the harsh reality of trench life was to prove something of a shock to them. The first battalions took over trenches that had been under observation by German snipers for months, and while constantly urged not to take glances over the parapet, many could not resist – with the inevitable consequences. Unlike most of their allies, the US Army had not entered the war totally devoid of sniping equipment, having a number of .30-06 calibre Model 1903 Springfield rifles, fitted with the same Warner and Swasey Model 1913 scope as the Canadians. This was an improved version of the original Model 1908, although 'improved' is a term the US Ordnance Board found questionable, tests having brought forth the following comments:

1. With the eyepiece offset ... the shooter is forced to assume an uncomfortable position for shooting.
2. There is insufficient eye relief, making the shooter liable to injury.
3. The magnification is higher than necessary, and the field of view correspondingly smaller than desirable.
4. Too small an exit pupil limits the sight's effectiveness at night.
5. Excessive weight and bulk make the sight awkward.
6. The glass reticle was easily obscured by film and moisture in spite of efforts to prevent this.
7. Lost motion in the windage and elevation adjustments made them subject to error.[133]

Unlike the Canadians, the US Ordnance Board considered it to be quite inadequate for combat use, and work had already begun prior to 1914 to find an alternative. Testing was still under way when America entered the war, and as a result some 1,530 Springfield/Warner combinations were issued for use from 1917–18. There was certainly no shortage of skilled marksmen to shoot the rifles, as in the ranks there were an abnormally high proportion of hunters and target shooters. With no sniper training programme of their own, American riflemen were trained at the British schools under the tutelage of experienced British snipers and soon began to account well for themselves. Major Penberthy saw a considerable number pass through and wrote admiringly of them:

> when the Americans arrived a large number of their officers and men passed through our schools and were distinguished by their passionate desire to learn all they could, in order, as more than one said to me, to 'make up for lost time'. They started schools of their own, modelled on ours, and in most cases partly staffed by British instructors in sniping. They even borrowed some of our officers to go to America and give instruction at the training camps there.[134]

New to the war, many American snipers took to their new profession with glee, one remarking in a letter home that 'Stalking Heinies [Germans] was like duck hunting'. It didn't do to underestimate the Germans, though, and the proportion of American snipers killed was abnormally high in the first months of their involvement in the war. Employment of snipers was on a company basis, broadly similar to that used by the Commonwealth snipers with men assigned to their own infantry sections and working in pairs on a specific area of front line. Inevitably, the US Marine Corps, who always took a very direct approach to combat sniping, had already adopted their own telescopic sight. This was the commercially produced Winchester A5 target scope, the same scope that Britain and Canada had been purchasing for fitment to the SMLE. First produced in 1910 it was an excellent target scope, of 5× with a tough body made from a solid bored-through length of steel bar, but it was handicapped as a combat scope by its narrow field of view of 3.2° and its rather delicate mounts. These used a spring plunger that pressed against the body of the scope, keeping it in line while still permitting it to slide forward under recoil. If the A5 did suffer from one design problem, it was the machined groove underneath its body into which fitted a stud in the base of the mount. This kept the scope horizontal as it slid in its mounts, but a knock could often unseat it, and if it became clogged with mud it could stick fast. The fine micrometre drums for elevation and windage, while more than adequate for the shooting range, were almost impossible to adjust in anything other than broad daylight and the Winchester A5's limited field of view made it a poor scope to use in bad light or on a moving target. Nevertheless the Marines liked the A5, and it was undoubtedly one of the best optical sights then available. They adopted improved click adjusters, and special Mann-Neidner type tapered dovetail bases for mounting the scopes and turned their Springfields into competent sniping rifles. However, this set-up too was inevitably criticised in an Ordnance report as giving 'too small a field of view, weak mounts, spaced too closely together, poor in low light conditions and a bolt that fouls the scope body unless it was slid forward on its mounts'.[135] While these complaints were undoubtedly valid in practice very few A5 scopes actually ever found their way to the front by the Armistice in 1918.

Marine sharpshooters were fortunate in that their rifle team Springfields, used for competitive target shooting and the annual Camp Perry matches, were available to them for combat use. The Springfield, like the Enfield, was to prove a tolerably good sniping rifle, even though it was never designed for the task. Hampered by the inevitable all-enclosing woodwork it could prove inaccurate at longer ranges. However, one great advantage was that unlike most British mounts the telescopic sight was fitted over the bore, providing a natural shooting position and quicker target acquisition than the offset scopes. It seems rather ironic, therefore, that the most famous example of accurate shooting during the war, by Sergeant Alvin York, was actually done using a service Springfield (some accounts state he used a Winchester P17) and open iron sights. A born marksman, who hunted game in the mountains of his native Tennessee, he also was a champion muzzle-loading match shooter. In October 1918 York had spotted a nest of German machine-guns that were invisible to his advancing comrades of the 82nd Division. As the guns opened fire, so did York, making head shots at a range of some 300 yards, and working his way along the line of machine-gun pits, ensuring no shot was wasted. At one point a squad of infantry rushed him and, with his rifle empty, he calmly used a Colt .45 automatic to shoot all ten, starting with the man at the rear, reloading and killing the leader when he was only 30 feet away. He then reloaded his rifle and resumed his sniping and succeeded in silencing four nests comprising 35 machine-guns as well as killing 25 Germans. Demoralised, they eventually surrendered to him, all 132 of them.[136] For this action on 8 October 1918, he was very justifiably awarded the Congressional Medal of Honor.

While America was unable to field large numbers of snipers during the war, those who did see action proved highly competent. It was unfortunate that after the war so many of the lessons learned were to be ignored by the US military, although in this they were by no means unique.

France's *Tirailleurs*

Pre-war, France had a small optical industry, mainly in Paris, based predominantly around the manufacture of telescopes, binoculars and opera glasses, as well as optical sights for artillery. Little thought had ever been devoted to the requirements of telescopic sights for infantry rifles, but because of the very high number of French soldiers lost to sniper fire in the early months of the war, the French commanders had to re-evaluate this position. Pre-war, there had been very popular 1,000 metre military shooting competitions, similar to those at Bisley or Creedmoor, which were open to civilians, and as a result the French conscript army of 1914 contained a number of competent long-range shooters. As with most of their allies, France did not possess a dedicated sniping rifle and its issue service rifle, the 8 mm Lebel 86/M-93, had its design rooted back in the old Chassepot needlefire rifle of the 1870s. There were no optical sights available so in desperation the War Ministry ordered tests to be carried out using a hastily modified sight taken from the Canon de 37 mm TR infantry gun. This was a small, quick-firing canon adopted in many different guises by most of the combatant powers during the war. Never having been designed for small arms use, the sights proved deficient in almost every respect. While there exists at least one example that has been modified with an improved, extended objective lens[137] there is no proof that they were ever mass produced for service issue. There was an early telescopic sight pattern, the Mle. 1907, which was based on a commercial scope, but it had never been adopted for military use. In late 1915, after experiments had been conducted using captured German telescopic sights the A.Px.-1915 (Atelier de Puteaux Mle. 1907-1915) was developed. This was a 3× scope very similar in design to that of the Gerard. It had a focussing ring on the scope body, crosshair graticule and a range drum graduated to 875 yards (800 metres).

The main problem facing armourers was in creating a suitable mount that did not prevent effective use of the bolt-action ejection mechanism. While few of these rifles now survive, those that have been examined all appear to have been hand-made using variations on a theme of mounting blocks on the left side of the receiver and a quick-release sidemount dovetail system. The methods of securing the mounts to the rifle all differ, some having a front mount that attached to a ring that was slid down the barrel onto the receiver, where it was soldered in place. Others had a front base screwed and soldered onto the top of the barrel next to the rear sight and rear mounts were either screwed to the side of the receiver or, in some cases, mounted on a steel trellis framework that was also screwed in place. As with other sniping rifles, all scopes were factory matched to rifles that had proved to be particularly accurate in testing; they were serial numbered to ensure they remained with the correct weapon and a leather carrying case was issued. By 1915, France had begun to realise that the Lebel was becoming outdated as an infantry rifle and belatedly adopted the 8 mm Berthier 07/15 rifle. It had a far more practical three round box magazine, later increased to five on the Mle. 07/16. As with the Lebel, selected Berthier rifles were set aside after manufacture to be fitted with scopes. However, the fitting method used either a two piece mount, similar to the Lebel, or a cast frame that screwed to the left side of the receiver. Most Berthiers appear to have been fitted with the modified A.Px.1917 scope, which differed primarily from the earlier pattern by being longer, at 11 inches (280 mm) as opposed to the Model 1915's 9½ inches (240 mm) and there does appear to be less of a mix of mount types on these later rifles. Issue of sniping rifles began in spring 1916 and they were supplied in small quantities to selected riflemen known as *Tirailleurs d'élite* (TEs). That these snipers proved their worth seems indisputable. In the dense forests of the Argonne the historian of the German Infantry Regiment No. 70, wrote:

at each step, death would knock. The French tireurs d'élite were solidly attached to the trees. Even if one or two were hit, we still could not get past. In this situation, the enemy positions could not be found. It was like machine-guns in the trees ... like fighting phantoms.[138]

On the Western front, French forces were issued scoped rifles on the basis of three or four per company, the riflemen acting on their own initiative to deal with German snipers, and while they were not used in the numbers that the British and their Commonwealth allies employed, they were able to offer some retaliation against the dominant Germans. Exactly how many scoped rifles were manufactured has been impossible to determine. Some French sources quote up to 50,000 but there is much doubt about this figure and the true number may be one-tenth of that.

The Beginning of the End

Britain had not been resting on its laurels for with the passing of 1916 and the failure of the Somme campaign had come the realisation that the war was going to be both long and bloody, and that the Allies would have to fight a war of attrition the like of which had never before been experienced. British sniper training schools now existed not only in France, but also in the UK and by 1917 the number of qualified men and sniping rifles the Allies could supply was outstripping the numbers that Germany could field. While British war production was reaching new heights of efficiency, Germany was beginning to face severe difficulties in replacing lost equipment. In particular the slow production of brass and optical glass was slowing down telescopic sight production and the superiority that the Germans had enjoyed up to the start of 1916 had all but vanished. The British attitude to sniping had also matured, with the acceptance by the high command that it was now a primary function of warfare and that dominance of No-Man's Land and the enemy's trenches were a vital element in achieving moral and military success. In early 1917 GHQ summoned all of the sniping schools' commanders and senior instructors to a conference. They believed that the employment of snipers should no longer rest with the commanding officer of the regiment. As Penberthy said, 'the number of snipers in any particular battalion depended on the keenness of the Commanding Officer. Some had as many as 30 snipers. Others were content with two or three.'[139]

The shift in emphasis away from scouting to intelligence gathering, was shown by the fact that it was also decreed that the command of sniping units was henceforth to be the function of the battalion intelligence officers and not scouting officers. There was a growing awareness in GHQ that the role of the British sniper had hitherto been limited to something similar to a gamekeeper. They patrolled the trenches to keep down the enemy, in much the same manner as keeping foxes out of a chicken coop. Valuable, if hard lessons had been learned from the German use of snipers for both defensive and offensive work. German tactical doctrine for snipers was that they were always to be used to the very maximum of their potential, and this included their use when taking part in an attack. While snipers would advance with their infantry battalions, their job was to establish themselves as quickly as possible on the flanks and as a priority shoot any observers or machine-gunners they could target. The gap was narrowing, however, as the skill of the British snipers now matched that of their counterparts.

By late 1917 the British had completely reassessed their sniping priorities. After the German offensive of March 1918 had been halted, Allied advances were now being made into occupied territory and British soldiers were suffering at the hands of German snipers who had been specifically positioned to fight as rearguards, which they did with exceptional skill and bravery. At Mametz Wood Penberthy recalled the Germans fighting an effective rearguard action using only snipers, enabling the main body of their men to retreat successfully. While there was no doubt that countersniper work was one of the priorities of the frontline sniper it was becoming clear that they had other, under-utilised skills. The British and Commonwealth snipers were proving to be increasingly invaluable for their intelligence gathering abilities. As Penberthy said:

> in the latter stages of the war every Platoon commander had at least two men in his platoon trained as scouts, observers and snipers, and these men did invaluable work. They were distinguished by a green band on the left sleeve.[140]

Frequently they didn't fire a shot at all in the course of a day. Private Jack Rogers recalled his typical working day:

> In the line we needed good observation posts so the Royal Engineers would come up and dig out a sniping post with a steel loophole. We'd always work in pairs and once in the post we'd stay there the whole day. We had telescopes and binoculars and we'd spend the whole day watching. If we saw a lot of German activity we'd inform Headquarters but we rarely saw a good target, though it was up to us if we wanted to take a pot shot or two.[141]

The Sniping Schools also began to teach a new doctrine, that of sniper employment during an attack and this meant that, as Penberthy said, 'the British sniper developed into a valuable controlled weapon'.[142] This comment was certainly borne out by Hauptmann Walter Bloem, whose Brandenburg Grenadiers were at the receiving end of a British fighting retreat in the Spring of 1918:

> I deploy the battalion and we pass obliquely over the crest quite unopposed. Before us is a wide plain on the right the captured wood. Not a shot. Suddenly … fire opens up from the left! Some Tommies have ensconced themselves as snipers in a group of trees. I order my leading company to take up positions and open fire. Good Lord! The Grenadiers of 1918 do not shoot like those of 1914, especially at long ranges. Practically all they know about is fighting in trenches. The scoundrels in the treetops continue to loose off merrily and the advance of the whole division is held up by that score of men.[143]

Bloem's comments illustrate an important point in the conduct of the sniping war, for the Allied snipers were now far better trained and equipped than the men of 1915 could ever have believed. There were now the 1st Army Sniping School at Linghem, the 2nd Army at Mont des Cats, 3rd Army at Albert, 4th Army at Toutencourt and 5th Army at Marieux. Training manuals for scouting and patrolling were being produced as well as technical booklets on the use and adjustment of scopes. While lecture notes such as Crum's *Scouts and Sniping in Trench Warfare* and Freemantle's *Notes of Lectures and Practice of Sniping* had been published privately and circulated among instructors in 1915 and 1916, the War Office had by 1917 finally begun to produce its own instructional literature. Much of the information these contained had been taken from course notes such as those produced by the 7th Canadian Infantry Battalion in mid-1916, which laid out clearly and in great detail, the care and adjustment of optical sights, setting up of hides, construction of camouflaged OP posts and other vital information.[144] No longer was there any excuse for a soldier to be sent into the line to fight with no practical sniping skills and a rifle and telescopic sight he didn't know how to use. As the Allies began to sweep eastwards across France, a new form of warfare began to appear in the guise of street fighting, something not seen since the early months of 1914. The Allies had had little chance to gain anything in the way of experience and learn this new and dangerous craft. It was a hard game, with the defending Germans always having the upper hand. Their successful tactics of leaving a cadre of snipers behind to cover their retreat made the British advance painfully slow, as Staff Sergeant A. Cook of the 1st Somersets later recalled:

> Our instructions were to mop up the village of Presau. We hurried forward … over the ground we had so recently captured and started mopping up the houses. Now, this is a dangerous and thankless task. You are an exposed target from all angles. Practically all houses in France have cellars, and these were the danger spots. Snipers began to pick off the men, and these are very difficult to locate and dislodge. Several shots were certainly meant for me, a sniper does not usually miss. One man came out of a house twenty yards away and fired – a miss – my turn – a bull. And so we worked our way around, death lurking at every corner.[145]

Many snipers dismounted their scopes, preferring snap-shooting and working in pairs, often in conjunction with a Lewis gunner, adopting the techniques that were later to become formalised during the hard fighting following D-Day. Mills grenades and smoke bombs were used to dislodge the Germans, while the small clearance squads watched out for each other. Staff Sergeant Cook paid the price for this work, receiving a bullet through the knee only nine days before the Armistice, although in many ways he could count himself lucky for British casualties in 1918 were higher than for any other year in the war.

The End of the War

Although the Germans were short of skilled men and equipment the resolve of their snipers did not waver, right up to the last hours of fighting, and a Canadian, Private George L. Price, 28th Northwest Battalion, holds the unfortunate distinction of being the last Allied soldier killed in the war, when he was shot by a sniper at 10.55am on 11 November 1918 as he patrolled the Canal du Centre near Havre.

While Germany had entered the war with a fully developed arsenal of sniping rifles, Britain and her allies had been forced to adopt, adapt and improve. Long and loud had been the complaints about the offset Aldis and PP Co. scopes. Whenever possible, captured German Mausers were used, sometimes in preference to the issue Lee Enfields and several examples had been sent to England for evaluation and comparison at the Enfield factory, but the Ministry of War had weightier matters to dwell upon, and it was not until 1917 that a solution to the sniper's problems appeared to be forthcoming. The .303 calibre Pattern 1914 rifle, originally designed to chamber the new high velocity .276 inch cartridge, was beginning to appear in substantial numbers, being mostly manufactured in the USA by Winchester and Remington in both .303 and .30 calibres. With its heavier barrel and Mauser based action, it was known to be more accurate than the SMLE so it seemed to be a natural platform for the development of a new sniping rifle. The question still remained, though, as to what sort of scope should be used and a broad range of German sights were examined, the best being deemed a 3× Hensoldt 'light' scope with a standard claw mount. These scopes were considerably more compact and lighter than the normal German patterns, and in comparative tests the Hensoldt provided a better image, particularly in low light conditions, than either the Aldis or PP, despite having a fixed focus and fractionally smaller field of view (7.25° as opposed to 8° and 9.5° respectively). In fact, variable focussing could be of questionable use, for recoil would more often than not loosen off the focussing adjuster on scopes, giving a gradually more blurred image. Both the Aldis and PP were rejected as unsuitable to be fitted to the new rifle, and it was decided that a new pattern would be designed, using the Hensoldt as a basis, by Lieutenant-Colonel L. Robinson, Chief Inspector at Enfield Lock, and Lord Cottesloe, Chairman of the Bisley Committee. This new scope, the Sight, Telescopic, Model 1918 was adopted for service on 11 April 1918, the rifle being given the designation Pattern 1914 Mk. 1* (W) T. Just how similar the designs of the two types of sight are can be gauged from the fact that almost all of the internal parts of the Hensoldt are interchangeable with the P18, including the lenses. Unfortunately the time taken to convert the 2,000 selected rifles meant that almost none were in frontline service by the time the war ended in November 1918. Britain had at last found the rifle it needed but it had found it too late for the war, for it was not approved until 31 December 1918. With wartime production winding down and demand having all but vanished, there was little incentive to continue with production.

Post-War Developments

By 1919, most people believed they had witnessed the war to end all wars. Understandably, few wished to be reminded of their experiences and both soldiers and civilians alike wanted to forget and move on to more peaceable pursuits. Many heeded the vociferous anti-war lobby that was clamouring for an end to militarism and politicians turned towards reconstruction and reconciliation, not rearmament. To this end none of the Allied powers were keen on retaining any more weapons or men than they had to. As a result, after the British Small Arms Committee sat in 1921, it was decided that the SMLE had outlived its use as a sniping rifle, and all stocks were sent to the Army stores depot at Weedon to be stripped for parts, while the Pattern 1914 sniping rifles were to be retained. This meant that of a total of 11,789 sniping rifles on charge, 9,788 were sent for destruction, this being the reason for the acute scarcity of original British Great War period sniping rifles today. The telescopic sights taken from the rifles did have a longer lease of life and continued to be commercially available until well into the 1930s, partly because demand for optical sights was not particularly high in Britain. Australian snipers had been largely unimpressed with the SMLE as a sniping rifle, and they did not retain those that had been issued, keeping only some P14s with the Pattern 18 Aldis scope. In 1923, a survey in Canada showed 211 Ross Mk. III (T) rifles held in store, with 357 dismounted Warner and Swasey scopes and a small but unspecified number of scoped SMLE rifles. A document from the Enfield factory, dated June 1927[146] gives an interesting insight into the patterns of scoped rifles that had survived the cull, listing some 13 SMLEs with Aldis scopes, four with PP Co. scopes, two with Winchester A5, two with Evans, one with Jeffrey, one with a German Goerz scope, two Ross rifles, one with Winchester A5 and one with a Warner and Swasey, and three P14s with Pattern 1918 scopes. It was not an impressive stockpile upon which to rely in the event of war, although fortunately some 10,000 Winchester manufactured P14 rifles were also held in reserve, and some were earmarked for future sniping conversion.

The fact was that in the early 1920s few nations really cared about the long-term requirements of their specialist army units, preferring to turn towards more pressing matters. For most countries by the end of the decade this revolved around economic crises, for it was the era of the Great Depression and the last thing any government had was the economic resources to squander on their armed forces. Britain still had, in theory at least, six snipers allocated per battalion but there was no training schedule or usable rifles. The decision of the Small Arms Committee to equip the Territorial battalions on the same scale as the regular Army, though laudable, served only to complicate matters, for there simply weren't enough rifles to go round. What was more pressing was the requirement for a better infantry rifle and the test work that had been interrupted in 1914 was continued. The experimental .276 inch cartridge that had shown such promise in 1913 was again resurrected and incorporated into a modified P14 design, known as the Ainley rifle. Six were manufactured at Enfield, and with their long barrels and cut-down fore-ends they closely resembled a commercial sporting rifle. Despite showing promise in terms of accuracy and producing an extraordinary muzzle velocity of almost 3,600 ft/sec, the cartridge was deemed unsuitable for military use so development work was stopped in late 1939. It is interesting to speculate on what the rifle might have achieved had an alternative sporting cartridge been adopted, for it would have been the first purpose designed, non-military calibre sniping rifle in service.

RUSSIAN SNIPING, 1936–45

Elsewhere in Europe, other countries had also learned some hard lessons after the Armistice. After a series of disastrous military defeats, Russia had been forced out of the war by the revolution of 1917. Under the guidance of Josef Stalin it had begun to rearm and re-equip in a series of Soviet Five Year Plans and as part of these improvements in 1932 it was recommended that the venerable 7.62 mm M1891/30 Mosin-Nagant rifle be modified for sniping use. For the Russians, this was not as difficult as it seemed as Russia had the basis for the manufacture of its own scopes, based on Zeiss designs. From 1926 it had started production of a series of simple, but very good, optical sights using as a pattern scopes manufactured by Zeiss-Jena and Emil Busch, these being designated the 2× and 3× respectively. The 3× scope was uniquely fitted with both elevation and windage turrets. Specially selected Mosin-Nagant rifles were taken from production lines and modified for sniper use by Gustaff-Werke in Berlin. It should be emphasised that in Soviet Russia, the army at this time was severely under-financed and much of this early development work was due to the money available from the comparatively well-funded internal security services, such as the NKVD, who could afford to develop improved firearms. The first Soviet manufactured scopes, an improved version of the Busch, appeared around 1932 and these are generally referred to in the West as the PE type. These scopes were over-bore mounted and had focal adjustment but were modified after experience gained in the Spanish Civil War, when the adjuster was omitted due to its penchant for letting in dust and moisture. The new scope, the PEM, was fitted on a side mount and was arguably the best used by the Soviet snipers. From 1932 to 1938, some 54,000 scopes were supplied and as a result, the cult of the sniper, *snayperskya* was widely promoted in the Soviet Army.

Russia and the Spanish Civil War

The cause of much political unrest at the time, the Spanish Civil War of 1936–39 has now largely faded from history, lost in the wake of the Second World War. In terms of advancing both sniping technology and methodology it was actually an important conflict, for it enabled two major powers, Russia and Germany, to test weapons and tactics in the guise of 'military aid'. The method was simple, involving supplying the respective sides with modern firearms and a suitable number of 'advisers' to make use of them. Once the war had settled into the inevitable trench fighting, there was great opportunity for sniping but there were no suitable scoped rifles, and little shooting expertise on either side. Unlike Germany or Russia, there was no hunting tradition in Spanish society to provide men for the army to draw upon. Indeed, it was a very young army with hardly any seasoned veterans so many soldiers only had the sketchiest idea of how to load and fire their rifles. It was the Nationalists, supported by the Germans, who first began to make use of the telescopic-equipped Mauser rifles. Some were of Great War vintage, while others were newly manufactured, short side-rail equipped K98ks. Under German tutelage the Nationalist army began to produce trained snipers who worked within their own infantry companies, soon totally dominating areas of the front, for the Loyalists initially had no sniping rifles of any description. It was not long before the Soviet advisers noticed this imbalance and numbers of Mosin-Nagant rifles with 4× PE scopes were introduced. Each Loyalist unit provided 15 to 20 of its best shots who were trained in marksmanship and began to take up camouflaged forward positions from where they could seek out enemy officers and soldiers:

> The sniper positions worked very well. In December 1937, the positions of the
> Ninth Brigade located on the front to the north of Huesca, killed 150 fascists

in two weeks. Similar positions were set up by another brigade on the river Ebro. Here the line of Republican trenches was 500 metres away ... shooting over that distance the snipers were able to put 5–6 of the insurgents out of action every day.[147]

Tactics were developed that were to be widely adopted in the Second World War, such as siting snipers near machine-gun posts, where the occasional well-aimed shot was masked by the rattle of machine-gun fire. Snipers were also sent to infiltrate enemy lines and prevent reinforcements and supplies from reaching the front:

> Three snipers spent five days in their post. In the end they had killed about fifteen mules and the same number of men. After this the Fascists completely stopped using the path and had to deliver food by a longer route.[148]

Both sides learned much about sniper deployment and the Russians, in particular, began to understand the tactical importance of using snipers in both defence and attack.

Rifle and Ammunition Developments

Since the First World War, the Russians had been interested in developing a better infantry rifle, and the idea of semi- or fully-automatic infantry weapons interested the Soviet high command sufficiently for the Army to develop a semi-automatic infantry rifle, the Simonov AVS36 in 1936.

It suffered reliability problems and was replaced two years later by the Tokarev SVT38 which was a 7.62 mm, gas operated, magazine-fed rifle with a rate of fire of about 20–25 shots per minute. There were great expectations for the SVT and in testing it appeared to function well, although accuracy was not as good as hoped. Several thousand were issued in time for the Winter War with Finland, and the Finns used as many as they could capture, prizing their rapid firepower in forest fighting. It had been planned that the Tokarev would also be fielded as a sniper's rifle, but the long-bodied PE and PEM scopes could not be fitted into the cradle designed to fit on the rear of the SVT's receiver, so a new shorter, lighter scope had to be produced, designated the PU. While the earlier scopes were undeniably better with greater magnification and 5° field of view the 3.5× PU scope provided sufficient eye relief for use on the SVT and was also simpler to manufacture, so it became the standard for all SVT models.

Ammunition for all Russian sniping rifles was the 7.62 × 54 mm cartridge whose origins stretched back to the late 19th century. It was a design that was rather impractical for modern magazine-fed small arms, having a rimmed bottlenecked tapered design similar to that of the French Lebel, although it was powerful enough, generating 2,836 feet/sec, and it was supplied in a number of types. Snipers initially used a light ball cartridge, with its 180 grain pointed bullet, or armour-piercing, which was also issued for use against lightly armoured targets, as well as tracer for spotting. The heavier AP bullet carried better and was routinely used. There was also special instruction in ballistics, which while normally covered in sniper training schedules had a special significance in the Russian climate. In extreme cold, the ballistic performance of the bullet would change in the thin air, which offered less resistance to its flight. This would alter its point of impact from the normal zero, and snipers were instructed in how to allow for these changes. It was not a simple procedure:

> At 100 metres the mean impact point will normally be higher than the aiming point if the temperature is 15°C and the atmospheric pressure is 750 mm. For the Model 1891/30 rifles it will be 17 cm.[149]

In practice this meant that at −35°C the zero of the rifle at 765 yards (700 metres) would have shifted by 105 mm (4½ inches), necessitating a higher aiming point, and tables were issued giving adjustments for both temperature and crosswind.

As the war continued, and the level of brutality increased, it became normal for snipers on both sides to use explosive ammunition. The Russians had introduced it as 'Observation Ammunition' for its detonation on impact made spotting it easy, and correcting the aim for machine-guns was greatly simplified. Survival of a hit from this ammunition was almost zero even with instant medical aid and by 1943 both sides were using it for sniping purposes. By 1939 the Russians claimed that some 6 million soldiers had qualified for the Voroshiloff Sharpshooters badge. This did not, of course, mean that they were all snipers, rather that they were trained to a certain standard of marksmanship which nevertheless would make them very dangerous at moderate ranges, up to perhaps 437 yards (400 metres), particularly in street fighting. It is almost impossible to know how many snipers Russia was able to field in 1939, but it was probably in the region of 60,000 men, more trained snipers than all of the other combatant powers added together. However, quantity does not equate to quality, as events were to prove.

The Russo-Finnish War

By the mid-1930s Russia had become both powerful and aggressive, and in late 1939 Stalin took the decision to invade Finland. This was to have unexpected consequences, not only for the Russians, but ultimately for the rest of Europe. The Winter War, as it became known, was expected by the Soviet command to be a short and sharp winter campaign but they reckoned without the Finns' natural ability to live and fight in temperatures as low as −50°F and their lengthy tradition of hunting and target shooting. Most Finnish duck hunters used rifles rather than shotguns to bring down their birds, and the task of dealing with the lumbering Russian soldiers was considerably easier than taking a fast bird in flight.

The Finns were materially aided by a decision made in 1927 to adopt a sniping rifle, and the Civil Guard, (the Finnish equivalent of Territorial or National Guards) undertook trials with the Japanese Arisaka but decided on the more logical path of using the Soviet Mosin-Nagant. It was easy to manufacture and the Civil Guard variant was designated the m/28. Some 36 rifles had imported Zeiss scopes fitted for testing but supply of these soon became a problem, and trials did not proceed further. Meanwhile, the regular Army, who had been relatively uninterested in the Civil Guards' attempts to produce a sniping rifle, suddenly woke up to the fact that Russia was posing a serious threat on their eastern border and in 1937 the Ordnance Department belatedly ordered 250 locally made prismatic scopes from optical manufacturers Oy Physica. These were not dissimilar in form to the US Warner and Swasey, and were fitted to the Army's service rifle, then designated the m/37 sniper rifle, (also known as the m/27PH). Some 150 found their way to the front and were used in the war, but were not robust enough as well as having optics that suffered badly from cold-related problems such as fogging. However, the Russians were well equipped and the Finns captured large numbers of sniping rifles which they turned on their invaders with a will. Many Soviet PE and PEM scopes were removed and retrofitted to the Finnish rifles, using the Soviet mount and base, the rifles being known as the m/39 SOV.

Finnish tactics were simple and effective. Two-man teams worked on the flanks or ahead of their own defence lines in prepared hides or infiltrated the Soviet lines, targeting mortars, artillery units and command posts. Their familiarity with the terrain, ability to move quickly on skis and fierce determination to defend their homeland gave a profound shock to the Russians, whose snipers were not highly trained for winter warfare and who were not as mobile in the snow as the Finns. When asked by a sensitive interviewer after the war if killing Russians had caused him any personal 'difficulties', one Finnish sniper paused thoughtfully then answered 'yes ... you see they tended to duck, try to get behind cover and run in a zig-zag'.[150] The Finns proved murderously efficient. Suko Kolkka achieved a confirmed score of over 400 while Simo Häyhä's score was in excess of 500. Of the Soviet Army of 1.5 million men that marched into Finland in 1939, fewer than 500,000 came home in 1940. In the wake of the huge casualties suffered at the hands of Finnish snipers, Soviet sniper training was changed. Greater attention was paid to teaching fieldcraft and winter warfare and snipers were given more freedom to work on their own instead of remaining as part of the field infantry units.

The Second World War – The Great Retreat

As the Germans rolled eastwards into Russia in 1941 the Soviet snipers began a fighting retreat that exacted a heavy toll on the invaders. Some idea of the Russian attitudes toward the Germans can be seen in the manual issued to Russian snipers, which stated that:

> Hitler's command pays special attention to selection of snipers, choosing them mainly from brutal members of the Nazi party – current and former criminals. They train killers and robbers who have lost human feelings. Fascist snipers kill women and children just for entertainment, by using them as targets.[151]

Exactly what the average German *scharfschützen* would say to this would be interesting to know as most were ordinary frontline soldiers but the implication was clear: German snipers were sub-human and should expect no mercy. There was sound reasoning behind this, as experience had taught the Soviet command just how dangerous snipers could be, for they had lost the Winter War largely through the resolve of Finnish snipers. Ridding the battlefield of German snipers was a priority and at the start of the war training for *snayperskya* was thorough, and snipers were all inculcated in their three primary objectives that were defined as:

> 'To destroy the fire assets of those enemy ... which by their fire can interfere with the advance of the platoon.' (e.g. counter-sniper work)
> 'To destroy the enemy's command component in order to disrupt ... and to introduce confusion.' (e.g. officers and NCOs)
> 'To find and destroy those enemy that are conducting fire ... and interfering with the advance of our own units.' (e.g. machine-gunners, mortarmen etc.)[152]

During the initial German advance, their primary function was to hold up the enemy as long as possible before retreating to take up new positions. This was a particularly hazardous occupation and the overwhelming impression gained from reading the sniping manual was that snipers should be prepared to sell their lives in defence of their country, and it was clear many of them were quite ready to do so. Some Soviet marksmen were inventive in the extreme, even at the cost of their own lives. A German *Panzertruppen* unit, resting to replenish fuel and ammunition supplies after a swift advance, came under accurate sniper fire from a number of different points, that claimed several lives. Patrols failed to find any clue as to the whereabouts of the sniper and men became wary of moving about in the open. In the cold of one early morning, a sharp eyed sentry saw through his binoculars what appeared to be steam rising from the wreck of a knocked-out T-34 tank several hundred yards away. A patrol found the Russian sniper living inside, with the dead crew of the tank for company. Each day he would crawl out to take up a new vantage position from which to snipe, then crawl back to his macabre lair, where he survived by using up the water and rations of the dead men. It was the warmth of his breath condensing in the low sun that eventually gave away his position. The fate of the man was not recorded, but it was undoubtedly ruthlessly administered. In fact probably nowhere else was the war fought with such savagery and disregard for human life, the Pacific campaign included. Prisoners were routinely executed, no quarter was given to the wounded and capture for a sniper invariably meant torture and a lingering death. Unlike sniping elsewhere, life for snipers on the Eastern Front was a combination of periods of exhausting marching, often in intolerable weather conditions, interspersed with ferocious close quarter fighting in which their rifles were replaced by sub-machine-guns, grenades and, at times, bayonets or fists. Russian snipers had a very broad range of terrain and climactic conditions to cope with, and were adept at using the landscape to its best advantage.

Sniper Training

Initially, training at one of the sniper schools (the biggest was near Moscow) over a three week period, covered all of the basics: shooting, observation, camouflage and map reading and also the specialist role of snipers during attack and defence, fighting in forested regions and, crucially, how to fight in built-up areas, a form of training that was initially lacking in any other European army. Probably unique among other snipers was the incorporation in the training schedule of the offensive and defensive use of various infantry weapons: hand grenades and anti-tank rifles, sub-machine-guns and bayonet work. All were to prove vital in city fighting and Soviet snipers worked as part of a regular infantry platoon, sharing the same work regime, duties and hardships. Vasiliy Zaitsev, fêted as one of the highest scoring of Soviet snipers, frequently mentions in his autobiography that in place of his sniping rifle he often carried grenades and a PPSh sub-machine-gun slung on his back, whilst fighting as an ordinary infantryman. Each sniper was issued with a standard 6 × 30 binocular, based on a Zeiss pre-war design which also had range graticules to enable distance to be judged from the size of the target. The gap between the crosshairs equated to 27.5 inches at 110 yards (70 cm at 100 metres) and snipers were able to calculate distance using the normal formula of comparing the size of target to the graticules. It required careful judgement though, and was by no means foolproof, for even experienced snipers could miscalculate, as Kulikov and Zaitsev discovered:

A machine-gun opened fire, we could see it well. The bullets began to skim over our heads. We set our sights at 300 metres and fired simultaneously. The machine-gunner continued his work, it's as if we were firing at him using blank cartridges. Nikolay and I were sitting quietly, I had many thoughts in my head; had I lost my sharp vision, was there a problem with my telescopic sight, perhaps my breathing pattern was broken, maybe I jerked the trigger? I look at Kulikov, who pushed his helmet back on his head and puffs his cheeks. He is also trying to guess the reason we missed. I curse myself like a trooper, for we were shooting downwards and in such circumstances the distance is not always obvious. One must raise the sights by one-eighth of the total distance. What's more the endless firing from all sorts of weapons has warmed and disturbed the air, causing an optical illusion that the target is nearer than it is. One must also correct for this. The machine-gun started firing again. Kulikov clung to the telescopic sight of his rifle. 'My sights are set to three-fifty metres, you move to four hundred.' I said. Taking aim we fired together. The machine-gun stopped firing. Nikolay had killed the machine-gunner, but my shot fell short.[153]

As the Germans pushed further eastwards, the training time for snipers became shorter and shorter. Casualties were high and the need for men outweighed all else. By late 1941 many Soviet snipers would be given a few days basic instruction before being sent to the line to ply their trade. These neophyte snipers were nicknamed *zaichata*, or leverets, and they were forced to learn quickly, usually being placed in pairs with an experienced sniper, who would try to teach them enough to enable them to survive and at least kill some fascists before they were themselves killed. The ruined towns, in particular the pivotal city of Stalingrad, proved an excellent training ground, for there existed a maze of tunnels, sewers and ducting under and around the industrial heart of the city that enabled the snipers to get very close to the German lines whilst remaining unobserved. It was hard work that required stamina, strength and iron nerves. Zaitsev recounted how he and Misha Masayev used a large waste pipe to get into a hidden sniper post:

We crept into the underground pipe. I go first, Misha behind me. It is damp and dark and stuffy, our hands are slippery and sticky. It is impossible to turn back, it's cramped. It is easy for me but Misha is heavily built and has broad shoulders. I can hear him gasping heavily for breath. The pipe turns. We can smell fresh air, it is apparent there is a break somewhere nearby. We crawl through an arm of the pipe to the right. We find ourselves in a brick pit covered with an iron lid ... one of the internal sumps which joins the plant's sewerage system. Where are we? Under the shopfloor occupied by the fascists? Misha threw back one of the plates of the iron lid. Bullets whistled through the shop, hitting the machines and cutting sparks. Collapsed on them dead soldiers are lying on their stomachs, on their backs and sides. Both the Nazis and our comrades. There is no movement at all.[154]

One lesson they learned early on was that as the sun set, facing into the west placed them at a disadvantage, permitting light to catch their optical glass. This worked both ways though, for in the early morning the German lines were sharply lit and a keen eyed sniper could make use of this:

We didn't have to wait long, something flashed. A small glass from a thermos, Aha, evidently they brought hot coffee to the sniper. One of them tosses back his head and drinks the last mouthful. I squeeze the trigger. His head topples back and the bright little glass falls in front of the sniper shield.[155]

As with any sniper units, the clothing worn was determined by the duties required on any given day, and men were free to use whatever was best suited to the task, including use of captured clothing on occasions. Soviet sniper teams worked mostly in the standard khaki combat clothing worn by the majority of infantry and had access to the practical and vital winter clothing, which for the most part the Germans lacked early in the war. There was a wide variation in issue uniform though, and Zaitsev, who was a marine, recalls his sniper section wearing their distinctive blue and white striped cotton shirt underneath blue marine tunics. However, practical consideration in the field soon had all marines dressed in the green gymnastiorka blouse and trousers that were normal summer wear for all infantry. Winter tunics were the heavily padded *telogreika* usually with matching trousers and in exposed conditions the thick felt overboots, which were about the only practical protection against frostbite. Many snipers favoured the protection of a helmet rather than soft headgear but a traditional item of winter headgear was the *shapka-ushanka*, a flapped fur-covered padded cap familiar to most people now as a winter fashion item. It was a practical and popular hat for the bitter winter, particularly when the sides were lowered. During the Finnish war a long one-piece white smock with hood was widely issued but it was cumbersome and by 1941 a thin white two-piece over-smock was issued. This gave the Russians a considerable advantage in winter fighting, providing vital camouflage in the heavy snow, something the German Army initially lacked.

Frostbite was a constant winter companion and especially dangerous to snipers who may be forced to occupy hides for several hours, with little chance of hot food or drink and no space in which to flex cramped muscles. Gloves, particularly sheepskin mitts, were an absolute necessity, and snipers often wore a one-fingered mitt which enabled their trigger finger to be used while protecting the rest of the hand. The triggerguard on the Mosin was thoughtfully big enough to enable a gloved hand to use it, and the adjuster turrets on the PU and PE scopes were large and easy to work with cold or gloved fingers. For summer, there was available a one or two piece camouflaged oversuit of 'amoeba' pattern in different shades of dark brown/black and green. It was large, light and thin with a folding hood, and was designed to be worn over the standard uniform and it had a face veil that offered not only good camouflage to the head and face but blessed protection from the swarms of mosquitoes that plagued much of the land in spring and summer. Rifles were camouflaged according to requirement, with bandages proving extremely useful in winter. Lengths of sacking or torn strips of old uniform were also used to bind the barrels.

Female Snipers

While there is a tendency in the West to be squeamish at using women in combat, the Soviets made widespread use of them in frontline roles as pilots, tank crew, medics and snipers. Women proved particularly adept at sniping, for they were small-statured, flexible-limbed and possessed both patience and cunning. Interestingly, they were also reckoned to be more resilient to combat stress than the men and more resistant to cold. They had their own training school, the Central Women's School for Sniper Training, near

Moscow, commanded by a female Red Army officer, N. P. Chegodaeva, who was herself a veteran of the Spanish Civil War. Many of the highest scoring snipers were female; Maria Ivanova Morozova was credited with 192, as well as being awarded 11 combat decorations. Any sniper with 40 kills was awarded the Combat Medal for bravery as well as the title 'noble sniper' and many earned the Hero of the Soviet Union title, the highest award possible.

Lyudmila Pavlichenko's story was typical of many. She was a history student when war broke out and had already qualified as an expert marksman. 'I joined the Army at a time when women were not yet accepted – I had the option of becoming a nurse but I refused.'[156] She began her career in August 1941 with the 'V. Ichapayev' 25th Infantry Division and in ten months scored 187 confirmed kills. She became very adept at counter-sniping, and had a preference for using the Tokarev SVT40 semi-automatic rifle. Moving to the Crimean region, she was again involved in heavy fighting and had 309 kills by the time she was wounded by mortar fire in June 1942, making her the highest scoring female sniper. Withdrawn from combat after being wounded, she went on a goodwill tour, meeting President Roosevelt in the White House and being presented with an engraved Winchester, which was presumably not intended for sniping use. She subsequently was promoted to major, lectured on sniping techniques and became active in veterans' affairs.

Unsurprisingly a female sniper's chance of survival was slim, and their fate if captured was particularly feared by them with many choosing to die by their own hands rather than surrender. Privates Mariya Polivanona and Natalya Koshova were both experienced snipers with over 300 kills between them when their unit was cut off near Sutoky in August 1942. They fought until they had run out of ammunition, kissed each other farewell and waited with grenades in their hands until the Germans crept nervously forward. As they entered the women's strongpoint, the grenades were detonated, killing everyone in the vicinity. They were both posthumously awarded the Hero of the Soviet Union title in February 1943. It has been calculated that the 1,061 graduates of the school and 407 instructors were between them responsible for the deaths of some 12,000 German soldiers during the course of the war.

Fighting Back

Sniper teams worked in pairs with the infantry under a platoon commander, and were frequently assigned specific tasks, priorities often being the targeting of enemy machine-gunners and observers. (German machine-gunner Franz Kramer elected for sniper training because he believed his chances of survival were far higher than if he remained a machine-gunner.) The fierce fighting that erupted often kept snipers heavily occupied, and on occasion sniper teams would combine for a specific purpose, and could prove to be devastatingly effective as a senior sniping officer recounted:

Our air reconnaissance determined that a [German] motorised column was moving … it was imperative that we prevent the enemy from occupying the next defensive positions. A small group of precision marksmen set off … these twelve bold men, comprising six sniper teams moved swiftly on skis. Their mission was to stop the fascist column, block its path of retreat, and delay it until the arrival of our rifle company. The snipers went to ground 328–437 yards (300–400 metres) from the road and carefully camouflaged themselves. The snipers placed their positions far apart from each other. This reduced their vulnerability.

Two pairs were to fix in place the lead vehicles while two pairs fired at the rear of the column. The remaining two pairs would select targets at their own discretion. Only Corporal Mikhailov, the leader of the group would fire at single targets. A staff car appeared on the road. Corporal Mikhailov fired … the car ran off the road into a ditch. A large lorry appeared on the road … with other vehicles trailing behind it. When the column closed within effective range, it was met with a hail of unhurried, well-aimed accurate shots. The lead vehicle was brought to a halt and blocked the road to the others. In several places lorries collided with each other and piled up. All enemy movement ceased. When the Germans were halted, our snipers didn't fire, but as soon as the enemy put himself in order and began to move, the convoy was fired on again. A traffic jam had been created. The Germans needed to push several vehicles from the road to clear the right of way, but hardly had the convoy moved forward when snipers opened fire again. The whole sequence was repeated. Only then did the fascists spot the snipers' positions from muzzle flash and open up on them with machine-gun fire. But our snipers tramped 1.5–2 kilometres and took up new positions to fire upon the convoy. Thus a small sniper group harassed a retreating German column for several hours, during which time it was only able to move forward about 3–5 kilometres. Soon it was overtaken by our infantry and routed.[157]

The Soviet Semi-Automatic Sniping Rifles

While the Mosin-Nagant 91/30 was to remain the standard sniping rifle for the Russian forces, there was continued development with both telescopic sights and other forms of rifle. Throughout the war Russian snipers used both the 4× power PEM and the newer PU. Developed for the ill-fated Tokarev semi-automatic sniping rifle, by 1941 the Mosin and PU had become the principal sniping combination, although many experienced snipers such as Kulikov, Vasilschenko and Zaitsev appear from existing photographs to have preferred the earlier PE set-up. Certainly the PU had some operational drawbacks, being of slightly less power, and with only a 4° field of view. Its positioning on the rifle, mounted quite high and set back, made it awkward for some snipers to use. In addition the position of the range and windage drums meant that it was impossible to move the scope forwards in its mounts to adjust eye relief.

While the Soviet snipers were operating in open country, the Mosin proved an adequate weapon. During the Winter War, the Russians had been impressed, and a little discomfited by the Finns' widespread use of their very efficient m/31 Suomi sub-machine-gun. During the Finnish conflict, the Russian infantry fighting in the vast forests found themselves severely disadvantaged in firefights as their long Mosins were cumbersome and slow to shoot, so demands were made for the issue of a semi-automatic rifle. This initially appeared in the guise of the 7.62 mm Samozaryadnaya Vintovka Tokareva, or SVT38, later superseded by the improved SVT40, known simply as the 'Tokarev'. It was not long before a sniping variant also appeared. The factory produced a simple mount that resembled a tuning fork, with a pair of hinged clamps enabling easy removal of the scope when required. Fitted with the PU scope, the entire assembly slid onto the rear of the receiver on side-rails, locking into place with a spring catch. As a sniping rifle it did not perform well, the internal construction proving fragile and accuracy at any range over 328 yards (300 metres) was unpredictable, although the manual optimistically stated that 'its effective sniping range is 800 metres [875 yards]'.[158] As the Russians were the first to discover, this inaccuracy was to prove an enduring problem where semi-automatic sniping rifles were concerned. Part of the problem was that of quality control for there are more moving parts in a semi-automatic rifle, and if accuracy is not to suffer their machined tolerances must be far tighter, and assembly must be done with the utmost care using carefully selected parts, which virtually necessitates hand-building. Triggers on automatics also tend to be heavier making a smooth pull difficult and the mass of the bolt and carrier moving can upset aim. In addition to this, there were a number of problems that resulted from design weakness, with mechanical failures, fouling and stoppages, so in 1940 the SVT40 was introduced in an attempt to remedy this. It was a more robust rifle than its predecessor and generally more reliable (although the manual still listed nine major causes of stoppage) but despite careful assembly individual rifles varied greatly in terms of accuracy. Clifford Shore tried some examples and remained unimpressed with their ability, commenting that while:

> many hundreds of these rifles were fitted with telescopic sights ... their wide use in this form does not indicate that an unusual standard of accuracy for a weapon of this type had been obtained; it merely confirms the repeated opinion that the Russian idea of sniping and sniper ranges (except for the true Russian sniper, the hunters from the Urals) was not consistent with the American and British conception.[159]

Nevertheless, the Tokarev saw considerable sniping use and seemed to have been particularly well liked by Soviet female snipers, as the cocking action of the bolt on the Mosin could prove awkward, unlike the single-cocking action required on the SVTs. While the extreme range accuracy of the SVT was questionable (German tests indicated poor accuracy over 546 yards (500 metres) with most SVTs) snipers such as as Lyudmila Pavlichenko were credited with a score of over 300 Germans mainly using an SVT, so clearly the army believed there was potential for a semi-automatic rifle in the sniping role, a belief they firmly adhered to in the post-war years.

THE GERMAN SNIPER & THE WAR IN RUSSIA, 1941–45

When German soldiers began to advance across Europe in the blitzkrieg of September 1939 they faced little in the way of organised resistance and virtually nothing in terms of sniping. This was just as well, for the Wehrmacht was not well equipped to deal with such a threat, having only a limited number of marksmen, mostly armed with First World War vintage Gew. 98 sniping rifles, some commercial rifles with telescopic sights and a very few short side-rail K98ks. Arguably, this shortage of suitable weaponry did not matter overmuch, for in the early months of the war Germany had little time or inclination to devise a sniper training programme, for rapid movement and overwhelming tactical superiority gave defenders little chance of effective resistance. It was not until Germany invaded Russia in June 1941 that reports of heavy casualties through sniping began to filter back to the Wehrmacht high command. In one instance the 465th Infantry Regiment, advancing through wooded countryside, began taking casualties from snipers. The advance slowed to a stop and in the course of one day the Germans lost 100 men, 75 of whom were shot dead by what their historian described as 'tree snipers'.[160] In his autobiography, Franz Kramer's notes deal with just such a defence, after five Germans were shot through the head. Using fire from his company machine-gun to mask his shots:

he watched the Russians' positions for marksmen ... they had to have a good view of the Germans' positions, so they had to be high, in this case the thick treetops. Franz could hardly believe they would make the cardinal error of shooting from a tree without the ability of retreat or taking cover. This proved to Franz that while they were good shots, they were tactically inexperienced. His plan worked frighteningly easily ... like sacks the Russians fell from the trees. Within an hour he had shot 18 enemy soldiers.[161]

The Germans were astonished to find the dead were all female snipers. The Russians withdrew under cover of darkness to take up new positions to harass the Germans and the whole process had to be repeated. Understandably, German demand for their own snipers grew quickly as did the requirement for rifles, but there were insufficient of both. Many German infantrymen made good use of captured Mosin-Nagant sniping rifles. Sepp Allenberger recalled he had 27 kills to his credit using a captured rifle before he was even selected for sniper training.

Training

German doctrine for sniper training also underwent a revision in the face of the fierce Soviet opposition and unit commanders were instructed to immediately select men who had proven to be both temperamentally suited to the role and good shots. Each battalion set up its own sniper unit, usually comprising 22 men of whom six (or more, depending on circumstance) would remain with the HQ company, while the rest were distributed among the line companies. Their duties were dictated by the requirements of the frontline company commanders, but they were generally excused normal fatigues. Although all snipers were supposedly volunteers, as was so often the case, in practice men who were simply good shots could be 'volunteered' without knowing. One recalled that while in a dugout 110 yards (100 metres) from the Russians he was ordered to leave immediately and report to sniper school.[162] The Germans also issued scoped rifles to a few selected marksmen in each company. These were not specifically sniper trained, but were good enough shots to ensure they could make consistent hits at moderate ranges. They served as regular infantrymen, but were capable of materially assisting in situations where trained snipers could not be obtained. As Helmut Wirnsberger commented, they 'were able to hit out to 400 metres and carried out a great deal of the work to be done by "actual snipers"'.[163] German doctrine required that the rifle each man was issued with at the start of his training would become his personal weapon and was not to be taken from him under any circumstances unless it required maintenance or replacement. Initially, rudimentary sniper training schools were set up behind the German lines and while these were to continue through the war, it was not long before a network of schools were set up all over Germany, one authority identifying no fewer than 30.[164] The syllabus was very similar in content to that adopted by Britain in the First World War. Weapon familiarisation, shooting exercises, range estimation, use of optics, map reading, observation and camouflage were taught. However, Captain C. Shore, who had the opportunity to examine the huge training grounds in Westphalia, noted some doctrinal differences:

> Their policy certainly seems to have been to merge weapon training and fieldcraft into its tactical application on the ground at the earliest possible moment and allow the two to … run hand in hand, instead of separate entities as was the British policy.[165]

German sniper training placed more emphasis on shooting from kneeling, sitting and standing positions than the British system and, while training was certainly thorough, Shore was of the opinion it was too prescribed and mechanical. There was some contemporary discussion about the effective ranges that the German snipers were taught to shoot at, Shore maintaining that he never saw a range that had classification beyond 328 yards (300 metres). That may have been true, but the training schedule certainly taught range estimation up to 546 yards (500 metres) and German scopes were zeroed at 328 yards (300 metres). When interviewed in 1967 Mathias Hetzenauer stated he could guarantee a head shot at 437 yards (400 metres), a chest shot at 656 yards (600 metres) and to hit a standing man at 765–875 yards (700–800 metres).[166] While he was undoubtedly a superlative shot, other snipers such as Allenberger and Wirnsberger confirmed they could achieve much the same results, although they did not often fire at extreme range, preferring to have the certainty of a kill by getting as close as possible. Some training schools had complete replicas of Russian villages built into them and German snipers were given a grounding in fighting from house to house, always the most difficult and nerve-racking of combat situations.

Rifles and ammunition

The extraordinary diversity of military patterns of scopes and mounts eventually in use by Germany (ten principal types, plus a host of variants) must inevitably have been detrimental to their war effort. Every unit, Wehrmacht, Panzertruppen, Luftwaffe, SS, had their own ideas about sniping requirements and as a result no single manufacturer was ever charged with their sole production. Rifles were made at various Mauserwerke plants – Steyr, Gustloff, Sauer, Berlin-Lubecker and others. Compare this situation with that in the UK, which adopted one basic rifle pattern, or the USA and Russia who had, by the end of the war, each adopted only two models of sniping rifle. It seems strange in view of the shortage of trained snipers and proper equipment, and the apparent lack of interest of the Army in training any, that much of the early German war effort was directed at manufacturing an optical sight that was never actually intended for sniper use. From 1941 the new short 1.5× Zielfernrohr 41 (Zf41) sight was fitted to some K98k rifles. The introduction of the Zf41 was in fact, something of a landmark in attempting to provide the ordinary infantryman with a rifle capable of being used, if not for pure sniping, then at least for sharpshooting, a concept that in modern armies is now widely accepted, most infantry rifles today being equipped with some form of simple optical aiming device. The initial idea was for these small sights to be issued in large numbers to combat units, but in the event only 6% of rifles were fitted with the special base assembly to which the scope could fit. Nevertheless, this added up to something in excess of 100,000 units supplied by 1945, making it the largest production of German optical sights during the war. It was viewed with distaste by trained snipers: 'the introduction of an aiming help in the form of a magnifying scope of 1.5 power was quite insufficient for precise shooting at long distances'.[167]

The sniping schools tested the Zf41 and generally rejected it as inadequate. Its extreme eye relief, poor functioning in bad light and low power rendered it unsuitable for accurate long-range shooting, although there is no doubt that for want of anything better, snipers were initially issued with this rifle and scope combination although many preferred to obtain captured Soviet sniping rifles. It is worth noting that, as in the First World War, there was widespread use of commercial mounts and scopes on military rifles. Such were the weapon shortages in the early part of the war, that any suitable rifle and scope combination was pressed into service, unit armourers often mating service rifles to commercial scopes and mounts, and making good use of captured rifles. A significant number of these commercially equipped rifles went to the Waffen-SS, who despite their later elite status, did not, at this juncture in the war, merit special treatment where any form of equipment was concerned. In the eyes of the Wehrmacht commanders they were no more deserving than any other unit, hence their frequent use of factory refurbished First World War Gew. 98 actions and scopes utilising the old single or double claw mounting system.

The first true sniping rifle to be produced was a pre-war design using a short, quick-release side-rail, that was screwed to the left side of the receiver. This presented a horizontal dovetail surface onto which the U-shaped scope mount was fitted. Once slid into place, it was retained by a spring latch. The scope was fitted to the mount by means of commercial type split rings. Scopes were a mixture of 4× by Ajak, Hensoldt, Zeiss, Kahles, Kohler and many others and usually graduated to 875 yards (800 metres). These short side-rail rifles were mainly manufactured by Sauer & Sohn and Mauser Oberndorf and early production examples mostly appear to have been issued equally to the SS and Wehrmacht. Early use showed a number of deficiencies in the design, with the scope sliding backwards in its rings under recoil. Perhaps the most serious problem was the tendency for the recoil to loosen or shear the three base mount screws. Three extra locking screws were added and from late 1943 two tapered pins were also inserted. These seem to have cured the problem, but by then an improved side-rail was already under development. As the war in the East became more protracted, the German sniper was gradually equipped with the weapon that was to become the standard for Second World War

German snipers, the Turret Mount K98k. Although a very small number had been used as early as 1940, during the Polish campaign it was not to become available in any quantity until 1942. Franz Kramer was not issued one until he went on a sniping course at the end of 1943. It had been developed to eliminate all of the problems associated with the old Gew. 98 pattern scopes and mounts, and it utilised a simple swivelling front 'turret' mount and a quick-release rear mount with a dovetailed mounting block that incorporated a screw adjusted windage mechanism. Adjusting this screw simply enabled the front mount to rotate freely left or right, without putting any strain on the scope body, as had been the case with the old system of fixed claw mounts. The base fittings were very solidly fixed to the rifle and the scope mounts had a hole machined through their centre, enabling the shooter to use the iron sights in an emergency. The turret mounts came in two heights, low and high, the low being slightly easier to shoot as it enabled the cheek to rest more firmly on the stock.

The turret mount rifles and scopes were to serve the German armed forces well up to the end of the war, and while the quality of manufacture declined noticeably in 1944–45 the ability of the rifles to do what they were designed to do did not alter. The problem was that there simply weren't enough to go round, so late in 1943 Gustloff Werke began manufacture of a new variant K98k, with a long side-rail mounting. These rifles had a larger left-side receiver upon which a flat was machined, to which a dovetailed base was screwed. This provided a horizontal mounting plate just to the left of the receiver onto which the telescope mount was slid. It then locked into place by means of the lever on the left side. As was often the case, a wide variety of telescopes were fitted, and surviving examples have been examined with Dialytan, Hensoldt, Opticotechna, and Sauer scopes, all of which have a recoil ring machined onto their bodies. This enabled either the front or rear scope mounting ring to butt up against it, and prevent the scope body from sliding. Some rifles have been found with double set triggers in an attempt to cure the notoriously gritty trigger pull of the K98k. The author's example has a trigger action that can charitably be described as similar to pulling two small pieces of concrete across each other and most others seem to have been little better. The problem was widely acknowledged and many unit armourers spent valuable time stripping and polishing the trigger assemblies of sniping K98ks to improve their action. A winter trigger was available that bolted to the standard triggerguard and enabled the rifle to be fired with gloved hands, but it did little to improve the trigger action. These long side-rail modifications seem to have been largely successful and they were manufactured in large numbers. However, with production facilities strained to the limit to produce enough service rifles to keep pace with losses, the requirement for sniping rifles was still falling well short of demand. To give some idea of the scale of production required, an extract from a report written to the Chief of the General Staff in July 1944 is worth reproducing. The writer, an unnamed member of the 2nd Infantry Brigade, stated that the current **monthly** requirement for sniping rifles meant that 'to cover losses of weapons by enemy and for supply of trained sharpshooters already at the front, an amount of 5,000 telescopic rifles are calculated'.[168]

In order to achieve something approaching parity of demand, the German Ordnance authorised a return to the claw mount system, a concept of mounting that had all but been abandoned after the First World War. The problem with the side-rail was the need for a modified receiver to be manufactured and this was expensive and materially slowed down production. The beauty of the claw mount system was that the bases could be retrofitted to any suitably accurate production rifle, using relatively simply assembly techniques. The fitting was identical to that of First World War rifles, and these rifles mostly seem to have been manufactured by Steyr-Daimler-Puch, being nothing more than a variation on a theme of the models of 1914–18. Regardless, they proved to be quite adequate for the job and some 10,000+ saw service from 1943 to the end of the war.

The single claw mounts were not the only type to see service, for in 1943 the Waffen-SS adopted a variation on a theme, with a double claw mounting system. This design actually owed nothing to German technology, but was copied from a very efficient pre-war commercial mount manufactured by the Ceskoslovenska Zbrojovka Company in Brno, Czechoslovakia. This comprised double-claw front and rear bases soldered directly on the top of the chamber and the bridge of the receiver. The telescopic sight was normally, but not exclusively, of the Opticotechna pattern with its distinctive centrally mounted range drum. Rifles may equally well be found with any number of variation scopes, including reused First World War makes. This system was peculiar to the Waffen-SS and it is believed that many of these rifles were converted by SS armourers at their own depots, hence the large variance of scope types, mounts and bases found.

The Semi-Automatic Sniping Rifle

It seems a curious anomaly that in the face of the generally poor performance of the Russian SVTs when used as sniping rifles, the Germans went ahead with development of their own version for sniping use. While the SVT may have been an adequate infantry weapon, combining a useful rate of fire with decent magazine capacity (ten rounds compared to the Mauser rifle's five) this did not make it a basis for constructing a good sniping weapon. The original Ordnance concept for the Selbstladegewehr 41 (Self-loading rifle 41) was not as a sniping rifle, but a practical self-loader for the infantry equipped with a basic optical sight, in this case the useless Zf41 scope. This, it was believed, would provide better accuracy as well as a fast-fire capability. In theory, this was fine, but in practice the Gew. 41 proved to be heavy, at 11 lbs (4.9 kg) and temperamental. It used an unusual gas system utilising pressure from the muzzle blast to push a cup rearwards and actuate a tubular piston that encircled the barrel. This drove an actuating rod backwards, re-cocking the action. Though it worked well on some medium machine-guns, it was not a reliable system for a rifle and the requirement for a special forging on the left side of the receiver to enable the scope to be fitted required what one Ordnance report termed 'excessive machine work'.[169]

In practical terms, the Gew. 41 was never issued on the Eastern front in any quantity but an improved version, the Gew. 43, was introduced in late 1943. Easier to manufacture, with a more conventional piston and gas cylinder mechanism, it proved to be an adequate, but not outstanding, sniping rifle. What was arguably more impressive was the 4× Gw ZF4 scope, a modern looking, compact lightweight instrument incorporating both elevation and windage drums adjustable in half-minute clicks with a range of 875 yards (800 metres). Manufactured by Voigtlander, Opticotechna and I. G. Farbenindustrie, it was located on the right side of the receiver by a simple machined rail and quick release spring-loaded locking latch, and had a scale graduated ranging reticle. The combination was effective, and in some situations the rapid fire ability of the Gew. 43 was unarguably effective as Franz Kramer proved:

> He swapped his K98k for a Model 43 with telescopic sight. He also took four separate magazines filled with B-cartridges [explosive] and put more in his pockets. As the Russians jumped up from their positions and attacked, he suddenly stood up and shot at a distance of 50 to 80 metres in his well-proven method, always at the last wave. With appalling effect his bullets tore into the Russians' torsos, tearing them apart. Every shot was a hit. The Soviets were utterly surprised at this flanking fire … the attack faltered. After ten shots the magazine was empty, and Franz inserted a fresh one. The screams of the injured were unnerving the others, and they aborted the attack and withdrew.

Using the dead for cover, he shot a further 23 Soviet soldiers as they tried to re-form. It is unlikely the rate of fire of the K98k would have enabled this feat to have been accomplished, and for it he was awarded the Knight's Cross.

The supply of special high quality 's.S' ammunition for snipers was something that had been considered during the previous war, but the logistics had proved too difficult to surmount and service ball was issued. The same principle applied in the early years of the Second World War, with the standard SmE 7.92 mm ball cartridge being issued. With its 170 grain bullet providing a muzzle velocity of 2,620 feet/sec (845 metres/sec) its performance was roughly similar to that of Soviet and British ammunition, and it was available in ball, tracer and armour-piercing. There were small batches of s.S ammunition available in limited quantity from 1941 which enabled long-range shooting to be undertaken with more confidence, but like all snipers, the Germans selected and carefully conserved their own favourite ammunition batches. Some idea of the problem of equipping frontline snipers with special ammunition can be seen from a note from The General of Infantry to the Quartermaster General, stating that 'the General of Infantry demands the production of suitable sharpshooter ammunition at a volume of 20 million cartridges monthly'.[170] As a result of the huge demands already placed on the German industry, and the setbacks caused by the Allied bombing offensive, it was not until the closing months of the war that supplies of s.S ammunition became plentiful, but in the interim a heavy ball, with 198 grain bullet had become widely available. What was more contentious was the issue of explosive ammunition. From the very earliest days of Russian and German sniping, the Soviet soldiers reported the German use of B-Patronen explosive ammunition and this was frequently cited in the press as an example of typical German inhumanity in waging war. Zaitsev continually refers to their use at Stalingrad:

> A shot was heard and the bullet passed over my ear. Yes, the fascist sniper had arrived … he was ready to meet us. Two more shots cracked out, one after the other. The fascist shoots well and quickly. I just barely move a little on the spot and an explosive bullet bursts near my head.[171]

There certainly was such ammunition available, for the Luftwaffe used it, its bright flash and puff of smoke giving a useful indication of bullet strikes, but Hitler, with his memories of the damage inflicted on men in the trenches by high velocity ammunition, had expressly forbidden its use on human targets. There were practical shooting considerations with such ammunition anyway, for its weight gave it a trajectory quite different to that of service ball ammunition, for which the rifle had to be re-zeroed. Nevertheless it became commonly used and it was eventually officially sanctioned, albeit solely for Eastern Front use, as a secret memorandum of 1944 stated: 'the brutal sort of Russian war-making demands similarly radical countermeasures, that is, every possibility for destruction of the enemy must be exploited'.[172]

There is good evidence that it was in use long before, for Allerberger, Hetzenauer and Wirnsberger all recalled using 'B.Pat' ammunition for observation:

> upon impact a small flame as well as a puff of smoke could be seen, which allowed good observation … we could force the enemy to leave wooden houses etc by setting fire to them. Observation cartridges were used up to a

range of about 600 metres; their dispersion was somewhat larger than that of heavy [ball] pointed cartridges.[173]

While there was little to be gained in practical terms by using it, the antipathy the two sides had for each other was well expressed by Franz Kramer:

> The Russians had this kind of ammunition before the beginning of the war and they had used it against infantry. The brutal effect of these missiles was greatly feared by the Landsers [the German's nickname for their infantry] in particular because the Russian marksmen liked to use it. According to the Geneva Convention explosive ammunition for small arms was forbidden, but war on the Eastern Front had slipped off the scale in terms of humanity by now.[174]

Cleaning of rifles was always vital, and the accepted method for any rifleman was to scrub out the bore when still hot, although this was seldom possible in combat. Boiling water and a steel cleaning rod with oiled cloth patches were the normal means, but the Reinigungsgerät 34 cleaning kit issued to all riflemen curiously contained an aluminium and steel-linked pull-through whose careless use over any prolonged period of time would almost certainly render a sniping rifle useless by premature bore or muzzle wear. Even the comparatively soft British regulation cord pull-through can damage the crown of a muzzle over a short time, affecting accuracy. Exactly why these metal cleaning pull-throughs were issued is a mystery as the rifle manual issued to Scharfschützen stated that the 'most important thing is the maintenance of the barrel'. One short rod was actually supplied with each Mauser rifle and most snipers combined their rods with two others to make a single, long, practical rod. In Russia, the full-length Mosin cleaning rod was a popular accessory for German snipers and many found space for one in their rifle cases.

Fighting the Russians, and the Cold

By 1943 the German snipers were becoming better equipped and armed, and they needed to be, for the Soviet troops surprised the Germans with the fierceness of their resistance, often preferring to die rather than surrender. Undoubtedly the toughest killing ground for snipers was the ruined cities, of which Stalingrad had become symbolic of stubborn Russian resistance. German ingenuity was pushed to the limit when dealing with Russian snipers in the rabbit warren of tunnels, collapsed buildings and trenches that the city had become. Frontal attacks were suicidal, so the war degenerated into sporadic localised urban warfare, comprising brutal raids, and the inevitable sniping. Erich Kern was a war reporter on the Eastern Front and watched the battle for Stalingrad unfold, gradually evolving into a ruined surreal landscape where the snipers dominated the shattered remains of the city and where killing simply became a matter of casual routine:

> It was a sniper's war. Rain fell in a steady monotony out of a pale grey sky. Undeterred by the weather, men [snipers] stood here and there in the trenches … sometimes alone, sometimes in pairs, one with the periscope the other resting to save his strength for the strike. We met … two boys from the Siebenburgen, Rudolf aged nineteen and Michael aged twenty-four. Rudolf's father was a hunter, his brother a hunter and he had it in his blood. Put a gun in his hand and his eyes looked for a target. Michael had seen his first hunt while still a boy. Now they were back in the butts, but here the quarry fired back. More hours of waiting and then at last a target. Another shot. The man on the other side stopped and tilted backwards. A pencil mark on the stockade, that one counted. I asked them what they thought about as they stood there crossing them off one after the other. 'Only that there's one more gone; one less to hold a rifle', they said.[175]

Most combat in the cities was at comparatively short ranges – under 300 yards (270 metres), and while there is a tendency to believe that all sniping during the Russian campaign occurred in and around built-up areas, this was far from the truth. The Wehrmacht advanced across thousands of miles of open country and fought in terrain that varied from rolling, heavily wooded countryside to mountains, tundra and vast wheat fields, all of which provided an excellent hiding place for the experienced Soviet snipers. During attacks, German snipers were often deployed ahead of their own lines, Hetzenauer commenting that his job was to penetrate the Russians' main lines at night. Then during the German pre-attack barrage, he was to silence 'enemy commanders and gunners because our own forces would have been too weak in number and ammunition without this support'. On occasions he also followed the advancing infantry, so that 'when the attack slowed down, I had to help by shooting machine-gunners anti-tank gunners etc'.[176]

Where lines were static, the Germans adopted the normal tactics of taking position in hides in front of their lines and waiting for targets at dawn or dusk, when the light was failing and the Russians became careless. This is when the optical advantages of the scopes came to the fore. Many snipers were able to work by bright moonlight and Hetzenauer recalled that he was 'often called into action when there was sufficient moonlight since reasonably accurate sniping is possible with a six-power telescopic sight, but not with standard sights'.[177] As the Russian advance gathered strength in 1944 the Germans found themselves retreating more often than advancing, and the snipers undertook the lessons learned from their Soviet counterparts earlier on, deploying snipers in pairs or groups of four to six to provide delaying tactics. Generally it was not so much the number of kills the German snipers made that made them invaluable, but the quality of hits. Russian troops were not good at advancing without leadership, and depriving them of control would usually lead to an immediate cessation of attack. The sniper's ability to target commanders or senior NCOs made this sort of tactic invaluable – one German sniper noting that he prevented an enemy advance by shooting eight Russian commanders in one day.[178] Franz Kramer adopted a cold but effective tactic during attacks, which was to shoot advancing Russian soldiers in the stomach:

In battles like these, against superior numbers … he waited until three or four attacking waves had begun to advance, then he started to put as many rounds as possible into the stomachs of the last wave. The startling cries of the wounded and the fact the attack was being demoralised from the rear unnerved the front ranks. The attacks started to falter. That was the moment he started to take the front rank into his reticle. Enemies nearer than 50 metres were hit with head or heart shots – men further back were shot in the trunk to create as many wounded as possible. In situations like this, Franz often had 20 hits in a few minutes, but he didn't count them.[179]

Although they adopted a similar technique to that of the Russians, the Germans, instead of using their snipers as infantry and arming them with additional weapons, preferred to use them specifically as snipers on flanks and in concealed positions to cover the infantry advances. By 1943, however, they were under no illusions as to the ability of their opposition and providing counter-sniping support was a particular priority. Training in the construction of hides and sniper positions was thorough, particularly as a result of the hard lessons the Germans had learned about the ability of Soviet snipers to detect and deal with their opponents. This was to stand the Germans in good stead after the Allied invasion of 1944 when the war flowed across Europe, as the speed of the Allied advance was held in check by the constant need to identify where sniper fire was coming from.

One problem for which their manuals provided no answers, was the Russian winter weather, for there had never been any requirement in European warfare for special equipment to deal with it. The scope turret drums would frustratingly seize up, preventing range or windage adjustment, and mounting screws commonly sheared under recoil because of the cold. One of the most widespread problems for snipers was with their scopes, for if taken from the comparative warmth of a dugout into the cold, they would fog up internally, rendering them useless. When marching, Kramer carried his rifle across his back, with the action and scope wrapped in waterproof tent fabric to protect it, and an MP40 sub-machine-gun across his chest. The problems with scope misting were constant and never really satisfactorily solved. Some scopes were sealed and marked K.f. (Kältefest – cold resisting) but even these were noted as being of use only down to about –4°F which, by Russian winter standards, was just a mild day. Many snipers dismounted their scopes and carried them on their bodies, trying to ensure that they left enough time for any temperature differential to adjust naturally before going on duty. It didn't always work and many adopted the Soviet idea of using sheepskin scope covers that provided some extra protection. Another problem was the oil used, as lubricants would turn to the consistency of thick treacle, often preventing the bolt from being cocked, or the firing pin from striking the bullet primer. The problem was initially solved by ensuring all parts were washed free of oil and grease in gasoline, and then reassembled and used dry. Eventually low temperature oil that would not solidify was developed, although it was not generally available until late 1942, and the winter trigger device at least enabled the rifle to be fired using thick gloves. The canvas carry cases supplied for the Mausers were worse than useless, turning to rigid boards in the cold, and being coated in mildew in the wet. Most were abandoned, with oilskin or camouflaged Zeltbahn ponchos being modified or, where they could be acquired, complete sheepskin cases being made to fit individual rifles.

Any soldier campaigning through a Russian winter needed to wear extremely efficient clothing, as remaining immobile for any length of time in temperatures of –40° or lower[180] would prove a death sentence. Even removing a glove to shoot was an open invitation for frostbite, for fingers would instantly freeze onto the icy metal of the trigger or bolt. The confusion of the German war effort is well illustrated where the subject of clothing is concerned, for German snipers had access to more uniform and equipment variations than any other country in the war. On the Eastern Front the supply of uniform and equipment was not what it should have been and, to complicate matters further, Army and Waffen-SS units were supplied with different clothing. SS camouflage being noticeably different, comprising a distinctive mottled or blotch pattern rather than the angular splinter pattern used by the Army. From mid-1938 the SS were among the first German units to sanction the issue of camouflage clothing, and the most popular early garment to be worn was the Tarnjacke manufactured from waterproof cotton. It was a pullover-style smock, with elasticated waist in Platanenmuster ('sycamore' pattern) or Rauchtarnmuster (smoke pattern) which was reversible, with green summer colouring on one side and brown autumn on the other. The issue of camouflage clothing was considered vital for snipers and one manual stated that 'if no camouflage clothing is available, fatigue dress must be imprinted or sprayed with appropriate camouflage colours. Camouflage dress must **always** be worn.'[181] This was fine in theory, but in practice obtaining any form of clothing was often impossible, and Kramer recollected paying his regimental tailor to make him both camouflaged and white over-shirts, which were roomy, thin and dried quickly if soaked. In late 1943 another variant of the smock, the Palmenmuster, appeared, with loops sewn into it for attaching foliage, and this appears to have been a popular garment particularly with Waffen-SS units on the Eastern front.

For most Wehrmacht soldiers the standard feld-grau (field grey) tunic and trousers had to serve, with field boots and grey painted steel helmet, often with wire netting over it into which foliage could be added, or a slip-on helmet cover, the Tarnhelmüberzug in army 'splinter' camouflage. It was retained by small hooks that clipped to the rim of the helmet. However, soldiers being what they are, any item that proved practical could be 'liberated' from its original owners. A universally popular head covering was the comfortable soft-peaked field cap, the Feldmütze which was not such a distinctive shape as the helmet and could be covered with scrim netting or a hood. Winter clothing became vital after the autumn of 1941, for no one was prepared for the harshness of the conditions. Captured Soviet winter uniform was worn when available, but a reversible padded smock, the Wintertarnanzug was produced, which had a white inner liner and hood, and winter trousers were also supplied. Although these garments were designed to be loose enough to fit over equipment, in practice most snipers appear to have worn at the least their ammunition pouches belted over the uniform, where they were easily reached. There was a problem with these suits though, as Kramer pointed out 'the thin covering cloth could be easily damaged and the padded lining soaked up every kind of wetness, so that it became not only unpleasantly heavy but also lost its protecting effect. When we had frost, the lining froze.'[182] Soon they had another problem, however. 'In the swollen material lice found nearly idyllic conditions and they were able to escape the persecution of their human hosts. You could only use these suits in dry cold and with little movement.'

In mid-1941 a roomy camouflaged pullover smock, the Tarnhemd was introduced, and many of these had a white interior lining that could be worn reversed to provide winter cover. Always individualists, the snipers occasionally pressed some unusual items into service. Sepp Allenberger said that 'for two years I used an umbrella which was painted to match the terrain'.[183] He would use it as a framework on which to put local foliage or painted fabric.

Despite the best efforts of the German Army, Russian tactics and an increasingly well supplied army took their toll, and by 1944 the German armies had been encircled. They were now in a full retreat fighting purely for survival, and the snipers were most often required to act on their own initiative to prevent the Russians from overtaking the fleeing German Army. How many died in this form of defence will never be known, for they have no graves, but they managed to prevent the wholesale over-running of the exhausted Wehrmacht. In June 1945, while victorious Soviet troops occupied Berlin, an emaciated Franz Kramer stood in front of his parents' house in Austria after nearly two and a half years of continual combat. As he poignantly said, he had survived the inferno of war almost unhurt, physically. 'But his soul would stay hard and scarred for the rest of his life. The ghost of war never, ever, let go of him.'[184]

8

THE WAR AGAINST JAPAN, 1941–45

The United States Prepares

In 1892, when the new bolt-action .30 calibre Krag rifle was adopted, it heralded renewed interest in the art of long-range shooting, and three Model 1898 Krags were fitted with optical sights from the well-established Cataract Tool and Optical Company of Buffalo, New York. In tests, the rifles and scopes performed very well indeed, enabling accurate shooting to ranges of 800 yards (738 metres). Yet despite a recommendation by the Chief of Ordnance that 'if found to be satisfactory, a sufficient number should be purchased to supply a number of the sharpshooters of each organisation',[185] none were ever ordered. While rifle shooting was taught as part of basic army training, the requirements for classification as an expert rifleman were quite low – a body hit on a man-sized target at 400 yards and a head shot at 200, about the same requirement as during the First World War, although this was hardly surprising in view of the fact the old Springfield Model 1903 rifle was still in service.

There had actually been a number of experiments undertaken between the wars to find a telescopic sight that could meet all of the Army's requirements. Examples tested included a copy of a German Goerz scope made by Frankford Arsenal, as well as scopes by Casey and Zeiss prismatic sights. Although large and well-equipped, the US Army had notable deficiencies with regard to its snipers. In practice it had few trained men or even any basic sniper training programme. There were some qualified marksmen, of course, for shooting had not been totally neglected and these few men were issued with a varied selection of rifles. These included the First World War vintage Springfield 1903 with a mixture of Warner and Swasey, and Winchester A5 and B5 scopes, none of which, post-war, were considered suitable for continued use as sniping weapons. The 2.5× power Model 1918 Winchester scope that had been developed would doubtless have proved more than adequate, had it ever been put into production. It had universal focus, a 9° field of view and external windage and elevation drums but despite a recommendation that it become the issue telescopic sight, no further work was carried out on it post-1925, and it vanished almost without trace. Tests by the US School of Musketry had actually favoured the German sight produced by Goerz and a report widely circulated stated that:

> in its opinion, the C. P. Goerz sight possesses all the essential requirements of such an instrument: power, definition, field, ready adjustment, simplicity, strength, rigidity and convenience to the user. For military use it is as such superior to the Warner and Swasey type as the latter is to the Winchester A5 model.[186]

No attempt was made to put it into production though. Meanwhile, optical technology had moved onwards, and what had been considered an excellent scope in 1920 was most certainly old technology twenty years later. However, the Army had not been entirely ignoring rifle development. John Garand had been working on a new design of semi-automatic rifle since the mid-1920s and Ordnance had also been experimenting with the potent .276 inch cartridge, but under orders from the Chief of Staff of the Army, Douglas MacArthur, Garand was instructed to redesign his rifle for the old .30-06 cartridge, which, as events subsequently proved, was probably a wise decision. In January 1936 a new rifle, the US Rifle, Caliber .30 M1 was adopted for service, becoming universally known as the 'Garand'. However, in the face of the difficulties the manufacturers were having with gearing up for mass production, no consideration was given to the design or production of a sniper variant.

In 1941 this put the US Army in the embarrassing position of facing a major conflict with no suitable rifle for its marksmen and the President of the Equipment Board wrote that:

> no special training program for snipers is contemplated by the army and no steps are being taken to procure special equipment. Special equipment is costly and requires special personnel to maintain and use it. Procurement problems at this time and supply problems in case of active operations would be difficult.[187]

In fact, no proper sniper training schedule was ever drawn up by the Army. As a result, the Ordnance Department and Infantry Board conducted urgent tests using the standard US Rifle, the M1903 Springfield, with a number of commercial scopes and by late 1942 it had decided on the Weaver 330-C hunting model. The Weaver had universal focus, a useful field of view of 35 feet at 100 yards and ¼ minute click adjustment for windage and elevation, with fine crosshair graticules. It was small and light but did suffer from low power and poor eye relief. However, it was to become the US Army and Marine Corps standard, being adopted officially in December 1942 and remaining in service until the end of the war as the M73B1. An improved and simplified rifle was introduced, the M1903-A3, and it had undergone some changes: the two groove barrels initially used were replaced with a four groove, and the beautifully sculpted 'C' type stocks with sporting pistol-grip were superseded by the plain 'warthog' stock. Remington were ordered to divert 20,000 of these rifles to be turned into the new standard sniping rifle, officially designated in February 1943 the Model 1903-A4. These also differed slightly from standard, in having forged concave bolt handles to clear the low-mounted scopes and, rather unusually, they had no iron sights. The lack of sights was to prove something of a handicap, but generally the 1903-A4 was considered an adequate, if not particularly outstanding, sniping rifle and, after manufacture of 28,365 rifles, it was relegated to second line in June 1944 in favour of the semi-automatic Garand M1-C sniping rifle.

The Marines' Rifles

The Japanese had little idea of the whirlwind of retribution they would unleash when they bombed Pearl Harbor on 7 December 1941 and brought the United States into the war. America was arguably less prepared for war than Britain and much of the equipment and training was derived from that of the previous war but if the Army was unable to field any trained snipers, at least the Marines did possess both qualified marksmen and some sniping rifles. The Marines had many dedicated target shooters in their ranks, and competition for the chance to shoot at the annual long-range matches at Camp Perry was fierce. However, the Corps, always the backbone of military shooting enthusiasts, was actually little better equipped than the Army. Their Springfield/Winchester A5 rifles had stayed in limited service until 1928, when the Lyman scope was adopted, following the company's take over of Winchester's optical production. Lyman had soon introduced an improved version of the old Winchester A5 scope, confusingly called the 5A. With lenses made by Bausch and Lomb it had an improved field of view, better light gathering qualities and its steel body was stronger, with a raised rib underneath that located in grooves on the mounts. This enabled the scope to slide more freely, while being less prone to being accidentally knocked out of zero, but it still suffered from the problem of the body fouling the bolt handle on cocking, necessitating the scope being pushed forwards each time a round needed to be chambered. There were also around 1,000 National Match target grade Springfield 1903s which, post-1941, Marine armourers soon modified into sniping rifles. Nevertheless, as war loomed, the Marines were only marginally better equipped than their Army counterparts, and they were woefully short of the skills needed to fight a long sniping war. Between the wars they had kept up some sniper training although it was primarily a shooting instructional course, with little in the way of field training, but the Corps recognised, with the coming war, that accuracy with a rifle was not in itself a sufficient skill. Fortunately for the Corps they had the benefit of men such as George Van Orden, C. N. Harris, C. A. Lloyd, and J. C. Smith. These were men like Britain's Hesketh-Prichard and F. Crum of a generation before, who were avid proponents of sniping and who pushed the Marine command to create a comprehensive training programme.

Van Orden's report, written prior to Pearl Harbor, stated succinctly the value of the battlefield sniper:

> his game is not to send a hail of rapid fire into a squad or company; it is to pick off with one well-directed, rapidly delivered shot, a single enemy. He must harass the foe ... hammer relentlessly upon the nerves of the rank and file of the opposing forces, until his rifle 'crack' becomes a menace feared more than the shrieking shells ... or explosive hail from mortars. His bullets must come from nowhere.[188]

He went on to recommend that the Marines adopt a purpose built bolt-action sniping rifle, and his recommendations, though ignored at the time, were to resurface again in the future. There was also a hard core of experienced gunnery sergeants, junior officers and men who were shooting enthusiasts, such as Gunnery Sergeant Charles Angus, who had won the distinguished marksman's badge (in fact, Angus was to put his knowledge to practical use early on in the war) and Lieutenant C. N. Harris, an NRA Championship winner, both of whom were dedicated competitive shooters. To its credit, the Corps responded to the demand and while in the early stages of the war the teaching programme was somewhat rudimentary, by late 1942 the Corps had set up a scout-sniper training programme based at Camp Lejeune, Camp Pendleton and Green's Farm in California. In theory all scout-snipers attending these schools were volunteers, but one ex-marine told the author how, after winning a company rifle shooting competition, he was congratulated by his lieutenant and promptly informed he had also just volunteered himself for sniper training.

Over a five week period, the men were taught the usual techniques of range estimation and wind judgement, map reading, camouflage, observation and fieldcraft and were taught to shoot at distances from 100 to 1,000 yards (92–923 metres). In this they were probably unique, for no other country gave their snipers such long-range training, and this practice was to stand many in good stead during the war, as Private Daniel Cass Jr. famously proved by knocking out Japanese machine-gun nests on Okinawa at a range of 1,200 yards (1,100 metres). He outlined the difficulties of combat shooting at extreme range when interviewed after the war:

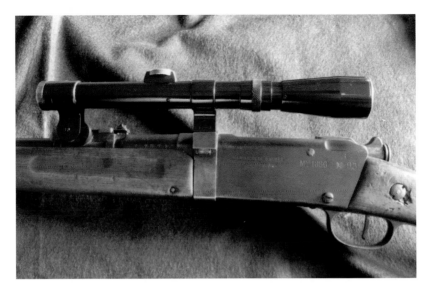

A French Mle.1886 Lebel rifle with APx. Mle1916 scope. Although the long-barrelled Lebel was a clumsy trench rifle, it was a competent sniping weapon, and the quality of the French scopes was excellent.

A British Rifle-Brigade officer instructs American snipers in the art of camouflage. (Imperial War Museum)

Few working snipers were ever photographed in the war, and this rare image shows a barn being used by British snipers. A relaxed sniper watches as another cleans his rifle. The SMLE propped up between them seems to have a PP Co. scope fitted. (Imperial War Museum)

By mid-1918 the German Amy was in retreat and they had evolved a highly efficient method of using snipers and machine guns as rearguards. The snipers watched for targets, which the machine-guns engaged. Any small groups infiltrating would be dealt with the by the sniper. Note the body-armour worn by the left-hand soldier.

On the left is Vasily Zaitsev, with two of his 'leverets' as his snipers were fondly known. They all wear winter smocks and Zaitsev carries his favourite sniping rifle, a Mosin-Nagant with 4x PEM scope.

Simo Häyhä, possibly the highest scoring sniper in warfare. He wears a winter smock and is holding his Mosin-Nagant rifle, which he used without any optical sight. Used to duck hunting in the forests, he was often able to creep so close to the Russians that a telescopic sight would have been useless.

Senior Sergeant Roza Shanina. A kindergarten teacher who attended the Female Sniper Academy in Podolsk. She went to the front in April 1944 and before her death later in that year had 54 confirmed kills and a similar number unconfirmed.

The US Springfield M1903-A4 sniping rifle, showing the tiny 2.5 x M73 Weaver scope and lack of iron sights. As an aside, the neat Marine posing in this often-reproduced image was in fact one of a new draft just arrived in the Pacific theatre, and was not even a sniper!

A marine cleans his Unertl-equipped Springfield. The 8x Unertl was an excellent long-range scope but suffered badly if poorly maintained. This combination was to see service until the end of the Vietnam War.

Sergeant Harry Furness, the highest scoring British sniper of the Second World War, Germany, 1945. He has his Enfield No 4.Mk. 1(T) rifle with No 32 Mk. II scope and is wearing an issue two-piece camouflaged sniper suit.

A Canadian sniper in full war paint cradles his No 4(T) rifle. He wears a two-piece camouflage smock, scrim headscarf and face paint, typical fighting garb for the advance across Europe after D-Day. (Canadian Archives)

Japanese sniping rifles differed in one fundamental point from those of other countries, in that all the scopes were fixed and pre-zeroed. One exception was this 7.7 mm Type 99 rifle, whose 4x scope has external elevation adjustment. (Courtesy of Fred Honeycott)

Russia, September 1941. A Waffen-SS sniper aims a Great War vintage Gew. 98 sniping rifle. Many of these were quickly refurbished and deployed when it was realised supplies of scope-equipped K98k rifles were quite inadequate.

A German Army sniper poses with a high-turret scope-mounted K98k, the most widely issued sniping combination of the war.

A sniper sights a Pattern 1914 Mk1*W (T) rifle. Arguably the best sniping rifle ever to see service in the Great War, many thousands were issued post-1940 and used by Commonwealth snipers in every theatre of war, with considerable success. (Canadian Archives)

The *bocage* country of northern France. Narrow overhung lanes with dense thickets of bushes and trees made it a favourite hiding place for enemy snipers. Here a British patrol is led by two snipers with dismounted scopes, the camouflage paint on the leading rifle is just visible.

The Korean war highlighted the acute shortage of allied sniping materiel and here an American marine aims a pre-Second World War vintage M.1903 Springfield with Unertl scope. The long ranges encountered in Korea made this a particularly effective combination. (US Marine Corps)

This publicity photograph extols the virtues of Zhang Taofang, one of the leading Chi-Com snipers. Accounts of his successes vary widely but Chinese sources quoted 214 kills in 32 days. Whilst doubtless this was highly optimistic, to the discomfort of the Allies, China did field some excellent snipers.

A lot of variables entered into shooting at a range of even 1,000 yards, the longest shot I had ever tried. Wind and heat waves, and in this case, fog, distorted the scope picture. The ammo we used was not great match grade; it came right out of the green boxes. Sometimes you got misfires with it; sometimes a round simply went 'pouf' and you had no idea which way it went. After some quick calculations, spurred on by hopelessness, I slipped a tracer round into the chamber of the Springfield and indicated to Carter I was going to use the telephone pole above the enemy placements as an aiming stake to try and get the range. Carter glued his eye to his spotting scope. 'Pick her up an inch' he curtly advised after my first shot. I adjusted the scope elevation knob and dropped cross hairs onto the Japanese machine-gun nest. I tried to remember everything I had learned at Camp Pendleton about long-distance shooting. So much depended on it. I worked the bolt with a feeling of elation. My hands and breathing were surprisingly steady. I fired and worked the bolt, fired and worked the bolt, pouring accurate fire into the Japanese defences, cross-hairing handkerchief sized targets momentarily exposed more than half a mile away ... even through his spotting scope Carter couldn't tell if I scored because the targets were so fleeting ... but he was all grins. The machine-gun fire ceased.[189]

The basis of Marine training was reconnaissance and aggressive sniping, although this was difficult to achieve in the early years of the war in the Pacific, where the jungle terrain often precluded 'normal' sniping activity. The Marines were primarily involved in seaborne assaults in the shape of what was to become their own specialised form of combat, known as 'island hopping'. Scout-sniper teams worked in three-man units, each attached to a company comprising a sniper, observer and spare man, who in combat with the Japanese was often occupied with rifle or sub-machine-gun, protecting his team unit. In practice though, wounds, illness or death often resulted in sniper 'teams' being a single man with infantry back-up.

Some snipers, such as Lieutenant John George, worked entirely unofficially. An infantry officer, sniping enthusiast and Camp Perry competitor, he was typical of the men who believed that sniping opportunities would present themselves to the well prepared. To his annoyance he had landed with the Marines on Guadalcanal, without his privately owned Winchester Model 70, which had been with him since his training days. It was fitted with a 2.5× Lyman Alaskan, but he had unwisely loaned the gun to a fellow officer for a hunting expedition. The officer had allowed the barrel to rust badly, necessitating its return to the factory for replacing. Landing on the beachhead without his rifle he subsequently wrote:

> I remember well … the mental kicking I gave the seat of my pants for being
> so careless with my Model 70. Actually, the only shooting items I had in my
> baggage were a few rounds of .30-06 hunting ammunition which I packed at
> the last minute.[190]

Eventually his rifle arrived and the marines in a frontline observation post welcomed his ability as their volunteer sniper. Nervous and unsure of the zero on his rifle, George found the experience more difficult than he imagined and left an honest account of how it felt for a sniper to miss with his first combat shot:

> My first shot went too high, at least a foot over his back according to Art [his
> observer]. The Jap … fell flat on his belly the instant my shot went past. Had
> Art not been there with the big telescope, I would have given myself credit for
> a hit, but he saw the bullet hit the sand in the wrong place. It was luckily one
> of those rare instances where a sniper is afforded a second shot after he has
> muffed the first one. The Jap … remained motionless on his belly, possibly
> thinking he was being fired on from our lines below … from my position
> above he remained an excellent target… I fired the four remaining shots in the
> rifle, getting at least two hits.[191]

The Marine scout-snipers who landed on Guadalcanal in August 1942 were armed either with the Springfield equipped with Winchester A5 or Lyman 5A scopes, or model 1903-A1 with Unertls, but the Marine command still viewed these as a stopgap measure. Colonel Van Orden was not only a proponent of a cohesive Marine sniper training programme, but had repeatedly demanded the introduction of a dedicated scope-equipped sniping rifle that was not just a modified service weapon. This was radical to the point of bordering on heresy, and Van Orden's views were regarded with deep suspicion by many senior Marine officers. However, when examined in purely practical terms, his logic was difficult to fault. The Springfield was a good service rifle, but was never designed for long-range accuracy, with its comparatively short, thin-walled barrel, and armourers were limited in the type of scope and mounts they could fit without extensive reworking, which was both time-consuming and expensive. As well as trying to find the ideal scope for the Springfield, the Marines had also looked into adopting a commercial sporting rifle and turned to what was generally regarded as the finest hunting rifle then available, the Winchester Model 70. Introduced in 1935 the Model 70 was available with three target barrel weights, designated Standard, Heavyweight and Bull Gun, weighing 9½, 10½ and 13 lbs respectively. It was a delicate but effective set-up, but after thorough testing the Marine Corps rejected the Winchester, as it believed it was 'insufficiently sturdy, non-interchangeable with M1903 and M1 rifle parts, replacement parts will be difficult to procure' and oddly, it was 'not fitted with sling swivels'.[192]

The Marines' main worry was the practical and serious one of keeping their rifles combat-effective in areas where no spares were available and hardly any Corps armourers had experience in the maintenance of such non-standard rifles. All M70s were factory prepared to enable the fitting of telescopic sights and many of the experienced target shooters in the Marines believed it to be the best available rifle for sniping purposes. Some Model 70s were fitted with the Unertl scope, which at the time was available in 8, 10, 12 and 14 power. With its distinctively long, slim tube and large recoil spring mounted half-way along the body it was described by John Unertl as a 'combination target scope', because its 1½ inch objective lens enabled it to be used as a spotting scope as well as for targets. The graticules were fine crosshair and the mounts were similar to those of the Winchester/Lyman set-up, incorporating front and rear rings in which the body of the scope slid under recoil, being automatically pushed back into position after each shot by a spring mounted on the body. There were external windage and elevation drums, mounted on the rear mounting ring. The Marine Corps Equipment Board had been impressed with the performance of the Unertl for it met almost perfectly their recommendation for a scope that 'was about 8×, with an object lens of about one and a half inches, medium fine crosshair reticle, and double micrometer quarter minute click mounts'.[193] Between five and six thousand scopes were procured and about 370 were fitted to Model 70s.

In March 1941, the decision was made to adopt the Springfield 1903 and to fit it with 8× power Unertl scopes as sniper standard, and these rifles were to be carefully assembled by Marine armourers based at the depot in Philadelphia, many of whom were peacetime gunsmiths. Parts received from the Springfield factory were examined, gauged and selected for assembly. Barrels were measured and checked for the slightest imperfection, then stamped with a star on the muzzle (star-gauged) to confirm their quality then mated to receivers, and Unertl mounting blocks were fitted. Close grain walnut Type-C stocks with flat-planed top surfaces were selected, as they were less likely to warp. These were loosely matched to the barrels and receivers before being carefully bedded. Internals such as magazine followers and bolt runways were polished, as were the bolts which were then numbered to rifles and blued, and trigger pulls adjusted. The scope was fitted and every rifle was test-fired for accuracy. The work on each rifle involved five armourers. These hand-built rifles were designated M1903-A1 but this combination was not to remain the Marines' chosen weapon for long. Early field reports received by Headquarters in 1942 stated that the Unertl suffered from problems and 'had not proved effective in combat'[194] although exactly quite what the Corps expected from these scopes is a questionable point. Although never designed for hard service use, the Unertl was inherently good but, like all optical equipment, it did suffer from problems due to careless handling, which could damage the delicate mounts, and sand, which could enter the mounts, preventing the scope from sliding on recoil and being returned to position. Many marines removed the recoil spring believing it trapped sand and grit, and used a short piece of elastic to pull the scope back into position. The lenses were prone to fogging from moisture and there were occasional problems with graticules failing but these were no worse than most other scopes and better than many. The Unertl's power, reasonable field of view (11 ft at 100 yards) and build quality gradually made it a favourite sniping weapon once the early problems had been ironed out.

Certainly, Unertl were not able to manufacture quickly enough to meet demand, and the Marines also purchased similar Fecker and Lyman Targetspot models, but it was clear it would not remain in general service for long. Ordnance tests with Lyman Alaskan and Weaver 330-C scopes had produced good results and the Marines appreciated that the new M73B1 scope with Griffin and Howe mounts was far more practical than the Unertl, as Colonel Julian Smith noted in a report in October 1940:

> these sights and mounts can be used under many conditions of light, target and background where iron sights would be entirely ineffective. [Scopes] can be mounted close to the barrel with the eyepiece in front of the bolt handle, so they can be used with the Springfield without modification of the bolt. With proper mounts they can be removed from the rifle and replaced in a few seconds in perfect alignment. All have internal adjustment in minutes for both elevation and windage.[195]

In late 1942, the Marine Ordnance Department recommended that their Springfields also be fitted with the Weaver M73B1. Its adoption by the Corps was logical for while it could not match the accuracy of a hand-built rifle such as the M1903-A1, it simplified production as there were vital elements of time and cost to be factored in. The Weaver was less than half the price of the Unertl, it was available in quantity, and service-trained armourers could build the new rifles as all were to be supplied via the Army and speed of production was critical. The commercially available Redfield Junior mounts chosen for mounting the scopes would also accommodate the Lyman Alaskan, although in practice almost none were ever fitted due to supply problems, as Bausch and Lomb were unable to provide lenses during the war. Some 28,365 M1903-A4 rifles were eventually completed by June 1944.

Jungle Sniping

In the Pacific, the Marine snipers soon appreciated that they could be at a serious disadvantage in carrying a scoped rifle in the dense jungles, a problem that would again rear its head in Vietnam, where speed of return fire could make the difference between life and death. Snipers, usually working in pairs or threes, soon adopted a practical compromise for jungle fighting, with one carrying a scoped rifle, his spotter having a light automatic, such as the .30 calibre M1 or .45 Thompson and, where available, the third man often having a heavier weapon such as the .30 calibre Browning Automatic Rifle. The .45 Thompson was devastating at close ranges of up to 50 yards, but its bullet lacked penetration in the undergrowth, which the more powerful .30 calibre round of the BAR had. The high power of the Unertl made close-range shooting difficult, although the M73 was slightly better in this respect, the lack of iron sights on the 1903-A4 was a real disadvantage for close combat.

Dealing with Japanese snipers was a difficult task, as they were patient, cunning, very well trained in fieldcraft and tenacious to the point of suicide. The first Army and Marine units to land on Guadalcanal met the type of resistance that was to become typical for the rest of the Pacific campaign. The Japanese were very well camouflaged and dug in and extremely hard to locate or dislodge. They also had an attitude to combat and death that was at variance to anything the Americans had previously experienced in warfare and often used the suicidally brave Banzai charge to close with the Americans, where they excelled in the use of the sword and bayonet. It was an effective and unnerving tactic, frightening and often successful. Sniper John George, who underwent a very rapid learning process once he had landed on Guadalcanal, was able to help out two Army riflemen from his sniper's position, when they were suddenly surprised by just such an attack:

'Banzai, Banzai', High pitched; blood curdling. I wrenched the forward half of my prone body round. As I did so I obtained a lasting mental picture of the two [US] riflemen putting weapons to their shoulders. The Japs were then out of view and below the riflemen's field of fire. These riflemen had not more than thirty yards in which to halt the attack with fire. Thirty yards space, and about five seconds time. As the first three Japanese loomed over the rise bounding towards the foxholes, the left rifleman fired as did I. My own first shot was fired in great haste, aimed frantically at the leading Japanese rifleman. A bound he had taken just as I fired carried him as much to the left as forward. My bullet sped through, missed but killed the last of the party, some twelve yards behind. My second shot timed perfectly with the first of the riflemen on the right, shared credit for slowing down, but not stopping the charge of the third member. The right hand rifleman's first shot hit the Jap I had missed, squarely in the chest at a distance of about eight yards. It took a second shot to finish the job. With only two cartridges in my weapon when the action began I was reduced to mere helpless watching (and fumbling to awkwardly load the magazine of my Springfield, occluded for clip loading by the damn bracket mount of the scope).[196]

Fortunately the Army riflemen dealt with the remaining Japanese soldiers, but it was a close run thing. Ever afterwards George habitually carried a loaded magazine and one round in the chamber. Even experienced shooters could find they had trouble:

We watched Sgt Angus ... when the Jap jumped up again and began to run. Angus was nervous. He fired several shots, working his bolt fast and missed. He inserted another clip of cartridges and fired one of them. But then the Jap had sunk down into cover again. It was a little disappointing – but only for the moment. He started to get up again – and that was as far as he got ... when Sgt Angus, now quite calm, took careful aim and let one shot go. The Jap sank as if the ground had been jerked out from under him. It was a neat shot – about 200 yards.[197]

In combat, very little special clothing was issued in the Pacific, the weather was too hot and humid and most Marine snipers simply wore the standard issue green two-piece utility fatigues of lightweight herringbone twill. An unpopular one-piece camouflaged suit was available from 1942, but the distinctive and more practical two-piece camouflaged utility suit was issued from 1943 onwards. Other equipment was basic; the M1 steel helmet and after 1942 the distinctive reversible (green one side, brown the other) camouflaged cover. Marine webbing altered as the war progressed, early-war snipers wore M1923 webbing ammunition belts but with the introduction of the M1942 pack system, a mix and match of later pouches and earlier equipment became common. Ammunition was often simply carried in cotton bandoliers slung over the shoulder. Water shortage was a constant problem and at least two water bottles were carried if possible, but travelling and fighting light were the general policy on the islands. In the early part of the war, the logistics of providing specialist clothing were almost insurmountable and few garments lasted very long in the climate. Keeping rifles clean was a constant problem, as sand found its way into every component and the salty air corroded all metal. Most snipers had to strike a balance between cleaning their rifles with oil to stop rust, yet using it very sparingly to prevent sand adhesion.

The Japanese Sniper

The Japanese Army had been looking at developing a practical sniping rifle since the 1920s and they had modified some Type 38 infantry rifles by mounting a basic 4× power scope on them. The Meiji 38th Year Type 97 had been developed after the Russo-Japanese war of 1904–05 and used a Mauser-style action with a 31½ inch (800 mm) barrel. It was chambered for the bottlenecked 6.5 mm round and a number were converted for sniper use. By 1932 the 6.5 mm was generally regarded as an inadequate combat round, lacking penetration, so the calibre was enlarged, the new Type 99 rifles being chambered for the more powerful 7.7 mm cartridge, which was almost identical in performance to the British .303 inch ammunition. Although it had virtually the same velocity as the 139 grain 6.5 mm (2,500 feet/sec) the heavier 181 grain bullet was more practical, having greater range and penetration through undergrowth. However, the old 6.5 mm did have certain benefits for sniping use. The Marine Corps Gazette outlined them as follows:

> practically all snipers still use .25 [6.5 mm] weapons. The .25 calibre weapon will not cut brush or penetrate like a .30 calibre weapon. It will however, penetrate our helmets at ranges of 150 yards or more. Its most annoying characteristic is that for practical purposes the ... powder is actually smokeless and generated little muzzle blast. Thus a sniper can 'hole-up' or 'tree-up' ... and although he may fire considerably, we will seldom, if ever locate him by smoke or muzzle blast.[198]

The Japanese had gained considerable experience in jungle fighting in Manchuria in the 1930s. They were taught to live as far as possible off the land, carrying only supplies of rice and water with them. As with the Vietcong, their self-sufficiency meant that a Japanese soldier was capable of staying hidden and surviving on a meagre food intake that would have had the average European soldier crawling to an aid post after a week. Snipers were not volunteers but were selected for suitability on the basis of shooting ability, and it was considered an honour. Motivation to succeed was based around the intense Japanese dislike of failure, and the consequent shame of being returned to the infantry ranks. Their training was intensely practical, with heavy emphasis on fieldcraft, camouflage and ambush techniques, but Japanese snipers were not used for intelligence gathering to the same degree as European snipers. As one Japanese sniper wrote:

> we were instructed that our job was to hold up the American advance, and to kill as many as possible before we too were killed. Dying in the service of the Emperor was an honourable thing ... but we should not take unnecessary risks for the longer we stopped the enemy, the greater the achievement.[199]

This is not to imply that the snipers were a form of kamikaze force although their tactics often appeared suicidal to the Allies, particularly their habit of adopting treetops for ambush. Once spotted, a treed sniper usually only ever reached the ground dead. There is a certain amount of myth surrounding Japanese sniping, the reason being the set-up of the 2.5× and 4× telescopic sights fitted to the Type 97 and 99 sniping rifles. These were fixed scopes, with no windage or elevation adjustment built into them. Any corrections had to be allowed for by the sniper's skill, to determine by how much to aim off for any given range or wind conditions. The scopes were optically very good, the 2.5× having a 10° field of view and the 4× a 7° field, with a fixed graticule, although some late war 4× scopes had elevation adjustment. Many snipers were equipped with nothing more than the standard Model 97 or 99 Arisaka rifles, with iron sights as the requirement for long-range shooting in the jungle was limited, and well camouflaged riflemen with open sights could deliver very accurate shooting out to 400 yards (369 metres), often far beyond the maximum required for jungle sniping.

Snipers were taught to completely familiarise themselves with the capabilities of their rifles up to 600 yards (553 metres), shooting in various weather conditions to enable them to understand how the point of impact would alter depending on wind, atmosphere and other factors. The training was not as technically theoretical as that of the Allies, but for the purposes of Japanese sniping it was not required to be, and the benefits of having non-adjustable scopes meant that its zero was fixed regardless of rough handling or fiddling by inexperienced hands. Many rifles were also equipped with a folding wire bipod that assisted in steadying the aim, and Japanese soldiers were taught to use a rest for the rifle whenever practically possible. Some snipers also carried a small piece of armour plate, about 10 inches high, with a spike for inserting into the earth and a 'U' shaped cut-out in which the fore-end of the rifle could rest. Practically speaking, little sniping was done at long range, due to limitations of vision rather than lack of ability on the part of the snipers. Accuracy of the rifles was also good, as testified by Lieutenant George, who thoroughly tested a captured 6.5 mm specimen:

> I fired at the short ranges – as near 100 metres as I could estimate. All the shots were bulls. At 200 metres the weapon kept everything inside 8 inches, even with some bad holding [on my part] involved. The gun continued to behave beautifully, not missing any of the settings for ranges up to 400 metres. To check the zero-return qualities of the scope mount, I took the scope off the rifle several times during the firing, with no noticeable change in the point of impact. There was no ready adjustment on the scope ... but at least the Jap soldier would not be able to ball-up what zero his rifle had been given at the arsenal.[200]

Exactly how many of the two major patterns of sniping rifle were manufactured is difficult to say with certainty, although from existing serial numbers it appears that it was about 20,000 Type 97 and probably 12,000 Type 99.

Fighting the Japanese

US methods of dealing with snipers varied, but generally the most effective forms were to rake the treetops with machine-gun fire or use 37 mm anti-tank cannon firing grapeshot canister, which shredded both the foliage and snipers, but this was a slow task. Where beachheads had been established, Marine and Army units would send forward counter-sniping teams, with observers who could spot possible sniper locations in nearby trees. Unorthodox weapons were sometimes used, with the US Army adopting some British Boys .55 inch anti-tank rifles, whose bullet was not hindered by something as puny as a tree trunk. Although the historian of the US 41st Infantry Division commented 'without tree cover no snipers could operate', this was not entirely true, for the Japanese made much use of 'spider-holes'. These were deep, well camouflaged one-man dugouts, usually sited to give a good field of fire, and nearly impossible to detect. If occupied by a skilled sniper using the 6.5 calibre rifle, with its almost non-existent muzzle flash, they were extraordinarily difficult to spot.

The Japanese snipers, both infantry and marines, were well equipped, their green uniforms being an entirely practical colour. A broad range of headgear was available. Steel helmets, usually covered with netting or foliage, the M1938 soft peaked cloth caps with protective neckflap, and lightweight 'solar topee' type bamboo helmets were all employed depending on preference, the cloth cap being the most favoured in tropical heat. Sleeveless cloaks based on the centuries-old rice-straw rain cape and made of palm *attap* were worn and camouflage netting was much used, which was a practical solution to providing cooling shade and cover in the fierce heat. Uniquely, Japanese snipers also had small spiked steel overshoes, that strapped to the *tabi*, rubber soled shoes with distinctive divided toes, and these made the climbing of trees simplicity itself. The men were incredibly patient and could remain undetected for long periods of time, as an American intelligence bulletin remarked:

A large number of Japanese wore green uniforms and painted their face and hands so they would be hard to see among the green vegetation of the islands. They also wore camouflage nets and wood fibre strands garnished with vegetation. Japs wearing these were hard to see, even at fifty yards.[201]

The tenacity of the Japanese did not diminish as the war progressed across the Pacific, for the closer the US came to the Japanese mainland, the more fierce the resistance. By the time the Marines reached Okinawa, they were being forced to use whole-scale demolition techniques to deal with the furiously defended bunkers, spider-holes and snipers' lairs. As Private Cass ruefully said:

> we were still fighting on Okinawa on May 8 1945, when Germany fell. At exactly noon every gun on the island and every ship's gun fired one shot to celebrate V-E day. I fired my victory round across a marsh at a battered tree trunk. It was a good thousand yards away. I hit it too. Then we got up and pushed on.[202]

British and Commonwealth Snipers

As was always the case when war threatened the 'Mother Country', Australians and New Zealanders flocked to the flag and providentially provided a hard core of experienced shooters who could be trained to become snipers. As in the First World War, there were a considerable number of men who were either professional hunters, or who had grown up on farms with a rifle in their hands. In the early years of the war, they had little chance to make use of their skills, and training was minimal, generally taking the form of lectures from experienced First World War snipers such as Ion Idriess, who had been appointed as instructors and passed on their hard-won skills to selected groups of men who were to become company snipers. Idriess had fought in Palestine and was an enthusiastic exponent of sniping. His lectures invariably began with an uncompromising warning that few could disagree with:

> The most dangerous individual soldier, and the world's best rifle-shot is the sniper. I mean the real sniper, the lone wolf. He is deadly. He is feared more than the tank, more than the aeroplane. He wages his own deadly little war regardless of the movements of battlefields, air fleets, panzer divisions, armies. If you decide to become a sniper then the die is cast ... your life will be in your own hands. There will be no-one to help you. Inefficiency, carelessness, over-confidence – just one little slip and you are a goner. So learn all you can before you venture out to shoot men.[203]

Not all men selected were given the benefit of training, though. Trooper L. T. Wright, Australian 2/4 Commando, recalled that he received no instruction at all, once issued with his rifle he simply 'learned by his mistakes'.[204] Though a few Australians had been able to put their skills into practical use in the desert of North Africa during the siege of Tobruk in 1942, their usefulness was limited by shortage of equipment – only a few P14 No. 3 Mk. I (T) rifles were available – and by the harsh conditions and the difficult terrain. It was not until the threat of Japanese invasion of the Antipodes loomed in 1942 that the Australian and New Zealand forces were able to begin to field snipers in some numbers.

There was clearly a shortage of suitable equipment and the old No. 3 (T) rifles were no longer in the first flush of youth, with worn barrels, damaged optics and no sources of spare parts; the rifles were no longer being manufactured. Fortunately in the early 1930s at the behest of the Army the Lithgow factory based in New South Wales had begun to look at improving the Mk. III SMLE, as they had been manufacturing them since 1913 and were well aware of their shortcomings, particularly with regard to accuracy. The old Mk. III was fickle in this respect and Lithgow improved matters considerably by manufacturing a heavy barrel, of the same profile as that fitted to the original 1902 Long Lee, but shorter by 5 inches. A special marksman's rifle, with a large 'H' marked on the wrist of the stock and fine aperture rear sight, was produced and many of the 50,000 rifle club shooters in Australia took to the new rifle like ducks to water, its superior accuracy making it the rifle to use for competition events, in much the same way as the Ross had become in Canada. When invasion threatened, many of these rifles were requisitioned (to the dismay of men such as Idriess, who believed they should have been retained by their owners for possible guerrilla use) and it was these guns that were to provide the actions for the new sniper rifle to be adopted. The old receivers of First World War or just post-war manufacture were reckoned, rightly or wrongly, to be made of better steel. They were refurbished, and all components including magazines were given a dull parkerised finish and the lower barrel under the woodwork was painted with a green rust preventative. As with the Canadians, the Australian manufacturers had a problem with optics, for there was no spare capacity in the UK to supply them with lenses, so their choice was limited by what could be locally produced. As a result they adopted the obsolete 3× Pattern 18 sight, for which drawings were available, and the Australian Optical Company of Melbourne was given the contract for their manufacture; 2,500 rifles were to be supplied and production began in mid-1944.

Two variants were produced, with either high or low mounts, both using the same German-style claw fittings and a rear-mounted quick release catch. The reason for these two variants is often misinterpreted but was a matter of practicality. The low mount made a better sniping rifle as the optical plane was so close to the bore of the rifle, and the shooter maintained a solid cheek-to-stock weld. This unfortunately precluded use of the standard iron sights, whereas the high mounts enabled them to be used with the scope mounted, which in jungle combat was often a very definite advantage. It was at the cost of an awkward shooting position though, as the head had to be raised off the stock to take aim through the scope. Most snipers overcame this as they had done in the First World War, with homemade cheek-rests made of field dressing or whatever else was at hand. Availability of open sights was certainly a godsend at times. Trooper Wright stated that when fighting in Borneo most of his combats were 'between 50 and 100 yards', not exactly practical scope distances, particularly when the P18 sight had only a 7° angle of view. Their first combat, on Timor in late 1942, was by independent companies who turned into guerrilla groups, each unit of which included at least one sniper, and in one year they accounted for over 1,500 Japanese for the loss of 40 of their own men.

By the time of the invasion of New Guinea the Australians and New Zealanders had developed their own jungle fighting tactics. The formal training that would normally have been given to them was bypassed in favour of basic instructional courses on care and handling and field tactics. Shore commented that the kangaroo hunters were remarkably good shots, used to the .303 rifle and seldom missing a target. In fact, in Shore's opinion, the Australians provided the most remarkable snipers of the whole war. In proof he quoted the instance of one kangaroo hunter on Timor who would not bother to put the scope on his rifle for shots under 300 yards and who was credited with 47 kills, and another who shot 12 advancing

Japanese with 12 shots in 15 minutes. As the Americans had found, actually identifying the whereabouts of a Japanese sniper could be a problem and the Australians found that forming counter-sniping teams was the best method. This usually comprised a spotter, sniper and sometimes a little unorthodox additional support. Russel Braddon, serving in the Australian Artillery, wrote of assisting in silencing a Japanese sniper with the use of a .55 inch Boys anti-tank rifle:

> Since the sniper fired from behind the top of the tree trunk, he could be shot through it – a Boys rifle was therefore essential for the job. With the barrel resting on my shoulder and the butt against his own, Harry took a long aim, apparently quite undeterred by the bursts of fire from all sides ... in fact as we stood there our feet spread wide apart to take some of the shock I was very deterred indeed. Then Harry fired and I was crushed to the ground ... and the sniper toppled gracelessly out from behind his tree ... I left Harry, still swearing volubly and rubbing his shoulder.[205]

Often the firepower of their service rifles proved inadequate and the ANZACs took a leaf from the Americans' book by hunting snipers using light automatics such as Bren guns, one member of the team exposing a piece of clothing on a stick to draw fire, while the others identified and dealt with the sniper, and it proved a highly effective technique, Shore recording that such tactics enabled one battalion's countersniper group to account for 35 kills in one day. In fact, some idea of the effectiveness of these techniques is the statistic that the combined Allied use of 48 snipers from two brigades accounted for an official tally of 296 Japanese over two weeks for the loss of only two of their own men.

> I thought I saw movement in the branches of one of the higher trees. Squirming behind the Bren ... I suddenly saw the unmistakable flash of an automatic weapon. Taking aim I loosed off practically a whole magazine into the tree and was rather surprised to see something thresh down out of the branches and begin to swing like a pendulum. 'You got the sod. He's on the end of a bloody rope.' Smith was jubilant as he leaned across to slap another magazine down beside the gun.[206]

This comment well illustrates the Japanese sniper's frequent habit of using weapons other than scoped rifles for the task, for this sniper appeared to be carrying a Nambu light machine-gun. Similar to the Bren gun, these light, efficient, fast-firing weapons were highly popular with the Japanese. Despite their best attempts at fulfilling the contract, by the end of the war the Lithgow factory had not managed to manufacture all of the 2,500 rifles specified in the contract. By the time production ceased in 1946, some 1,131 high mount and 481 low mount rifles had been finished. However, when war broke out again in Korea some seven years later the Australian Army found itself in the same position as it had been in 1939, with few rifles and even fewer trained snipers.

THE WAR IN WESTERN EUROPE, 1940-45

Britain's Rifles

If Britain was not keen to allocate either the time or the money to developing specialised sniping rifles, there was at least an awareness of the shortcomings of the old SMLE design, and since the early 1930s there had been considerable work undertaken to modify and improve the rifle. The final result, ratified by the Board of Ordnance in October 1939, was the Enfield No. 4 rifle, which went into production in early 1940. It had a heavier barrel and good quality aperture rear sights and was as accurate as any comparable military rifle of the period. The knotty problem of how to produce a sniping variant without adding to the demands of an already overburdened wartime economy was solved in typically British 'adopt, adapt, improve' fashion. A Mount, Telescope Sighting, No. 32, had been authorised as a straight-line sight for the Bren light machine-gun adopted in 1937. The scope had both windage and elevation drums mounted on it, and its cast-iron mount was simple but solid. Only a couple of prototype Bren mounts had been made by 1939, and the idea was officially dropped the following year. However, there was a burgeoning requirement for sniping rifles, particularly as some of the few P14 No. 3 (T) rifles issued had been lost during the retreat from France in 1940, and there was almost nothing left in store with which to replace them. Returning soldiers told of suffering at the hands of German snipers yet being powerless to retaliate, a sad repeat of the situation in 1914–15.

Corporal Eric James, who survived the Dunkirk retreat recalled that on one occasion 'I had the men either side of me shot through the head, we didn't even know there were any Germans about and we had no idea where the shots came from'.[207] Even if they had known, they had no means of dealing with them.

As a result of pressure placed on the authorities by the Army, some 1,403 Enfield No. 4 trial rifles, dating from between 1929 and 1933 were taken from stores and converted to sniping rifles at Enfield, the first batch of 100 being issued to commando units. As an interim measure this was barely adequate, the supply of rifles being nowhere near that required, so 421 Winchester made P14s were drawn from stores and converted by Alex Martin of Glasgow to No 3 Mk. 1* (T) A rifles, the A indicating pattern 3 or 4 Aldis scopes, although in fact examples with PP Co. and Watts scopes have also been noted. The mount was a non-detachable type and the scope was soldered into it; two examples of these still exist in the MOD Pattern Room Collection.[208] The new sniping rifle was known as the Enfield No. 4 (T) and with its No. 32 Mk. 1 scope it was to become the primary British service sniping weapon for almost 25 years. First issued in small numbers in North Africa in late 1942, they saw limited action, in the main because of lack of supplies and the simple practicality of attempting to use such weapons in the desert. As with the sniping rifles of the First World War they were largely issued to untrained soldiers; what rifles were available had no spare parts and there were problems with the method of adjustment of the Mk 1 scopes, which sometimes refused to retain their zero or focussing – or both. The hot dusty conditions played havoc with the rifles, jamming actions and filling the scopes with fine dust. Worse still, as sniping instructor Captain C. Shore noted:

> considerable trouble was experienced by the lenses of the sights becoming completely blurred due to the melting of the Canada balsam which joined both sets of the rear lenses.[209]

What worked well in the temperate climate of damp Europe proved less than practical in the 100 degree heat of the desert. Interestingly, while the new rifle was giving the British some teething troubles, some Commonwealth troops fighting alongside were using the old Pattern 1914 No. 3 Mk. 1* (T) rifles with good effect in the defence of Tobruk, holding out against overwhelmingly superior German forces for eight months. The Australians were born to a hot climate, and maintained their rifles completely free of oil, preventing the damaging build-up of sticky abrasive paste, as well as carefully covering the muzzles and actions to prevent ingress of sand. Even so, wear rates on sniping rifles were rapid, with most being no longer fit for sniping after 200–300 rounds. Despite this, they exacted a steady toll on the Germans, firing from concealed foxholes dug in front of the Allied lines. However, hot weather sniping was difficult for it meant that men invariably shot in shirtsleeves, which was uncomfortable, and the contact between the shoulder and buttplate was never firm, as the metal would rest on the shoulder joint and collar bone. Using the popular American M1907 sling didn't help because:

> without sufficient clothing round the arm a throbbing of the arteries will be set up and consequently steady holding will not be maintained – some form of padding where the sling bears on the arm is necessary.[210]

It was obvious that demand could not be satisfied by half-measures and the Enfield factory could scarcely divert the necessary expertise or manpower to hand build sniping rifles. As a result a contract was issued in September 1942 to the highly respected London gunmakers Holland and Holland to undertake conversion of some 12,100 No. 4 rifles to No. 4 (T) specification. The conversion was fairly straightforward: rifles that had proved exceptionally accurate when being factory zeroed were marked 'TR' on the left of the butt socket then stripped, two mounting pads being screwed to the left side of the receiver. The barrelled actions were then carefully re-bedded and a matched scope and bracket were fitted and zeroed. Despite some theories to the contrary, it was not possible to fit any scope or mount to a No. 4 (T) and expect to hit your target. As with all true sniping rifles, the scopes were carefully collimated to the barrel on assembly and it is almost impossible to replicate this without the assistance of a very competent gunsmith. The conversions cost £2 8s 6d each (£2.42, $5.00) and in February 1943 another contract for a further 12,100 was issued, with an expected turnover of some 800 rifles a month. In all some 26,442 rifles were produced by Holland and Holland.

The No. 4 (T) was capable of good long-range performance; although it proved to be an unremarkable sniping weapon at short ranges, beyond 400 yards it was highly accurate in skilled hands. Captain C. Shore recounted the tale of the British sniper in Italy who was scouting with two GIs prior to a British unit taking over from the Americans near Mt Grande. When he spotted Germans 700 yards away, he opened fire from a ruined house and scored at least two hits, the sniper commenting that the Germans' attitude afterwards 'was not half so cocksure and brazen as formerly'.[211] Harry Furness noted that his battalion snipers could make head shots out to 400 yards but only body shots beyond that, but this was due more to the limitations of the 3× power scope than to deficiencies on the part of the rifle. The great benefit for the snipers over the old telescopic sights was in having easily adjustable range and windage drums. Where circumstances permitted, most preferred to make use of them in conjunction with elevation and wind tables, rather than the old tried and tested method of aiming off, although this was still inevitable in some situations.

As always, a vital component in the sniper's arsenal was his ammunition, for accuracy depends on the standard of ammunition used. The Army determined that the standard Mk. VII ammunition was perfectly adequate for sniping use, but as always snipers had their own preferences. Shore always used Winchester made .303 inch and Harry Furness, Sergeant sniper with the Hallamshire Battalion, Yorks and Lancs Regiment, made a point of swapping cigarettes for the Mk. VIIz streamlined long-range ammunition used by his battalion Vickers gunners. This had a heavier 175 grain bullet and slightly larger charge that produced a muzzle velocity of 2,400 feet/sec, and was generally not recommended for sniping rifles, but it had its uses, as Sergeant Furness commented. 'It had good qualities for extreme range sniping and I considered it no more corrosive than the AP [armour-piercing] or occasional incendiary rounds I used at times.'[212] Using this ammunition he was able to pick off a senior German officer who was involved in a conference with fellow officers, at a range in excess of 600 yards (553 metres). In fact most snipers developed a quiet obsession about their ammunition, and Shore wrote that he:

meticulously cleaned and polished all my ammunition before use. At first the men used to find this highly polished ammunition of mine something of a joke, but later I found a number of them, a bit shamefacedly, following my example.

Canada and Long Branch

The British were not alone as they waded up the wet beaches of Sword, Juno and Gold in 1944, for there were also large numbers of Canadian troops alongside them. Following a recommendation made by the British Army Council the previous year, the Canadians had begun to take their shooting skills more seriously and in 1938 militia HQ had authorised the issue of '8 rifles, No.3 Mk. I* (T) to each Infantry Battalion'. These were the old P14 rifles equipped with Pattern 1918 scopes, and they were adequate but hardly the latest in sniping technology. There were insufficient to equip the Army, which comprised 58 infantry battalions that up to this date boasted on their combined inventory only two scoped Ross rifles for sniping use with a further 385 scopes and 208 rifles held in stores. A further recommendation was made that they be issued for training purposes at the level of two per battalion. In practice, when the first Canadian units went overseas in 1939, their sniping equipment consisted of 80 Warner and Swasey sights that had been mated to No. 3 Mk. I* rifles which while an odd combination, proved effective enough. Other patterns were also fielded including No. 3 Mk. I* rifles fitted with offset Aldis and PP Co. scopes on Purdey-type mounts, and Ross rifles with PP scopes on offset mounts. While these rifles were certainly useful as a stopgap measure, they did not provide the Canadian Army with the modern sniping rifle they required.

The setting up of the Small Arms Limited production facility at Long Branch, in August 1940, paved the way for the manufacture of Enfield No. 4 rifles under licence. Initially the first batch of Long Branch sniping rifles were ordinary production arms specially selected for accuracy after test firing, and set aside for conversion. This proved difficult, for the finished rifles had case hardened receivers, which as the Inspection Board noted resulted in:

considerable difficulty in drilling and tapping the holes in the body to fit the rear telescope bracket, and in consequence it was found preferable to select certain components in the early stages of production and to follow them through as a special order.[213]

As a result, later batches of No. 4 (T) rifles were specifically allocated blocks of serial numbers. The telescopes were to be manufactured by a Canadian optical company called Research Enterprises Limited (REL) based in Leaside, Ontario and were made to the No. 32 Mk. 1 standard, but unlike the British production facilities where optical glass was supplied to one of six telescopic sight makers[214] by specialist manufacturers such as Chance Brothers, REL had to manufacture their own. This is a difficult process at the best of times, even more so under wartime conditions, yet by May 1941, only an extraordinary nine months from its inception, the factory was producing optical glass from its own furnaces. However, it had to supply not only glass for telescopic rifles, but also for artillery and tank gunsights, dial sights, clinometers and observers' telescopes – some 7,000 instruments of eleven different types in total. The fact that they lagged behind in the supply of scopes for the No. 4 (T) is therefore hardly surprising, and by the end of the war they produced some 326 No. 32 Mk. 1, 255 No. 32 Mk. II and 113 No. 32 Mk. 1A scopes. Despite occasional claims to the contrary, there were no Mk. 3 scopes manufactured until after the end of the war.

From the outset the engineers at REL were less than happy with the performance of the British scopes, and others were tested including the ubiquitous Weaver 330-C and Lyman Alaskan, fitted to Griffin and Howe mounts as well as REL made 3.5× scopes and 5× Gimbals. The Lyman and Gimbal both proved very effective and four Gimbals were produced, which after 500-round trials were deemed suitable, but after some argument the Canadian Ordnance decided on a 3.5× power, as 5× was thought to restrict the field of view too much. This went into production as the No. 67, although many early ones were marked as 'No. 32 Mk. 4'. Aside from improved adjustment drums and simpler construction the new scope weighed 10 oz less than the portly British No 32. Later rifles were also modified with the addition of a Monte Carlo sporting stock, with a built in rubber recoil pad and sculpted cheek comb, as the screwed-on British cheek rest was not considered comfortable. Despite the efforts made to supply them with their own rifle during the fighting in 1944 and 1945 most Canadian snipers used the Enfield made No. 4 (T), as only 1,141 Long Branch sniping rifles were constructed in time, with a further 350 still awaiting assembly by end of hostilities. Development of the Canadian sniping rifle was not to remain static, however, and it was to re-emerge in Korea a few short years after the war.

America's Sniping Rifles

Although the United States was still relying on a rifle that had been designed pre-First World War, the Ordnance Department had been busy in the wake of the adoption of the M1-Garand and by mid-1941 a large proportion of the US Army were equipped with them. This excluded the few serving snipers as no work had been done in developing a telescopic sight or mounting system suitable for use with the M1. With echoes of the problems faced by British snipers in the First World War, the Garand could only be clip loaded and this meant that any scope had to be heavily offset to the left, placing the shooter's head at an awkward angle on the stock, so not only a mounting system but a compatible scope had to be found. Therefore, in late 1943 the Ordnance Department began testing to find a suitable system. They had initially discounted the 330-C Weaver because of its fragility in the less than caring hands of the snipers, allied to the fact there was almost no latitude for moving it forward to give increased eye relief. HQ Army Ground Force put forward a demanding set of recommendations among which were that whatever system was chosen must:

> Lower the telescope [and bring it] on a level with the standard iron sights.
> Bring the axis of the scope to the vertical plane through the axis of the bore, and still permit clip loading.
> Bring the rear of the telescope … to a position one quarter inch in front of the … elevation knob on the rearsight.
> Permit fore and aft adjustment of the scope … to fit the individual.
> That an adjustable cheek-piece be supplied.[215]

Two mounting designs emerged from the Springfield Armory in Massachusetts, the M1E7 and M1E8. The former used a mounting block that required three holes to be drilled and tapped into the left side receiver wall, while the latter needed a machined block pinned to the chamber, with a threaded hole in it to accept a mounting screw, with consequent shortening of the rear top handguard. The M1E7 was chosen, initially partly for ease of fitting but also because of the availability of the practical Griffin and Howe mounts, which used two locking levers that held the base securely in place by means of a pressure plate. This enabled the scope to be easily removed and refitted, which left only the problem of what optical system actually to adopt. The Ordnance Board returned to the Lyman company with a request that they furnish a modified Alaskan telescope fitted with a sunshield at the objective end and rubber eyepiece at the ocular end of the scope body, and a cross-hair reticle. This was designated the M81 and was approved in October 1944. A scope fitted with a slightly modified reticle using a tapered post was also adopted soon afterwards, becoming the M82. The Lymans were of 2.5× power with fixed focus and provided a useful field of view of 35 feet at 100 yards which remained unaffected regardless of the eye relief. The scopes were produced in commercial blue finish and were issued with a web carrying case. The designation of the rifle was to be the M1-C and from its inception there was controversy over its suitability as a 'sniping arm' as Springfield-armed Sergeant William Jones commented: 'I might have been slower with my rifle than the other boys with their Garands, but I knew I was a great deal more accurate. I could hit what I shot at'.[216]

As both the Russians and Germans had discovered when attempting to modify semi-automatic rifles for sniping, assembly of standard components, no matter how carefully done, will not give the same levels of reliability or accuracy as that achieved with a hand-built bolt-action rifle. Even the Office of the Chief of Ordnance in Washington accepted this, and wrote to Springfield Armory that:

> the office fully appreciates not only the desirability but also the necessity of selecting not only components with preferable dimensions ... but eliminating from possible assembly into M1-C rifles all components that are not within drawing dimensions.[217]

In other words, to build a good sniping rifle, all parts had to be blueprinted (selected and scrupulously measured for exact tolerances as specified in manufacturer's drawings) then hand-assembled to provide, as the Chief of Ordnance put it, 'the best artisan skill of the Armory and it must live up to all the expectations of the soldier receiving it'. Early problems with the Garands included jamming, failure to eject spent cases and the apparently insoluble problem of ejection of the empty ammunition clip:

> When you fired the last shot, the damn clip would eject with a clang that sounded like a ringing bell. If I were out [sniping] I always made sure I had a full magazine and I never, never fired my last shot without another full clip right next to me. It was a real problem with the Garand.[218]

Generally it was thought that the Garand was a good sniping rifle out to medium ranges of 500–600 yards (461–553 metres), but of little practical use at longer ranges. Army Sergeant John Fulcher reckoned he could hit anything up to 500 yards (461 metres), and when US forces landed at Salerno in Italy in September 1943 he and his fellow snipers finally had a chance to put their skills to the test. They were faced with a very different situation to that of the Marines who were island-hopping in the Pacific. Many of the German units facing the Allies contained men with a great deal of practical sniping experience, often gained in Russia, and in particular their paratroop units held many good shots, and were to prove extremely stubborn during the campaign. The US snipers were deployed, 'to establish a presence' and they took up the challenge with a will, working on the flanks of their advance and often ahead of their own men, seeking out enemy snipers and machine-gun units left behind by the retreating enemy to delay the advance. The Americans had little experience and at first suffered grievously from the effect of the German snipers, who would occupy advance positions before dawn and shoot any enemy they observed, before silently withdrawing, leaving confusion, fear and an understandable reluctance to advance. Oberst Karl Krauss recalled that:

> my spotter and I would take a position to overlook a crossroad or vehicle park, then shoot officers or NCOs or sometimes the drivers. In this way we

managed once to stop a whole column because the road became blocked and all the Americans were forced to take cover. I made only five shots and we withdrew. I think we held their advance up for hours.[219]

The Americans learned quickly and Fulcher and his men began to copy the German tactics. He and his No. 2 had settled onto a ridge one early morning and watched in astonishment as a whole company of fresh German troops led by an officer marched along the track:

I looked at my partner. He had his rifle scope trained on them. He looked back at me. He shook his head. A whole company? I nodded at my partner. Let's take them. They're green. Even if they organised an assault, we could be off the ridge before they got halfway across the field to us. As cool as could be, I cross-haired the officer and shot him through the belly. He was dead by the time I brought my rifle down out of recoil and picked him up again in my scope. His legs were drumming on the road, but he was dead.[220]

After his partner also shot a German, Fulcher decided to wait, partly out of curiosity and the two sat silently, cradling their Garands. Led by a junior officer, the Germans retreated at speed back down the track, straight into the rifles of another pair of snipers stationed further along the road. Fulcher made an interesting comment about his first kill. 'After I killed the officer … I felt something inside me start to change. You become a predator. I got to where it hurt more to kill a good dog than a human being.'

In the Army there existed little in the way of proper sniper training. One Regiment, the 42nd Armoured Infantry did establish a five week course under the tutelage of its enthusiastic commander, but it was a rare example and other units provided the minimum of shooting training, and almost no field training, so snipers were frequently turned loose with little idea of how to operate and only the most basic knowledge of the care and maintenance of their equipment. Army Sergeant William E. Jones recounted the typical experience of how he became a sniper, after attaining the highest score on the rifle range during training. 'Because of that, and no other reason I know, I got volunteered to be the company sniper. We had only one for each company.' He was issued with a new 1903-A4 Springfield, for, as he said:

my job was to shoot folks 'way out there'. I heard some of the other divisions had sniper schools to learn that, but I guess the brass didn't think I needed any schooling, the way I could shoot already.[221]

Such amateurism must have puzzled the German snipers, and Karl Krauss, himself a veteran of five months in Russia, had some pertinent comments on the subject:

Sometimes we came under fire from the GI snipers, but they were often not good shots, and their hidings [hides] were usually very easy to find. They were not trained well I think, and once we captured two. They had good rifles with small telescopes but they did not know much of camouflage and they fired too many shots from their hiding place, so we found them. We kept their rifles and sent the men back to the rear as prisoners. I do not think they were real snipers.[222]

Krauss's comment about taking prisoners is almost unique for nowhere else in his research did the author find any evidence that a captured sniper was not summarily dispatched on the spot, so perhaps those lucky Americans were saved by professional courtesy. Thousands of Springfield 1903-A4s remained in service throughout the war, many snipers swearing, with some justification, that their 'bolt rifles' were inherently more accurate than the semi-automatic Garand. Despite the fact that the rest of his Eighth Infantry buddies carried Garands, Army Sergeant William E. Jones held on to his 1903-A4, partly because of its abilities, and partly because of its uniqueness:

Everyone else in the company had either the standard issue M-1 Garand or the shorter .30 calibre carbine. Because of 'the rifle' everybody knew who I was. I was the sniper. That's how I thought of that relationship too – the rifle; the sniper.[223]

During the advance through Italy, the US Army snipers would pay a heavy price for their lack of training, but by the time the Allies reached Rome there had formed a hard core of battle-hardened snipers whose skills would be put to the ultimate test in the fight across Europe, following the Allied invasion of Normandy in June 1944. The hardest part was yet to come.

Invasion

By 1944 the fortunes of the Allies had turned around. Rommel had been defeated in North Africa and the Allies had fought their way up through Italy. Germany had suffered the fate of all who attempted to invade Russia; a winter campaign where their armies had eventually been encircled and fought to a standstill. The survivors had withdrawn west and Hitler was facing a war on three fronts, which even the superbly equipped German Army could not sustain, for it was battle weary. Allied bombing and the defeat of the U-Boat threat had turned Germany into a country beset by shortages of raw materials, food, clothing and increasingly, able bodied men.

The decision taken by Allied high command to invade Normandy was certainly a gamble, for there were some very tough German troops stationed in France, including Panzer units and Waffen-SS troops. The longer the Allies waited the more likely their plans would be discovered and the vital element of surprise lost. When the troopships put to sea on 5 June 1944 it was to be the biggest gamble of the war, played for the highest possible stakes. For many of the snipers who huddled in the pitching landing craft, they faced the unknown, having done no more than train endlessly, but they were at least well equipped, which was just as well, for the Germans were not going to give ground easily.

The British and Commonwealth snipers who had landed on the beaches of Normandy had received a mixed reception. Wading ashore with their rifle barrels and scopes covered by condoms to protect against the sea water, the first wave were met in some places not by withering machine-gun fire, but an almost surreal lack of response from the Germans. This was not to last long, as German units were rushed forward and the weary British soon found themselves having to contest every house in the small coastal villages. One sniper recalled his first kill being a reflex snapshot at running Germans, his bullet bringing down a young corporal.[224] As the men moved through the open farmland, they began to meet stiffening resistance, and as they advanced it became clear that the Germans were prepared to contest every inch of ground. Initially snipers were ordered to 'dominate the battlefield'. As one wrote:

This was accomplished not by shooting at every movement, but by highly selective shooting of what we termed 'priority targets'. The effect of killing with one shot only their officers, senior NCOs, etc caused such confusion ... that it was a decisive factor in who controlled that area.[225]

Not all British commanders understood the value of their snipers, however, and one unit commander issued scoped rifles to a number of 'riflemen' in his unit, sending them forward en masse with instructions to 'pot jerries'. With no sniper training or rifle instruction they achieved little and proved easy meat for the opposing German snipers and an ideal target for mortars and artillery. One skilled shot in the unit commented that he was more accurate with his rifle using iron sights than any of the 'snipers' were with their scopes. Generally speaking, though, most snipers were prized for their abilities even if their service lives were to prove brief – the Green Howards regiment had in excess of 100% losses during the Normandy campaign and Private Francis Miller, 5th Battalion East Yorkshire Regiment, became known as 'Borrowed Time' as one by one, his fellow snipers became casualties. He was the only one to survive long enough to serve with the unit until it reached Germany.

The routine of fighting through occupied country was exhausting, both mentally and physically and it became more so as they moved into the central Normandy region known as the bocage. Fighting was constant, and even in rest the men were targets for mortars, artillery and sniping. Harry Furness wrote that his memory of Normandy is disjointed, for:

we never seemed to get much sleep ... any chance of a brief rest meant putting your head down for a few minutes, often in a waterlogged slit-trench. We were always fully equipped ready to move so rarely got out of our uniforms, including boots and gaiters. Getting hot food anywhere near the frontline was a luxury.[226]

Sniper Training and Equipment

The British high command were well aware of the need to produce trained snipers, many of the officers and training NCOs having fought in the trenches 25 years before. There were sniping schools in existence, although few and far between, and the 1941 Notes on the Training of Snipers was almost a copy of the notes issued in 1918, although there was a more noticeable emphasis placed on open warfare sniping. In view of the course the war would run, this advice would prove particularly prophetic. However, in the early years of the war training was haphazard and could vary widely. In theory, it was determined that a British sniper section should comprise 8 men under the command of an NCO and, as in the First World War, their duties differed significantly from those of the infantry. Harry Furness commented of their duties: 'snipers do not take on the role of line infantry, neither are we expected to take ground, take P.O.W.s, or lead attacks'.[227]

The Army, having at last understood the importance of having snipers with the right mental attitude, accepted only volunteers. No longer was the best shot in the platoon, or a man with Bisley target experience, to be handed a rifle and informed he was a sniper, for as Clifford Shore pointed out:

> During the training of snipers there were many instances of men being excellent target shots but failing in the role of sniping... In 1943 I had a fellow in my own unit ... and a range shot of considerable skill and experience. When I took him out on some elementary sniper shooting I was very disappointed. He was slow and his shooting at sniping targets lacked a good deal. In other phases of sniper training he was useless.[228]

Finding enough men with the right skills was difficult. Training was undertaken in various schools in the UK, most notably the Small Arms School, Sniping Wing at Bisley in Surrey, The School of Musketry at Hythe in Sussex, the Army School of Sniping at Llanberis in North Wales and the Commando School in Scotland where the large estates were ideal training ground. As the war progressed there were additional schools set up in Lebanon, Palestine, Italy and eventually northern France and Holland. The training course differed little from that of the previous war, although more emphasis was placed on intelligence gathering, fieldcraft and open warfare sniping, where the construction of hides in open land would prove of vital importance if a sniper was to survive. Specialist equipment was issued to snipers, comprising the camouflaged Denison smock of the same type as issued to paratroopers, a prismatic compass, a notebook from which patrol details would later be entered into a logbook at battalion HQ, maps of the area, chocolate, chewing gum, two full water bottles and, if there was a chance of very close enemy contact a couple of No. 36 grenades. Cigarettes were seldom carried by snipers, the smoke being, quite literally, a dead give-away and the temptation after hours sitting cold and bored in a hide too great.

Clothing, as was the case in the First World War, was whatever the snipers deemed practical but they generally adopted the roomy camouflaged Denison smock, issued to airborne troops, with standard fatigue trousers and issue boots. Headgear was varied, Harry Furness always wore a steel helmet, camouflaged with netting and foliage, while Francis Miller preferred a brown army beret. Others opted for the woollen cap comforter and there exist some photos of Canadian snipers wearing eminently practical bandanas made from camouflage scrim. Unlike the Germans, Britain did not issue anywhere near as much in the way of specialist clothing, and it was not until 1944 that a camouflaged suit was issued. This mattered little to the snipers, who would fabricate their own ghillie suits and adapt them in a way only the frontline soldier can. One sniper said of his working uniform and kit:

I always wore a Denison smock … it had large pockets in which we kept our prismatic compass, notebook from which we later wrote (always in capital lettering so that it could be easily read by the intelligence office) the patrol details. We had a survey map of the area in which we were operating. During the winter snow and frost I also had a white snow suit to wear, and I wrapped my rifle and telescopic sight in white bandages. Later in the campaign I was issued with a complete camouflage suit, a smock and trousers of a very unusual disruptive pattern … it had very mellow colouring and was in addition windproof so I found it very useful indeed as snipers get very cold. Frequently over my boots and gaiters I found it helped if I slipped an unused sandbag and tied it with string, it disguised the outline of my boots and was a help in preventing me slipping if I hurried over smooth pavements with my steel studded boots, it also muffled the sound. Camouflage cream was available at some Sniper Schools but not often in the frontline so we just wet some mud and smeared it on our face and hands.[229]

Harry Furness always carried a Fairbairn-Sykes dagger with him, which aside from making a useful utility knife, was vital for probing for mines and booby traps, and he had his Denison smock modified with the addition of two large pockets sewn onto the back so he could reach them while lying prone. Colonel Peter Young, commanding No. 3 Commando, noted of the resourcefulness of his snipers:

> Trooper Fahy, made himself a camouflage suit from denim overalls, hessian strips and odd pieces of material that came to hand. Then nothing would do but he must go off and try his luck. He and Trooper Needham, a cool resolute Irish Guardsman similarly attired, showed me their suits and persuaded me to let them loose ... they were back within half an hour, having shot two Germans. In 3 Troop Corporal Hanson and Trooper Hawksworh were the star performers ... they once accounted for five Germans in one day. After this the enemy became so careful that it was hard to find targets.[230]

On patrol, snipers soon learned that the slightest carelessness could have fatal repercussions, and most carried the absolute minimum of equipment with them. Shore wrote that 'occasionally snipers went out looking like shabby old poachers, carrying only their sniper rifles and no equipment'.[231] Food had to be carried and making hot meals was a serious problem, particularly in cold weather, for any fire and consequent smoke was likely to prove to be a death sentence. A sniper, recalling his time in the frontline said of his rations that he carried:

> hard-tack, hard black chocolate and a real treat was that we had cans of soup and sometimes a mash which could be heated by pulling a tab which heated it internally ... but we had to be careful to see that the cans were not badly dented or damaged as that way they would explode. We usually had two full water bottles, and I never knew of any sniper taking alcohol with them, the risk is too great not to be fully aware of all of the dangers.[232]

Carrying tins and the issue metal cup was dangerous, and all ranks were exhorted to ensure these items were wrapped in spare clothing or socks to prevent them clanking.

The *Bocage* and Beyond

To anyone passing through the benign, pastoral northern French landscape today it is hard to imagine the hell that it became for the Allies in summer of 1944. The farming system had altered little since the middle ages and fields were still separated by dense thickets of hedge, small trees and wild undergrowth that give the country its name. Unlike the thin, neatly trimmed British hedgerows, the *bocage* can be over ten feet thick, 20 or more feet tall and so dense that access can only be gained by cutting into it with an axe or machete. It proved to be the natural environment for the sniper, particularly so from the point of view of the defending Germans, who were provided with the best cover nature could offer. From the outset of the invasion, Allied casualties as a result of sniping were so severe that some battalions were reduced to no more than a couple of officers and a few NCOs, a situation reminiscent of that in 1914.

Counter-sniping became a vital tool in the advance and a cat-and-mouse war within a war began. Whole sections of the advance were at times halted by a combination of German sniper fire and the use of carefully concealed light machine-guns. Opening up harassing fire at the advancing troops, the German machine-gunners would then fall back to new positions, while one or two well-concealed snipers ensured there was no further movement from the Allies before slipping back to join their comrades when darkness fell. However, even the Germans were not infallible. Arthur Hare, a regular soldier of the Cambridgeshire Regiment, was a company sniper, and had learned a few things as he fought through Palestine, Greece, Crete and the Western Desert. In July 1944, with his newly arrived subaltern occupying his own position some yards away, Hare and his partner Packham lay watching for signs of movement from the thick hedgerows. One single shot broke the silence, then peace returned to a landscape that appeared utterly devoid of war. Eventually the sun sank and they stealthily moved over to collect their officer:

'I do believe the blighter's gone to sleep', Arthur thought to himself, and shook him gently by the shoulder. The Lieutenant's face swivelled round and between the staring eyes, drilled with minute precision was the entry hole of the bullet that killed him.' Hare and Packham returned the next day to their hide and lay in wait, watching. Hare suddenly whispered 'See that dead tree standing to the right of that hayrick, just on the edge of the wood? Two fingers from there to the right.'

'What am I looking for?' 'Smoke', was the laconic reply. 'The bastard's having a fag.' 'Got it', Packham rasped …

'You fire', Hare replied. 'I'll watch and make sure you get him.' But the German didn't move. For two days the pair returned to their hide, patiently lying still until, at 6.10am on the third morning, the German's head and shoulders briefly appeared, framed in an archway of foliage. Packham's rifle fired a single shot. All that Arthur saw was the German's rifle pirouetting in the sky.

'Got him', he said with satisfaction.[233]

As the Allies crept forwards, the conditions deteriorated, with supply becoming more difficult and German resistance more organised. Burial of the countless dead was almost impossible and a sickening stench pervaded the whole region, which became overrun with millions of huge flies. So bad was the situation that the pilot of a Hawker Typhoon fighter-bomber recalled that even flying over the area at 2,000 feet 'you could smell the battlefield below, a mix of rotting corpses and the horrible smell of burnt flesh and burning fuel. There was a pall over the region that could be seen from several miles away as we flew towards it, and it was a hateful place'.[234] The flies spread dysentery, from which none were immune and Sergeant Furness said of the problem 'I leave it to your imagination what it was like coping with dysentery when you are in a concealed position for hours at a time and even the slightest movement could lead to discovery'.[235] One German Eastern Front veteran recalled that he thought the weather conditions were often more unpleasant than in Russia, due to almost ceaseless rain.

The inexperience of many of the Allied soldiers made German sniping easier. Young officers were particularly easy meat, for despite their uniform and equipment being identical to that of an infantryman they were frequently victims of snipers' bullets, the average lifespan of a subaltern being three weeks. This was not due to any uncanny ability on the part of the Germans but simply, as in the First World War, a failure on the part of officers to comprehend the observation skills of snipers. As one British regimental historian commented, when interrogated, 'German snipers told us they could always pick out the officers by their moustaches'.[236]

Much of the advance was spent in attempting to deal with German snipers, and while many were very experienced, a large number were not, having been rushed to the line as soon as their training was complete. One German sniper commented that:

We had only just finished our training when we were sent to Normandy. In the first week four of my comrades were killed and I was wounded by a grenade that was thrown into the roof in which we were concealed. I hid my rifle and surrendered my pistol and so I survived. I was eighteen years of age.[237]

The Allied snipers invariably had to do things the hard way, watching for tiny clues and occasional carelessness. Despite taking great care over their camouflage, snipers often overlooked one basic item of equipment, their telescopic sights:

The worst reflections from the optical sight really needed careful handling. It was my standard practice to wrap my entire rifle and T/S [Telescopic sight] in green and brown scrimmage wrapping ... I left just enough uncovered to load my rifle ... and I left sufficient space to operate my two [range and elevation] drums.[238]

Taking such care often provided the fine line between living and dying. Hidden in the rafters of a damaged roof Sergeant Furness was tasked with finding a German sniper inflicting bad casualties on his forward company. Despite careful observation:

over a long time no further shots were fired, I continued to search for signs using my more powerful scout telescope, and one house I watched for a while

... had broken windows and damaged exterior wooden shutters ... but now and again one of the shutters moved as the wind caught it. I must have been watching the area and that swaying shutter for hours when I caught a little movement – quick movements of any kind draw your eye to it if you are looking. I switched from my telescope to pick up my rifle and it seemed to me to be a hand reaching to get hold of the shutter by the edge. I fired immediately into and near the edge of the shutter, and even with the rifle recoil I felt sure I had seen an arm inside the house slide down and bang on the sill. I waited and watched until dusk before I left but saw no more movement nor had any shot been fired all the time I was there. That night a fighting patrol was sent out and they brought back for me a semi-automatic G43 rifle fitted with a telescopic sight. On the floor next to the window was a dead German.[239]

As the Allies advanced across France and Holland, the winter began to settle in, and snowsuits were issued to snipers, rifles being covered with white bandages to camouflage their outline. The Germans knew that defeat was only a matter of time, but they still made life as difficult as possible for the advancing Allies and Holland and western Germany were to be extremely hard fought, with mounting casualties on both sides. By this time, the Allied snipers had become both more wary and cunning, and the experience gained during the advance stood them in good stead. Few German snipers survived capture and of those who survived, most prefer to remain silent about their experiences. One Waffen-SS veteran who did speak of his experiences said of this time:

our unit morale was good, we understood the war was lost and most of us had no homes because of the bombing, but we were not going to surrender. The enemy would pay for every metre of ground. In these months I gained very much experience and made many scores but the British snipers were well equipped and hard to fight. Usually, we made a position and fired, maybe one or two shots, then left quickly for it was dangerous to remain. One bullet smashed the sight on my rifle and I could not get another for some time so I was a sniper without a telescope. I was very lucky to return to Germany, but there was nothing left, everything was gone and I was angry for many years about this.[240]

The US Advance

It wasn't just the British and Canadians who were having a hard time advancing through Europe, for since they had landed in June, the Americans had had an equally tough fight, constantly using their snipers to the maximum of their ability. Equipped with a mixture of Springfield 1903-A4s and Garand M1Cs they too had to contest every inch of foreign soil. Of the 6,896 M1Cs manufactured from late 1944 to August 1945, exactly how many reached frontline snipers is a moot point, but certainly enough were in service to warrant some modifications to improve performance. The muzzle flash, particularly in low light conditions was deemed excessive and an M2 flash-hider was provided which clipped to the muzzle and eliminated 90% of the flash. Unfortunately it was soon discovered by the snipers that this attachment altered the zero of the rifle and few were used operationally. The comparatively low power of the scopes was also a limiting factor, but as maximum effective range was generally agreed to be no more than 600 yards (553 metres), this was not the problem that it could have been. In reality, the Garand proved an extremely useful combat rifle in the *bocage* country for its semi-automatic ability meant it could be employed quickly for close combat, a factor that was to re-emerge when the US became involved in the conflict in Vietnam. Nevertheless, at times the snipers might almost have been in the Pacific jungles:

> The countryside was a patchwork quilt of little fields enclosed by hedges of hawthorn, brambles and vines tangled together to make walls ten to fifteen feet tall. A lot of these hedgerows grew out of big mounds three to four feet high, with drainage ditches on either side. They grew out of the roads, which were nothing but wagon trails ... and made it seem like you were going down through a tunnel ... and all you could see in front of you was the gloom and dripping, shaggy walls of the hedgerows.[241]

Sergeant William E. Jones also recounted how the undergrowth could conceal all manner of surprises such as when one astonished GI walked round a bend into an equally amazed German. Neither had the ability to shoot and they could have reached out and touched one another. 'The GI yelled "Shoo! Get the hell outa here!" And the German took off.'[242]

The Americans were forced to learn their trade the hard way and by the time Sergeant John Fulcher and his M1-C had fought their way across Italy, he had become a tough and experienced sniper. The scarcity of trained snipers meant that most combat units contained their own unofficial snipers who, despite not having specialist training, proved to be extraordinary shots with their iron-sighted rifles. A member of Colonel Howard Johnson's Airborne Intelligence and Recon. S-2 teams, Private Roland Wilbur, practised obsessively on the training ranges in England with his Garand M1 rifle. As fellow Private Carl H. Cartledge was later to recount:

> because of our secret status, Roland Wilbur's legendary skill with an M-1 languishes in obscurity. It should not. Gifted with extraordinary eyesight ... each round that Wilbur fired served as practice to improve his skill. Wilbur fired tens of thousands of rounds to push himself to the limit. After Normandy a man identified to us as a factory representative came to ... watch Wilbur shoot. He watched with powerful binoculars what Roland Wilbur did with the naked eye. He stated 'this man can shoot his rifle further and faster than our calculations say it can be done'. Wilbur could snap shoot between five and seven hundred yards. He later recorded kills at that distance at Bastogne. Wilbur never fired from the same place twice. He never exposed himself longer than to roll over. If no-one lined up in his sights, Wilbur disappeared. When Wilbur fired, there was one less of them.[243]

During the Normandy campaign men such as Wilbur were worth their weight in gold, for their abilities as combat infantrymen combined with their shooting accuracy meant that they were able to protect comrades from enemy snipers while also being on hand to perform as an integral part of a tight-knit group of specialists.

Snipers understood their importance in protecting their men and William E. Jones looked after his rifle like a child. It needed it, for in the constant wet weather of Normandy in late summer and early autumn 1944 everything, men, weapons and vehicles, suffered in the unending rain:

> I kept a little can of oil, a cleaning rod and some bore patches. Steel rusted in that climate overnight. I fought the rust constantly. No matter how beat I was

... every time I got the chance ... I broke out my cleaning rod and attacked the rust before it got a good start. I disassembled the parts on a spread-out poncho and looked down the bore and felt in the chamber ... I would have liked some wax for the stock but I didn't have any, so I oiled it down using an old sock.[244]

Sergeant Furness wrote that in the heavy rain the snipers made sure to keep their ammunition dry in the magazine:

If it was raining general technique was to tip the rifle to the right, towards the ground and use the bolt that way to keep the rain out. Wet rounds are bad news for snipers, they fire badly, they are inaccurate and you can lose a killing shot that way.[245]

Taking such care of their rifles and ammunition was second nature for a sniper for his life, or that of a comrade, could depend on its accuracy with just one shot – perhaps the only one he would fire all day. Private Jones was soon called upon to deal with an enemy sniper and surveyed the foliage in front of him through his telescopic sight. After patient observation he spotted what he took to be a bird in the knot in a tree:

The next time the knot moved, I knew it was not a bird. The sucker had shot at least two of our boys. With that in mind and nothing else I drew in a deep breath filled with the smell of the rich soil on which I lay, let half of it slowly escape and then gently stroked the trigger... I saw the tree shaking violently. I quickly bolted in another round and put my cross hairs back on target. I squeezed off another round. The German turned loose his perch just like a squirrel does and bounced off the limbs down through the tree until his body hit the ground. That was my only 'confirmed' kill if 'confirmed' meant you had to go up and look at his teeth shining between his lips and pick out the bullet hole.[246]

The rain also caused a problem with the widely used Pattern 1907 rifle sling. This American-designed shooting sling was still the most practical type available, but in wet weather its oiled leather became slippery and it would not stay in place on the upper arm. Frustratingly, if it were not kept oiled it cracked as it dried and some British snipers found that the extra-long webbing sling for the Bren gun made a very acceptable substitute.

Germany Retreats

The Allied troops slowly began to roll up the defending Germans before them, pushing back through the infamous Falaise Gap and eastwards towards Germany. The onset of winter did not make life any easier for either side, the snipers suffering particularly from the cold. They were forced to lie static for hours at a time and lack of hot food and drink, or the means to restore their circulation, made creaking old men of them. In later life many would suffer as a result of the conditions they endured during these months. There was also a new threat being faced, which at the time appeared inexplicable. Casualties were being taken but no shots heard and various theories abounded about secret equipment the Germans were testing. In fact the technology being used was nothing new, for sound suppressors were being issued in limited numbers probably in conjunction with subsonic 7.92 mm ammunition. A very few suppressors have been recovered from Normandy over the last few years and Sergeant Furness recalled one of his company officers finding cases of specially marked subsonic ammunition, although whether this was for exclusive issue to snipers is not known.

The problem with any form of suppression is that it cannot mask the supersonic 'crack' of the bullet, even if it muffles the sound of the discharge, so to be truly effective, low velocity ammunition must be used, which introduces one of the major drawbacks of such technology for it severely limits the range of the bullet to about 200 yards. In the towns and villages of northern France and the *bocage* this was actually practical for close-range sniping but of no real use once the fighting moved into the open land of rural France. As the front line moved steadily eastwards into the more densely populated areas so the shattered houses proved a haven for snipers on both sides. It was quite possible for snipers to move from house to house through their internal walls using the holes blown through them by tanks. One sniper commented that it was possible to traverse entire streets without emerging into the daylight. Much of a sniper's time was spent doing nothing but observing, particularly in situations where the strength of the enemy was unknown and a shot could bring about massive retaliation.

Arthur Hare had taken up station in the roof space of an empty house and by afternoon had been silently observing troop movements for five hours, but he was human like anyone else and he found himself increasingly irritated by a German sentry who apparently kept staring directly at him. Without fixing his scope, he drew a bead on the German and fired. All hell then broke loose, as rifles, machine-guns and mortars laid down a torrent of fire on the house. To compound matters, British artillery began to return fire, and the first two shells landed smack on the house, badly shaking Hare, but his coolness, which was later to earn him the Military Medal, reasserted itself and he quickly screwed his scope into place as a shell landed on the roof of a house opposite:

> The front door was flung open and a hefty German officer, minus hat or helmet, rushed out. He made three yards before Arthur's first bullet hit him … a second German appeared. Again the bullet smashed home, the unfortunate recipient seeming to leap high into the air. The third man made twenty yards before Arthur caught him. He slumped to the ground, tearing at his throat … this time two Germans ran out, so that the fifth man got away. It was easier than knocking down rabbits in a harvest field.[247]

Sergeant Furness recalled this period of urban warfare as the most dreaded by his men:

> As our rifle companies fought house-to-house, and room-to-room in close combat, all of us snipers were kept hard at it in support. This type of fighting is horrendous … as the retreating Germans fought us every inch of the way. With their infantry inside every house and their tanks and SPs [self-propelled guns] roaming the streets they fired high explosive shells into every building we occupied, so often our snipers were shooting from burning buildings … there were so many places which concealed German snipers that … it was difficult to judge where the shots were coming from.[248]

Snipers worked closely with their infantry and frequently took on Soviet infantry tactics, using sub-machine-guns and grenades:

It was common practice to fire a long burst of Sten-gun fire into the floorboards and the ceiling above to try and flush out the enemy troops. We used very many hand grenades, throwing them first before entering rooms, cellars etc, as we had the short 4 second fuses we tended to pull the pin let the lever fly off and then say 'and one' before we threw it. That way it gave no time for anyone ... to throw it back.

One element above all else that the snipers hated was the menacing squeak and rattle of tracks, for they had little defence against tanks. A good sniper with strong nerves could smash the driver's prism, or even put a bullet through an open visor slit, but, like wounding a tiger, this often made matters worse. German snipers had the advantage that, in dire circumstances, stick grenades could be bound together to provide a makeshift demolition charge that would disable a tank, but the Mills grenade could not be used in the same manner. Many snipers chose to adopt a wait-and-see approach when a tank was around, for the commander would often open his hatch to get a better view down the rubble-strewn streets, and could provide an easy target. Sometimes the vehicle was simply used as a bulldozer to demolish a house or merely to open up a different, less hazardous route, and if a sniper was concealed inside, that was unfortunate for him.

Occasionally snipers simply made a mistake. Sergeant Furness was moving up one side of a street with his rifle company, clearing houses as they went. He spotted a German with a *Panzerfaust* anti-tank projector and made short work of him, losing sight of his men as he did so. Arriving on his own at a junction he zig-zagged toward a derelict tank, diving underneath, only to hear the voices of the crew inside the vehicle. Sure he must have been spotted, he rolled out behind the tank and ran as fast as he could to get around the corner. This didn't stop him pausing to see if he could take a useful shot at the tank, however. Sometimes not doing anything was worthwhile. During the Normandy advance in 1944 the Yorks and Lancs Regiment were alarmed to hear the sound of tanks being driven behind the German lines. They had virtually no means of dealing with armour and a concentrated attack would break their own thinly held lines. Before decisions were made resulting in either the line being pulled back, or artillery being rushed up to support it, two snipers were sent out to reconnoitre. They returned grinning, to report the noises were one very small German vehicle equipped with a tape recording device and large loud speakers, being driven up and down a road behind the lines.[249]

If conditions had been uncomfortable in Normandy, as the war spread across Holland into the waterlogged polders it became worse, with troops unable to dig trenches in land that had been deliberately flooded by the Germans to slow the Allied advance. The Hallamshire Battalion, Yorks and Lancs Regiment fought across an area in Holland known, notoriously, as 'The Islands' where the only points of high ground were some farm buildings that had been constructed on low ridges and poked up just above the floodwater. Snipers had to wade waist deep (or deeper) across to these islands, in the full knowledge that each would have been carefully registered by enemy artillery and were often swept by German patrols.

The war gradually progressed into Germany and by early 1945 it was becoming obvious that German resistance was beginning to fade from all but the more fanatical Waffen-SS units. Despite the wavering resistance, the snipers found their skills still being called into use, sometimes by acts on the part of retreating Germans that were apparently suicidal. One machine-gunner took refuge in a small outhouse to wait for an advancing patrol to enter his field of fire. His choice of concealment was the last place any experienced soldier would have chosen. He was spotted by a British sniper as he made himself comfortable and the shed was literally riddled with bullets:

> I was told later that this much shot-up soldier proved to be a senior NCO of the Waffen SS. His choice of hiding place must have been obvious to him that he would never leave it alive.[250]

In addition to the hardened combat veterans, the Allies were being faced by younger and younger troops, some no more than 14 years old, and few had the experience, or desire to deal with the by now battle-hardened US and Commonwealth soldiers, even less the will to die for the now crumbling Reich. Units of Free French soldiers were also fighting the Germans, equipped with American uniforms and weapons, and they also had their own snipers, using Garands or Springfields. Able to fight on their home ground once more, they proved reluctant to take German prisoners. One French sniper shot the entire crew of a troublesome machine-gun position, even though several had stood up and attempted to surrender. When this was angrily pointed out to him by an observing British officer his reply was unanswerable: 'if your family had been shot by the Germans as a reprisal, would you have spared them?'[251]

The gods of war can work in a curious manner though, for as Arthur Hare and partner advanced cautiously into the town of Susteren, and moved silently through a shattered building, they turned down a corridor and walked, quite literally, straight into the muzzle of a Spandau machine-gun. The two German soldiers crouched behind it stared blankly at them over the sights and Hare knew he was but a split second from death. Both snipers dropped instinctively to their knees, awaiting the smashing fusillade of bullets, at which point both Germans burst out laughing, stood up and surrendered to the astonished men. The gun proved to be cocked and loaded but the Germans were worn out, dispirited and hungry and deeply gratified to be offered cigarettes by the two very shaken men.

Casualties among all snipers were high and very few who fought in Normandy survived to arrive in Germany as part of the occupying or retreating armies. Those few who did, such as Private Francis Miller, were often the sole survivors of their original sniping companies, and all were battle-weary. Miller was hospitalised because of battle stress and was nearly killed there when a flying bomb landed on his hospital building. In fact, Miller found that his ability as a sniper worked against him:

> I kept going out and coming back again, I was the only one left out of about 12 of us snipers in the Regiment, all the others had been killed. My old regiment had gone into what they called 'suspended animation'. They came home because they had done enough ... but I was unfortunate to get posted to the Royal Scots because I was too good a soldier to be sent home.[252]

He finished the war with the DCM and MM and reckoned it took him four months of recuperation to return to something approaching a normal mental state. Tired of killing, Arthur Hare became a gardener and devoted the rest of his life to watching things grow, and any injured animal or bird found locally was assured a refuge in his cottage. He died in 1970 aged 71. Harry Furness fell for a young German girl whilst stationed with the occupying forces and eventually returned to England with her as his wife. Karl Krauss returned home to find his family missing and nothing left of his house but rubble. He never traced his wife or small son and eventually emigrated to Canada, then to the United States. Others came home, resumed their pre-war careers and quietly got on with making a life for themselves, trying to forget their experiences. Unlike other veterans, few ever appeared to want to return to the battlefields in later years. Perhaps Harry Furness stated the reason most succinctly. 'I haven't the words to really describe the sheer horror of fighting as a sniper in Normandy. That is why I never went back for fifty years, you don't go to places that were nightmares.'[253]

10
LIMITED WARS, 1945–85

Driven back into Germany from both the east and the west, the German armed forces had eventually been forced to surrender in May 1945. In the Far East, the war against the Japanese lingered on, with the Allies facing the pressing problem of how to invade the Japanese mainland without incurring wholly unacceptable losses. It was fully appreciated that the Japanese would, quite literally, fight to the death rather than surrender their homeland and estimates of probable Allied casualties simply to gain a foothold on Japanese soil were around one million men. The problem was effectively solved by the dropping of two atomic bombs on Hiroshima and Nagasaki and the Japanese quickly sued for peace. The greatest conflict in human history ended on 14 August 1945. For the snipers of the combatant countries this was none too soon, for most were war-weary, but they found themselves suddenly both unemployed and unemployable, their highly evolved skills now of no use to occupation armies geared to helping the shattered economies and peoples of Europe and Asia.

Some few British snipers in occupied Germany found new, if somewhat unofficial, employment as their battalion gamekeepers. This was strictly against orders, for the Army believed any form of hunting would antagonise the local populace, so soldiers were not permitted to take rifles into the open country. Nevertheless, Arthur Hare regularly used his Enfield to pot game for the company's cooks and on his return from foraging one day, was charged by his regimental sergeant major for 'improper use' of his rifle. To the fury of the RSM he insisted on seeing the colonel, whose affection for his sniper section was well known. Hare explained he had just been reprimanded for shooting rabbits:

> The colonel's face began to harden ... he turned to the R.S.M.
> 'Did you prefer a charge against this man?'
> 'Sah' the man roared.
> 'Then you ought to be bloody well ashamed of yourself. If this man can't be trusted with a gun, I don't know who can.'
> The sentence was cancelled and the documents torn up.[254]

Understandably, both the civilian population and the soldiers were sick of war, and only too pleased to hand their rifles in to stores and return to civilian life. Commonwealth soldiers, Americans, Russians and others simply handed over their rifles and were quietly shipped home, their fighting finished, although for many the war did not end there. While some slipped seamlessly back into civilian life, others suffered from what is now termed post-traumatic stress, suffering illness, nightmares and paranoid behaviour. One told the author that he was fine for 30 years, then broke down totally one Christmas after witnessing two small boys playing soldiers in his street. Some stayed in the Army but few were able to use their hard-earned skills. Based as a weapons instructor with the British Army of the Rhine (BAOR) Harry Furness was a rare exception and he entered for, and won for his regiment, the 'All Comers Snipers Competition' in August 1946. This was to the huge delight of his battalion, most of whom had bet heavily (and illegally) on his winning. Many of the thousands of returned rifles were quickly offered as surplus. In England in 1947 a complete Enfield No. 4 (T) rifle with its chest and all accessories could be had for £20 ($36) but there were few takers.

Korea, the Forgotten War

If the rifles were no longer needed, the same can also be said of the skills of the snipers. Post-war, sniping had once again become a taboo subject, as a wave of anti-war feeling swept across Europe, and few snipers of any country were still gainfully employed in their respective armed forces. It was not surprising, therefore, that when a little-known country called

North Korea invaded South Korea in June 1950, the multinational force assembled under the aegis of the United Nations contained soldiers from all over the world, including the United States, Britain, Australia and Canada, armed with the weapons they had carried through the Second World War, but lacking almost any snipers. Never more accurately could the saying 'those who cannot remember the past are condemned to repeat it'[255] be applied to the abandoned skills of sniping. As the war turned into the inevitable stalemate of trenches and bitter winter weather, the UN troops found themselves under disturbingly accurate aimed fire from the communist lines. The commanding officer of the 1st US Marines had the binoculars shot from his hand as he surveyed the enemy trenches. When he enquired where the battalion snipers were he was informed that there were none and immediately called for his 'gunnies', (senior gunnery sergeants) to select and train a sniping squad as soon as it could possibly be organised.

Men of the Royal Australian Regiment took frequent casualties from shots fired from the high ground in front of them known as '614', which was some 600 yards (553 metres) away. Exactly who was shooting at them was a matter of some conjecture, but the rumour abounded that several Soviet snipers were at work. This was not as improbable as it sounds, for Russian 'advisers' were assisting the Chinese-communist forces (Chicom) and most of the weapons captured by the UN were of Soviet manufacture, including a small number of Mosin-Nagant rifles with PU scopes. Whilst there is no proof that imported Russian marksmen were at work, there is ample evidence of Chinese soldiers being trained for sniping and sharpshooting duties, some of whom were certainly very good. Their sniping appeared to be mostly done with iron sights, and while scoped rifles existed they appear to have been used in very small numbers. Zhang Taofang was a sniper situated near Hill 614 and publicity photographs of him tell of his bag of 214 hits in 32 days. As with many such claims, high figures must be treated with extreme caution, but there is no doubt that soldiers such as Zhang were certainly competent enough to seriously worry the Allied forces in front of them.

The response of the Americans and the Commonwealth line officers was to form scratch sniping squads using men who had previous sniping experience or were marksmen. Typically, the Marines were the first US forces to be organised and their main requirement was the most basic of all, to procure scoped rifles capable of accurate shooting. Many old Springfield 1903-A4s equipped with a mix of scopes were hurriedly sent to Korea and some precious 1903-A1s with Unertl scopes were taken out of retirement despite the Springfield no longer being in service, and the practicality of their outdated scopes under close scrutiny after the experience of the Second World War, but anything was better than nothing. The existing combinations were already old technology, with scopes that were too prone to ingress of moisture, adjustment drums that were small and fiddly, and scope positioning that provided poor eye relief when the shooter was wearing a steel helmet. There were certainly stocks of new Garand M1-C sniping rifles held in store, for the bulk of them had been produced too late for issue during the Second World War, and their production had continued throughout the last months of the war. As Ordnance Sergeant Roy Dunlap said, 'they were beautiful outfits and I would have given anything to have one during the war, but they arrived in the Philippines just before the Japanese surrendered. The rifles were selected, the best finished and tightest M1s I ever saw.'[256] Oddly, in order to procure the numbers of service rifles required for the infantry, a number of M1-C rifles were taken from stores, had their scopes removed and mounting holes plugged, before being reissued as ordinary service rifles. Between 1,500 and 4,000 such rifles were modified and they can be recognised by the marking 'SA-52' on the receiver.

In fact, the Marine Corps didn't even finish its evaluation of the M1-C until August 1945 and although approved for Army issue, the M1-C was not accepted by the Marines until February 1951. Their rifles had similar Griffin and Howe quick release mounts as on the Army M1-C, but the mounts were slightly longer, more heavily constructed and designed for the 4× Stith-Kollmorgen scope which was not itself actually adopted until early 1954. Meanwhile a new scope, the M84, had been authorised for issue with the M1-C. It was a 2.2× straight tube design with vertical post and horizontal cross-hair graticule and lenses sealed inside rubber gaskets that protected them from moisture. Manufactured by Libby-Owens-Ford, the M84 was distinctive, with its forward placed adjuster drums covered by rectangular rubber weather covers, but it was, like the M81 and M82, still woefully under-powered. At the outbreak of the Korean conflict, the US Army Infantry Board were still engaged in the testing of more commercial scopes to find, in its words 'a more suitable sniper rifle scope'.[257] The improved Garand M1-D rifle also began to appear; it was cheaper and faster to mass-produce than the C, and it utilised mostly standard parts but with the addition of a special heavyweight barrel. It also had an improved scope base using a tapped hole on the left of the receiver, and a mount with a large threaded thumbscrew. This could be retrofitted to earlier models and from December 1951 the Springfield Armory was instructed to convert some 14,325 standard M1 rifles to M1-D specification as well as taking a further 3,087 for conversion to M1-C specification.[258] This order was against all previous procedure and these rather bewildering conversions of sniping rifles to ordinary specification, and vice versa, gives some idea of the haze of confusion that surrounded the supply and issue of these weapons.

There were also a number of Winchester M70 target rifles, with both standard and heavyweight barrels and commercial Unertl and Lyman scopes with their useful 8× magnification. The ability to extend their effective range was an important consideration for the US snipers, for the mountains and open terrain of the front along the 38th Parallel gave ample opportunity for some very long-range sniping. One exponent of this form of shooting, using a specially converted target rifle, was Ordnance Captain William S. Brophy, himself a fine target shot. He would visit field units and demonstrate the effectiveness of using his own Model 70, with its 28 inch Bull barrel and 10×, 2 inch objective lens Unertl scope, by inflicting casualties on Chinese troops at ranges in excess of 1,000 yards. Despite this, he failed to persuade the Ordnance Board that a purpose built bolt-action sniping rifle was a necessary requirement. In fact the Marines reiterated their reluctance to move away from a modified service rifle in a report published in 1951, in which they had said the same as they did in the Second World War, namely that:

There is no Marine Corps requirement for a special rifle for use by snipers ... it is undesirable to inject a new rifle into the system, and if another rifle [were adopted] it is necessary to inject non-standard ammunition into the supply system ... in order to exploit fully any gain in accuracy. The US Rifle Caliber .30 M1-C is sufficiently accurate for use by snipers in the Marine Corps.[259]

However, Brophy had sown the seeds of a change in military thinking that would have important repercussions for sniping that reverberate to this day.

The First Long-Range Rifles

Not only did the men shoot with their .30 calibre rifles, but a number of .50 calibre Browning heavy machine-guns on ground tripods were set up, and mounted with Unertl or Lyman Targetspot scopes of 8, 10, or 20 power. These guns are particularly significant for they were the first large calibre service weapons specifically modified for long-range shooting. Some years earlier, Major F. Conway, supporting the Ordnance Board at Aberdeen Proving Ground, had modified a German PzB39 anti-tank rifle in late 1946 by fitting a Browning barrel to it and a telescopic sight from a German PaK anti-tank gun. It weighed 46 lbs and Conway commented that 'recoil was never a problem, but with that muzzle brake, ear protection was highly recommended'.[260] During the Second World War, Russian troops had used 14.5 mm PTRD and PTRS anti-tank rifles as impromptu sniping rifles to deal with lightly armoured vehicles, emplacements, well dug-in German snipers and for occasional long-range shooting. The Americans had long been interested in their efficiency, and a few Soviet anti-tank rifles had found their way to Korea where unit armourers had mounted a number of different scopes to them. How effective they were is sadly unrecorded, but the fact that the Marines were prepared to field some Brownings gives a clue as to their potential usefulness. Major N. W. Hicks wrote of the training of the 1st Marines' snipers:

> Each student trained not only with the .30 calibre M1 rifle (or the '03 depending on his preference) but with the .50 cal. Machine-gun, fired single shot. Scopes were mounted ... and they proved to be effective for ranges up to and beyond 1,200 yards. At the time the snipers finished their special training ... enemy snipers seemed to be in control. The whole area of the 1st Marines was a hot spot of sniping. Then, the Marine sniper teams were sent out to the various outposts. All hands turned to helping the rifle experts in

spotting the enemy snipers. The change in the situation was fantastic. 'In nothing flat there was no more sniping on our positions', recalled the Battalion's Colonel, 'and nothing moved out there but we hit it.'[261]

Experience with the PzB let to a dozen British and Canadian manufactured .55 inch Boys anti-tank rifles being converted to shoot .50 Browning ammunition. This work was undertaken in Korea by the military adviser to the Nationalist Chinese Ordnance Corps, R. T. Walker, who had been a gunsmith in civilian life:

> After severe proof firing with loads made by pulling .50 bullets and packing the cases with powder, we concentrated on smoothing out the action somewhat. Finding it necessary to load rounds singly, we installed a block of steel in the magazine well, which served to strengthen the action and function as a loading block.[262]

He made up external mounts to enable two-inch diameter, 20× spotting scopes for tank use to be fitted, and after hand loading .50 cal cartridges on site the rifle was tested:

> Although the Boys had a bipod in front and monopod on the rear with a small built-in recoil system, it really rattled you to fire it. Three to five shots was about all a man could stand at one time even from a prone position.[263]

The Nationalist Chinese were impressed enough to put the Boys to use and they frequently used them to shoot at, and hit, communist troops bathing out of rifle range at ranges in excess of 1,100 yards. Although these experiments were along similar lines to the German use of scoped T-Gewehr rifles in 1918, at this period there was not any official interest being shown in the use of such novelty toys by the Military Ordnance Department. However, the pioneering work undertaken in Korea by men such as Conway and Walker was to be looked at much more closely before too long.

Although often quoted, the experiences of the 3rd Battalion, 1st Marines were typical of the situation that the Allied forces found themselves in. After their Colonel's near miss when his binoculars were shot from his hands by a Chinese sniper, he instructed that six two man sniping teams be allocated per company and a training facility be built. A 600 yard range was constructed and a three week course devised that basically copied the training schedule used in the previous war, under the tutelage of experienced gunnies. Targets were man sized wooden boards salvaged from packing cases and painted white or 155 mm shell cases packed with earth and placed prominently at 100 yard intervals.

This impromptu training paid off and within a month the first snipers were working along the front in conjunction with rifle squads. Before long it was possible for the marines to walk unmolested along their front lines in view of the enemy. The Chicom soldiers became very wary of exposing any part of themselves to the Americans, and some US snipers became frustrated at the lack of target opportunities. The front lines became a trench world reminiscent of the Great War, to all intents devoid of human life, but the snipers were patient. Army Corporal Chet Hamilton had watched the enemy lines from his bunker for days without the slightest opportunity to shoot:

> The Chinese had been fortifying their positions for almost two years. Their trenches were a maze that presented few targets. One night I was looking through my rifle scope across the valley to the chink positions on the opposite hill, when something flashed in the wash of the Airforce searchlights. One of the Reds was doing a little home improvement, digging in his trench and throwing the dirt up ... he patted down each shovelful twice before going back for more. I couldn't resist it. The next time the shovel came up and started to pat, I put a bullet through it. I heard the bullet strike the metal. The shovel vibrated and hummed in the Chicom's hands, it must have shook his teeth loose. He didn't do any more digging that night.[264]

The Commonwealth Forces

British, Australian and Canadian forces had small numbers of snipers working with their rifle companies, and they were mostly armed with the same Enfield rifles as in 1945. Of the Commonwealth armies, it was the Canadians who had most usefully spent the brief post-war years examining their sniping rifles, for they had never been entirely convinced that the performance of the Enfield was all that it could be, and despite the modifications Canada had made to the No. 32 scope and mounts, the Army was dissatisfied with it as a sniping weapon. Nevertheless, the Canadians were still using their modified 'Rifle C No. 4 (T)' with its No .67 scope, as well as some Enfield No. 4 (T)s.

The Australians had arrived expecting the conflict to become a sniper's war, and all infantry companies had snipers allocated to them, equipped with their Lithgow manufactured SMLE No. 1 Mk. III* sniping rifles. For some of these men who had fought in the claustrophobic jungles of Borneo and New Guinea, where shooting distances were normally under 100 yards (92 metres), the terrain in Korea appeared almost perfect for sniping, with huge tracts of open land. This enabled Allied snipers to create hides from which they could dominate the surrounding country. Private Ian Robertson, 3rd Battalion Royal Australian Regiment was occupying a high point opposite an enemy-held ridge, which he estimated to be 600 yards (553 metres) away. Estimating ranges at higher altitudes and across valleys is always difficult and, trying to ascertain the point of impact of his bullets, he found that he had to set his scope to maximum elevation, 1,000 yards. Firing into a steady, light headwind, he discovered he could place his shots quite accurately and began to take an interest in the steady flow of Chicom soldiers moving up and down a steep path to the ridge, so he began shooting:

When I saw these blokes suddenly drop or fling themselves away or something like that I thought that most of the time it was a near miss – that they were flinging themselves out of the way to give the impression I had hit them ... I was able to do it time after time, every time I fired, the figure would disappear. I nutted [worked] it out that when they passed a particular spot, if I fired then, they would run into the bullet. They had to come down at the same speed because of the rough terrain. I tried an experimental shot low down and saw blast of the bullet above the bloke ... then I got the measure of them coming up the hill as well. I kept on doing this between other duties ... all this went on for a week. They were mortaring a tangle of rocks not far from where I was ... I could see through the scope that there were a number of important figures in control of all this, so I cheerfully waited and put another shot in amongst this group, and they'd all disappear. When we finally took the hill I thought 'I've got to have a look at this thing'. It was only a [rifle] pit that would hold a few fellows but there was a steep drop in front of it. There were about 30 bodies down there in front of the pit. I went a bit like jelly for a minute and thought 'oh shit, I'm in a grisly business here'.[265]

British units also found it necessary to form scratch sniping squads and, equipped with their venerable Enfield No. 4 (T) rifles they did sterling work. The Enfield had proved to be a robust and accurate rifle with few faults but there had been problems with the scope, so work on improving the sight continued post-1945. The Mk. I scope suffered from being able only to be corrected to within 2 minutes of angle (MOA), which equated to 2 inches at 100 yards, and this was a problem for fine adjustment at longer ranges. It required a special tool and three pairs of hands to reset the range drums when the rifle was re-zeroed and, when adjusted, either drum might well slip back to its lower setting. Snipers learned to over-correct by one click then drop the back one click to ensure it remained on the correct setting. By late 1943 to early 1944 testing proved that there were three major problems with the No 32:

1. Alterations in optical focus.
2. Chipping or cracking of the eye lenses.
3. Failure of the mechanism for adjustment of range and deflection.[266]

As a result, the method of assembly was modified. The eye lenses, which mounted directly into the tube body, were replaced by a screw-in assembly and the Mk. II scope was further redesigned so it was adjustable in 1 MoA increments. In October 1944 an improved Mk. III scope was introduced, remaining in service until the 1960s. Probably of greater importance was the recently adopted practice of using coated lenses, a process known as blooming. It was possibly pioneered within the German camera industry, although both the Russians and the Swiss have subsequently claimed the invention as their own. Whatever the truth of the matter, blooming was certainly being used by late 1944. Coating the lenses with magnesium fluoride to a thickness of one wave-length of light (5 millionths of an inch) gives it a distinctive blue-purple colour, which is invisible when viewed through the lenses. This cuts down the amount of flare (reflected light) from around 5% to 1%, which does not sound very impressive until translated into practical terms, for it increases the light gathering properties of a scope by about 15% over an untreated lens.

The harsh winters caused operational problems though. One Commando sniper commented that, while their rifles were adequate for the campaign, the scopes still gave trouble, with adjuster drums freezing up, and clothing to cope with the bitter winter was not adequate. One major problem, as the Germans had found in Russia, was the need to wear heavy clothes to protect against frostbite, but the small triggerguard on the Enfield made it impossible to use a gloved finger. One solution adopted was to wear mitts with a small flap cut into the area of the forefinger, allowing it to be used on the trigger with the minimum of exposure. It could truthfully be said that by the end of the war the technology of sniping had not moved forward one inch from that of 1940. The eventual uneasy cessation of hostilities in Korea in 1953 brought an end to the need for serving snipers.

Small Wars

If global conflicts appeared to be becoming a thing of the past, there were more localised wars than ever. Indeed, it has been calculated that there has not been a single day's peace since 1945. Most of these conflicts were very localised indeed: political and inter-tribal wars in Africa, power struggles in South America and simmering discontent in the Middle East. As with the Spanish Civil War in the late 1930s, many of these small wars were used by the major political players, such as Russia, China and the United States to promote their own brand of politics or simply as a testing ground for new weaponry.

After Korea a few snipers stayed on in the various Allied armed forces to become career soldiers and tried, with little success, to ensure some vestiges of sniper training were continued. While America became obsessed with the Cold War and the spread of communism, Britain and the Commonwealth were feeling the wind of change blowing around the world as colonies began to demand the rights to self-government. India, Egypt, Cyprus, Aden, Rhodesia and others had become more politically aware and less dependent on the benevolent dictatorship of the Europeans. While this did not sit well with many British politicians, it was a hard fact that post-war Britain was in no state financially or militarily to support and rule the large portions of the globe that it had traditionally done. Additionally the new left-wing Labour government was more concerned with the immediate welfare of a worn-out nation. Nevertheless, Britain was still to become embroiled in a number of limited-war conflicts. As with the United States Marine Corps, the British Royal Marine Commandos managed to continue with the tradition they had started in the Second World War of training their men to a high standard of marksmanship and maintaining sniping as a skill. When wars broke out in hot spots around the ailing empire, it was often the Marines who were able to field the only snipers, and they achieved some notable successes.

Malcolm Fox, in receipt of a letter in 1953 requesting him to join Her Majesties Armed Forces as a conscript, opted to join the Royal Marines, and as an enthusiastic shot in his school army cadet force, volunteered for a sniping course at Browndown in Hampshire. Issued with that old workhorse, the Enfield No. 4 (T), he successfully completed his training before being sent to Cyprus with 40 Commando where he spent his days in a hot camouflaged hide observing the activities of the Greek-Cypriot community, who were supplying EOKA rebels living in the hills.

In the Middle East, where Britain still retained considerable political and trading influence, the conditions were far harsher, with blistering daytime temperatures and freezing nights. The Special Air Service (SAS), had men dotted around on hilltop look-out posts, called sangars, watching for enemy movement. An ex-SAS trooper recalled of this period:

it was absolute hell, as we couldn't move in daytime and temperatures were over 100 degrees. Issue kit was not much cop [use], so we adopted whatever we could scrounge that was useful. I wore a commercial brown cotton shirt, a lightweight hooded parka, which was German I think, US combat trousers and a mix of British webbing and pouches with some American and German pouches and stuff. We carried three water bottles each, which wasn't enough and we had to fill up at nights. I often used to wear an Arab style turban which was very practical and provided good camo for the head. When it was cold we wore the old para Denison smock over it all.[267]

The Irregular Sniper

Into this arena of what was becoming known as Limited Warfare, came a combatant whose skills were as old as warfare itself, the mercenary. The ever increasing number of specialists who had been trained in the Second World War or after – demolition, logistics, AFV crews, snipers – meant that highly skilled men were available to any government that had the money and the desire to employ them. The Spanish Civil War had witnessed the use of multi-national forces in this role, and after the Second World War, there were huge numbers of men with no ties (and in the case of many Germans and Russians, literally no homes or families to return to) for whom warfare was a way of life. Not for them was the dullness of peacetime routine, and they travelled the world as guns for hire. While their stories are fascinating, they are somewhat outside the scope of this book, but there was another breed of sniper who also began to appear in the late 1960s who served in a more – or less – official role, the irregular sniper.

Some of these men were recruited without even the benefit of any military training, or even a definable army to fight for. At the height of the war in Angola in 1973 one talented young American competitive long-range shooter, having finished graduate school, had embarked on a shoestring African trip before settling down to the normal routines of work, mortgage, marriage and all of the other dubious benefits that maturity bring. While enjoying the rare treat of a cold beer on a 100+°F day in the port of Dakar, Senegal, he was approached by two Americans who began a friendly conversation, as expats do in foreign lands. The small talk drifted over a number of topics and eventually ended up on shooting; the new graduate had been a small bore shooter at one university and latterly a large bore 1,000 yard competitor. 'The wording was very delicate and deliberately ambiguous, but they asked if I might want free transport and well remunerated short term employment in a nearby country.'

Approaching penury, he listened, and was startled to realise that they apparently knew more about him than strangers should. The offer was simple: in exchange for payment in any manner he desired (a numbered Swiss account was chosen), he would be briefed and more or less equipped by them and inserted in the bush with instructions to target the foreign 'advisers' working with the Angolan rebels. For a young man, the lure of sufficient money overcame common sense and rationality. Armed with little more than the optimism of youth and a limitless confidence in his own ability, he agreed. His instructions 'make a nuisance of yourself and kill anyone white' were succinct, and his only way home was to ensure he arrived at a pre-arranged rendezvous point to meet a helicopter. His training for bush warfare had been nil, he carried no identification and he had with him a standard Winchester Model 70 sporting rifle equipped with a commercial telescopic sight. Within a couple of weeks he was in the African bush, with food, water and a map and compass. His knowledge of sniping techniques was learned from manuals and his practical experience was nil, but he adopted the best possible approach to staying alive, which was extreme caution and detailed observation, and his rifle began to take a toll on the Soviet and Cuban military personnel; they were easy to identify both by their physical appearance, and by their habits. 'I would watch their camps, sometimes for days, planning how to shoot, and then take cover until they became tired of looking for me.' With nowhere to run to, he became expert in vanishing into the bush:

You had to hole up in a pre-prepared hide, with somewhere to use for a latrine without exposing yourself and maybe sit it out for two days or more. Sometimes there were centipedes sharing the hole with me, as well as snakes, spiders and things with no names. I'd get bitten half to death; you couldn't scratch or wiggle, or swear a long blue streak, especially in an exposed lay, and those long days baking in the tropical sun, feeding a wide variety of insect life, seemed eternal. Although most of my time there was spent alone, crucial skills, both military and survival, were acquired during the rare occasions I was in encampments. Although I loathed these degenerate gatherings, I had to deliver intelligence, receive new orders, be re-supplied, or possibly head off for R&R in Senegal. Camps were a good opportunity to get news of the rest of the world, some idea of how the 'war' was going in the wider theatre, and to trade or swap for luxuries such as a clean towel.

He was very fortunate in finding a mentor:

A well educated Dutch man who had been active in the Congo during the '60s was very fatherly towards me just after I arrived, and over several days while awaiting equipment and orders, taught me crucial skills and thinking processes. I pray for him even now, for without him, I simply would not have survived.[268]

The young man had one useful skill, for having grown up on a farm had provided him with observational skills in the outdoors, such as quickly recognising a bush that didn't fit in with the landscape, or slightly disturbed ground concealing a land mine. As each new scene came into view, he had only seconds to analyse it, from his feet to the horizon. 'The Soviets owned the skies and although not frequent, any individual on the ground was on the short end of the stick if it came to duelling with a helicopter gunship.' On at least two occasions he was forced to jettison every item of equipment, short of clothes and boots, to keep ahead of pursuing trackers, and tried to always carry small hand grenades, which he used to booby trap his rifle and other choice items he left behind. This form of lonely warfare was incredibly trying on the nerves and stamina:

Re-supply was **the** major problem – it took a long while, it was sometimes defective, or was not what you had asked for because some clerk knew better than I did what was needed! My second rifle for instance, a Winchester, had a scope that either was not mounted properly or the cross-hairs drifted. Ammunition might be decades old based on the head stamps and inconsistent from cartridge to cartridge, especially if they had been stored in the African heat for years. On the rare occasion where the target was solo, after searching for documents and maps, the next question was whether his weapons/ammunition might be suitable replacements for mine. I did not trust their food or water, but at least once, someone else's canteen contents probably saved me from certain collapse from dehydration. The obvious supplies of surface water were full of parasites but you did not dare build enough of a fire to boil water in most circumstances. I might utilise any number of captured items such as compass, flashlights, matches, water treatment tablets, socks, skin lotion, soap, camo paint, etc. Equipment was precious. It would not matter if I was captured with enemy items – being captured with a scoped rifle was a death sentence anyway, and I carried a pistol on occasion. I always kept a round in a breast pocket, to be certain there was always one left, for it is not easy or fast to use a rifle on yourself.

In general, the entire Angolan situation was degenerating and the unexpected was becoming too common as chaos reigned. He became increasingly uneasy about who exactly was employing him and why, and after slightly less than a year in-country, decided to leave while he still could. 'My decision to take an early retirement was assisted considerably by the bomb blast that destroyed my ancient car in Dakar whilst there for R&R, which left me in no doubt as to my eventual fate.' The entire experience left an indelible mark on him, and he admitted that 'for years I never really slept properly, I would wake at the slightest sounds, and I was without doubt paranoid for a good part of my younger adult life'.[269]

Weapons Improvements

If there was little change in the issue of clothing and equipment for the snipers then some advances were at last being made with regards their weapons. In 1957 Britain had at last abandoned the Enfield rifle and adopted the Belgian designed FN-FAL self-loading rifle in the new NATO standard calibre of 7.62 mm. While it was a good infantry weapon, its design, with a sliding sheet steel top-cover over the receiver meant that it did not provide a stable platform for any optical devices, although many means of mounting were tested. As a result a redesigned sniping rifle had to be created that could chamber the new ammunition and was simpler and more accurate than its predecessors. The availability of rifles was limited, and there was great reluctance within the Board of Ordnance to adopt a brand new rifle, if for no other reason than the sheer cost and the time it would take to test, approve and then produce. As a result they took the basic Enfield No. 4 design and fitted it with a heavy grade target barrel, chambered for 7.62 mm ammunition, with redesigned magazine, a cut down fore-end that left the barrel completely open forward of the front sling-swivel, and a factory fitted wooden cheek-rest. This was then equipped with the No. 32 Mk. III scope, of which hundreds were still held in store. This interim rifle was called the L42A1. The equipment issued with these rifles remained virtually unchanged from the Second World War, with the same wooden transit chests, cleaning kit and steel telescope carry-case as issued with the No. 4 (T).

Canada too had undertaken a series of trials in late 1956 to find a replacement for their No. 4s and they too decided on the FN design. As with Britain, this decision also posed them with a problem regarding securely mounting a scope on the fragile top cover. Some commercial scopes had been acquired, for comparative testing, such as the American Stith/Kollmorgen, Canadian Leitz and Beaconing Optical Products (BOP) manufactured No. 67. It was the Leitz, mounted onto a reinforced top-cover that eventually won, after it proved superior in cold weather trials. The eventual weapon adopted, the Rifle 7.62 mm C1A1 Sniper was something of a compromise, for the basic FN design had never been to produce a rifle capable of being used in a sniping role and, as with most semi-automatic rifles, it did not have the capability for accurate long-range shooting. Despite the reinforced top cover, the design of the FN meant that the scope could be dislodged by rough handling, with consequent loss of zero. However, it did work and provided reasonable accuracy up to around 656 yards (600 metres), although it often proved inconsistent. Not that this appeared to matter too much to the Canadian Army, for post-Korea they had deemed sniping to be an outmoded and irrelevant skill for modern warfare.

In the United States there were still a few serving officers whose passion for advancing the science of accurate shooting remained undimmed. If Captain William S. Brophy's expertise in Korea had won him support from the ground troops, it had achieved little in persuading the armed forces that it seriously needed to reassess its position with regard to sniping. Neither was his voice the only one in the wilderness, for Brigadier-General George O. Van Orden, USMC (now retired), had long been unhappy about the limitations placed upon snipers by the military's insistence on using nothing better than converted service rifles for sniping. As far back as 1942 when he had recommended the adoption of the Winchester Model 70 sporting rifle for issue to snipers and he had written a summary entitled *What is the most efficient Sniper's Rifle Available in America Today?*[270] He had certainly not changed his mind by the end of the Korean war, and was years ahead in his recommendation that rifles be chambered for more powerful non-standard calibres, such as the potent .300 Winchester Magnum. There was sound reasoning behind this, for this specially designed hunting ammunition used heavier, more stable bullets, with greater range, penetration and a flatter trajectory that that of the normal .30 calibre military calibres, with only a small penalty to pay in terms of increased recoil. However, for reasons of logistics (and one suspects, inevitably, cost) the Marine Equipment Board at Quantico had rejected the idea, stating that if another rifle were introduced 'it is necessary to inject non-standard ammunition for this rifle into the supply system in order to exploit fully any gain in accuracy'.[271]

It is perhaps worthwhile noting that the underlying implication in this statement was that the Board were fully aware that both the service rifle and the issue .30-06 inch cartridge under-performed in a sniping role, they were not prepared to sanction any means of improving the situation. Meanwhile, the Army was looking at replacing the old M1 rifle but had opted to continue with the Garand system, in the guise of the 7.62 mm M-14, adopted in 1957. There were a number of internal design changes to improve reliability and aid production, but one of the most practical alterations was the simple adoption of a 20-round detachable box magazine, which alleviated the knotty problem of topping up the ammunition that had so plagued the M1. In terms of its use as the basis for a sniping weapon, the M-14 had been designed from the outset with a machined screw recess on the left side of the receiver that could accept a scope mount, although there was no actual system approved for use with the rifle. Some ad hoc commercial scopes and mounts were used, in particular by Captain R. Wentworth, who used with great success a selected M-14 equipped with Weaver K-6 scope in the Running Deer World Shooting championships in Moscow in 1958. It proved to doubters that a carefully assembled semi-automatic could be used for very accurate shooting and for three or four years an assortment of tests were carried out with a varied range of scopes and mounting systems.

The United States Army was not the only army which regarded semi-automatic rifles as the way forward, for the Soviet Bloc had adopted the gas operated semi-automatic rifle as far back as 1940. In 1943 they had introduced the Simonov carbine, firing a short 7.62 cartridge inspired by the German 7.92 Kurz round used in the MP43/44 assault rifles. It soon led to the introduction of the Kalashnikov Model of 1947, or AK47 as it is now universally known. This was of no practical use to snipers, but it was to spawn what became the only front-line purpose-designed semi-automatic sniping rifle then in front line service, the Dragunov SVD.

The Dragunov was adopted earlier than many people suppose, between 1965 and 1967, and its 24½ inch (622 mm) barrel is chambered for the old, rimmed 7.62 × 54 mm cartridge, that dated back to the 1890s. At a time when Britain was still relying on a bolt action designed in the late 19th century, and America was still musing over modifying its service rifle, the Russians did what they do best, developing a simple piece of equipment that was easy to manufacture, robust, powerful and equipped with an effective telescopic sight. The SVD is not, as is often quoted, simply a carefully built AK, for it does not use the same rotating bolt and gas piston system found on the Kalashnikov. It has a redesigned bolt to deal with the more powerful rimmed cartridge and utilises a short-stroke gas piston that strikes an operating rod to initiate the opening cycle of the breech, and is better suited to the pressures generated by the larger cartridge. The SVD's short-stroke system also has less mass than the AK and creates less inertia on firing, thus affecting aim to a far lesser degree. The PSO-1 sight is a 4 × 24 scope with a field of view of 6°, simple adjusting turrets for windage and elevation out to 1,100 yards (1,000 metres), and excellent optical qualities. However, one of the oddities of this rifle is the inclusion of a bayonet lug on the muzzle, which is generally of little use to a sniper. The first appearance of the SVD caused some puzzlement to western observers who were unsure as to its precise purpose, not believing Russia would adopt the wholesale arming of its snipers with such a rifle, but they soon found out that this was indeed the case.

The Rise of the Terrorist

After the Second World War, a new global threat was being witnessed, that of terrorism. The early terrorists were often disenchanted local groups who were demanding an end to foreign intervention in what was increasingly viewed as local, not colonial politics. These eventually led to the formation of hard-line groups who are, depending on one's point of view, either freedom-fighters or terrorists. Although the large majority of these groups wage clandestine war using explosives, there has always been an element of face-to-face confrontation, particularly in urban environments. Normally, terrorist groups will recruit local men as irregular snipers which is seen not only as a propaganda coup but also a valuable means of harassing the foreign soldiers with little risk to the attacker. For regular army snipers, fighting in built-up areas (FIBUA) has become another skill to be learned and as the 20th century has progressed it has become one that is being used with increasing frequency. The sniper in an urban environment will not necessarily be facing another rifleman as skilled as he is, but that doesn't make his job any easier. Urban areas are particularly difficult to work in as the risk of injury to innocent civilians is high, the areas from which incoming shots may be coming is almost impossible to locate, because of echoes from surrounding buildings, and a rifleman has almost limitless deep cover in which to hide.

In Beirut during 1983, the US forces were subject to frequent hit and run attacks, and one Marine base was taking continual fire from a maze of damaged buildings, making any sort of routine task dangerous. A two man Marine sniper team was detailed to solve the problem, and settled down to watch. Two days of patient observing had brought them no nearer to finding the source of the shots and they were hampered by the fact that many buildings still had civilian inhabitants trying to scratch a living, so they had to be perfectly sure of their target. The snipers examined bullet strikes on the buildings and spoke to men who had had near misses, but could not pinpoint the shooter, despite his regular every-five-minute shots:

A bullet clanged against something metallic nearby and a voice cursed, before suggesting a battleship drop a few 16" shells on the already shattered building.

The observer said 'Oh Oh … I think I got his muzzle flash.'

'No shit. Where?'

'Wait a minute till I work it out.'

'OK, find the building with the upper floor gone. Come down it and go off the left edge. A block deeper is a stucco ruin. You got that? See where it's split open like an axe laid into it?'

'OK.'

'Focus in there and you'll see a bunch of opened up walls. I think he's shooting in there, maybe four or five rooms back in.'

'Man, what a maze, no wonder we couldn't find him.'

The sniper got ready. He shoved a sandbag forward as a steady rest … and adjusted another bag under the M40A1s butt.

'Just like a bench rest. How far do you figure?'

'Eight hundred, maybe eight-fifty.'

The sniper nodded. 'I'll cam on 8 and raise one click.'

'We'd better be right. One shot will be all there is. We get him or he'll be gone from there.'

The sniper practice sighted. 'When he shoots this time I'll get an exact aiming point.'

'Go an inch or two high. You don't want to ricochet off his rifle or scope.'

They again saw the flash. The sniper said, 'OK, next time. Just one more buster.'

The observer studied his watch. 'Any time now.' They waited.

Flash.

Crack!

The sniper slid down, ejected the empty and chambered a live round.

'How'd it feel?'

'He won't shoot again.'

There was no further incoming fire from that area.[272]

This was typical of the type of engagement that occurs in urban fighting and illustrates not only the patience that snipers must show, but also the care that must be exercised in determining the exact place of the shooter, as there is a limited chance for retaliation. Yet there are times in terrorist warfare that the situation is totally opposite, with targets so openly visible that they clearly believe they are beyond the reach of any retribution. This happens rarely, but when it does, it is invariably because the range is so extreme that few believe there is any threat to them. This happened to a British sniper in Londonderry, Northern Ireland in 1972, as he and his observer watched an IRA ambush being sprung on a British armoured car on the edge of the city. A civilian car arrived close to the disabled vehicle, and a man began unloading weapons from it. More arrived to help and they began to arm themselves. The sniper knew he had to open fire to keep the ambush under control until foot patrols could reach the scene, but there was a problem. His 7.62 mm L42A1 rifle was considered effective out to 1,000 yards, but from their map, he and his partner calculated their nearest target was some 1,200 yards (1,100 metres) away. They did have one aid however, and that was black flags hung in the streets to mourn an IRA man who had recently died. These proved invaluable in judging the wind speed, as the distance was beyond that for which the sniper's pocket book gave corrections. 'We'd trained at 1,000 yards on the sniping course but this was different, the bullet would be in flight for about three seconds, and the targets were moving.' In fact, his first shot would have missed, as he had misjudged the wind speed, but his target unexpectedly walked away from the car, and slap into the bullet:

> The men assumed that they were being fired on from down the road, and took cover on along the side of the car. One dived into a cemetery and I got him eventually, and two more were taken out from the side of the car. One ran across the road and dived through a front door. My sergeant fired and the bullet smashed through it and killed him as he leaned against it. My sergeant and I were working beyond the limits of our equipment, and it was calculated that my furthest shot was over 1,470 yards [1,300 metres]. We fired 83 rounds between us, and I was credited with seven, he got three. The silly thing was that Brigade HQ was on the radio at the time demanding to know what weapons we were using![273]

The Falklands War

Basking in the reflected glory of Prime Minister Margaret Thatcher's iron premiership, the last thing Britain expected was to find itself embroiled in a conflict concerning a small group of islands situated far out in the

Atlantic Ocean. However, the British administered Falklands had long been a thorn in the side of the Argentinian government, and under the leadership of its military Junta, they invaded the islands in 1982, claiming the Malvinas for themselves. Affronted by this challenge to Britain's political authority, a task force was hurriedly raised and dispatched to the islands. It was not expected that the conflict would last long, as the conscript Argentinian Army was not thought to have the stomach for a war, but the level of resistance by all Argentinian forces proved to be much higher than expected, and British casualties mounted accordingly. One of the main problems for the invading British forces was the barren, windswept and wet landscape, covered with rocky outcrops, deep fissures and well sited Argentinian positions. The defenders had excellent fields of fire and it was a sniper's paradise, one Argentinian held up an entire British company for four hours. This was a chilling experience for the Royal Marines and Parachute Regiment soldiers, many of whom had only ever experienced the close-range, and usually ineffective, urban sniping that occurred in Northern Ireland. Some Argentinian snipers were in a different category, and the British soldiers were powerless to deal with them:

> I have some advice for you and it's good advice, so try to take it in. If ever you are walking down your local high street and suddenly come under sniper fire, here's what you do. Try not to panic, and dive for the ground. Then look for a phone box and crawl to it. On reaching the phone box pull down the Yellow Pages and look under 'S' for sniper. Then give one of them a quick call. In other words you set a thief to catch a thief. There were no phone boxes on Goose Green, but we did have radios. The call was made.[274]

They were certainly causing problems for the advancing British, pinning down units and causing casualties. Sergeant Jerry Phillips, a sniper with the Parachute Regiment had worked his way up to a mountain strongpoint and was determined to silence the Argentinian snipers and machine-gunners:

> I fired 100 rounds at targets over a two hour period. My shooting was accurate. If something moved and I fired it didn't move again. I don't know if I killed and I don't want to know. But the shooting from those positions

stopped. At the end of it there were two particular snipers I was after. They were diehards just like us.[275]

Some of the Argentine snipers were equipped with infra-red night sights, that gave off a tell-tale red beam, and Sergeant Phillips was quick to spot one:

> One of them had an infra-red beam coming from his scope. We shot him and his beam suddenly pointed upwards towards the sky. That's how it stayed; a small red beam pointing upwards and doing no more damage to us. The other one I never got.[276]

The identity of the snipers employed by the Argentine Army has always been somewhat shrouded in mystery, as there was virtually no training programme within their armed forces for snipers, and whilst some special forces did have limited access to military pattern scoped rifles, the few that surfaced after the battle were all of FN/FAL type, with low power scopes fitted, which classified them more as sharpshooters' rifles than as dedicated sniping weapons. There were, however, certainly a number of Remington 700 rifles with optical sights of unspecified types examined after the war that appeared to have been purchased commercially. The men who used them were certainly competent and from conversation with British Falklands veterans, there seems little doubt that some, if not all, were employed as mercenaries by the Argentine forces. Certainly most appeared to have previous combat experience and may well have been of Spanish-American descent with experience in Vietnam:

> We caught two at Goose Green, they had proper scoped rifles, and they had caused some heavy losses but neither spoke Spanish – they spoke English with American accents but didn't say much. They knew we were pissed off with them. Some of the lads took them away and we never saw them again.[277]

The British snipers were using the Enfield L42 but it was an ageing design and the Army were already investigating its replacement. While it served throughout the Falklands it was not always with success:

I had no oil for mine and in the constant wet the bolt got stiffer and stiffer. It lost its zero, then the scope fogged up. I got so exasperated with it that I dumped it in a stream and carried a captured Argie FN for the rest of the battle, which worked just fine out to four or five hundred yards.[278]

Some British infantry marksmen carried their issue FN/SLR rifles equipped with AN/PVS night sights, which proved useful during the fierce night attacks, where they were used at comparatively close ranges, but for the huge open spaces there was only one solution for pinned down infantry, and that was to wait for the arrival of their own sniper. This brought about a heated exchange from those under fire:

To my rear I noticed a bush. Not that surprising, we were in a field, but this bush was different, it was moving. As the bush got nearer to our position it became apparent it was not a bush but a member of our Sniper Platoon. The bush reached our position and stopped. Another shot rang out.

'Where is he?' asked the bush.

'Where is he? Where the fuck is he? If I fucking knew that ... I'd be trying to kill the bastard.'

The bush always had a reputation for being something of a madman and true to form he did not let his reputation down. He jumped up on to the top of the hedge. Two more rapid shots flew over. These were followed by more cringing and yelps on our part but the bush remained still. He obviously had not heard them.

'It's a sniper' shouted the bush.

'Oh really! Did you hear that boys, it's a fucking sniper. What am I? Am I talking in Czechoslovakian or what? I know it's a fuckin' sniper.'

The bush remained on the wall and from under one of his branches pulled out a pair of binoculars ... and slowly began to survey the landscape.

'I see him.' said the bush and with that he finally jumped down off the wall and crawled off to our right. After about twenty metres he stopped, aimed his rifle and fired a single shot.

'Think I got him' said the bush.

Again slowly one by one we started to look over the hedge. There were no more shots. We began to rejoice; a man had just died and we were happy.

I was later told that after the battle the British bush had gone in search of the Argentine bush. On finding his corpse he discovered that he had shot him clean through the head from a distance of 1,000 metres.[279]

After experience gained in the Falklands and Northern Ireland, it was clear to the British Army that the days of the old L42 were numbered, and that a new design of rifle would have to be adopted before very long. Exactly what type of rifle this should be was the subject of considerable debate, but there is some evidence that the eventual decision was influenced by events that had unfolded half-way across the world in Vietnam.

11

VIETNAM, AMERICA'S NEMESIS

As small conflicts waxed and waned around the world, the problems in Indo-China that had been simmering for more than two decades began to drift towards a major escalation. The carefully organised warfare that had finally driven out the French after the debacle of Dien Bien Phu had left the south of the country wide open to communist invasion, a scenario that the United States, suffering from acute cold-war anxiety, was not prepared to countenance. From December 1961 direct military aid was given to bolster the weakly armed and poorly led Army of the Republic of South Vietnam (ARVN). As the military balance tipped further in favour of the North Vietnamese Army (NVA) and local guerrilla forces (Vietcong – VC), drafts of American soldiers were sent into South Vietnam to 'stabilise' the situation. By the late 1960s there were some 540,000 US troops in country. The two sides were set for a confrontation, both military and cultural that would have repercussions to the present day. Since the end of the Second World War, there had been a shift in emphasis on the part of the US Army with regard to shooting training. This was due in part to the adoption of new weapons technology, and to a lack of will on the part of the US armed forces to instruct their men in the basic discipline of accurate shooting. This had been engendered by the decision to introduce an automatic weapon, the M-14, as the standard for all military units. Of improved Garand design, it was re-chambered to use the new 7.62 mm NATO standard cartridge that was a less powerful cartridge than the old .30-06 inch round and it fired a lighter 145 grain bullet. Nevertheless, it was a perfectly capable calibre for most combat situations, without the penalty of the recoil of the larger .30-06 cartridge. The M-14 was not destined to remain the frontline rifle for long though.

In 1956 Eugene Stoner had developed the AR-15, a light automatic rifle, to military specifications. This was chambered for the tiny .223 inch (5.56 mm) cartridge, which had hitherto seen only limited use as a small-game hunting round. The new military rifle, the M-16, soon developed a reputation for having little knock-down power unless a head or heart shot was made, which was unlikely in view of the existing state of marksmanship in the Army. It was also unable to penetrate foliage, which was something of a shortcoming in jungle warfare. In addition its limited combat range, of about 328 yards (300 metres), was wholly inadequate for any long-range shooting and these limitations would have posed the Army snipers with a real problem – had there been any snipers. In an article in the Army's journal in 1954, the writer pointedly commented that most commanding officers ignored the basic requirement of offering a ten-day sniper course to selected men, complaining that '[the Army] has not produced snipers in the past and it will not produce them in the future',[280] and things clearly had not improved a few years later when a survey showed that the majority of infantry companies still had no trained snipers.[281] To compound the problem, in 1956 the US Army had introduced the 'Trainfire' system of shooting, which they adopted in the light of their experiences in Korea, whereby soldiers were trained to hit pop-up targets in simulated battle conditions, at a stroke totally by-passing the basic shooting skills they needed to enable them to become good marksmen.

In the wake of the general issue of the new rifle in 1966–67, the situation was further worsened by the adoption of another policy known as 'Quick-kill' whereby the burst-fire capability of the M-16 was used to provide volume, rather than aimed, fire at the enemy. Soldiers no longer took careful aim, but sprayed the vicinity with fire in the hope of hitting something, and marksmanship skills continued to decline. As Lieutenant-Colonel L. Wagner, director of the US Shooting Team, pointedly said:

We are fooling ourselves if we believe the American soldier can shoot. Two major obstacles must be surmounted if military marksmanship is to be saved;

the first is bureaucratic resistance ... the second is the fact that most Army officers and NCOs think they know marksmanship. They do not know that they do not know.[282]

Indeed, even the American firearms magazines were demanding to know what had happened to the traditional shooting skills of the American soldier and in 1969 the *American Rifleman* magazine, voice of the National Rifle Association, plaintively asked:

'Can the American Rifleman Still Shoot?' That our average rifleman is something less than a sure shot with his weapon is indicated by what happens in a chance collision along the trail ... quite suddenly the target is there and in the clear, not more than seven to 15 metres off. Our man fires, four times out of five he misses and the target scuttles away.[283]

Some men already serving in Vietnam were competent hunters and target shooters, but were so frustrated at the lack of availability of a suitable sniping rifle that they had commercial scopes shipped from home and begged or bribed unit armourers to fit them to their M-16s. At least one lieutenant in the 25th Infantry Division, angered at his inability to return long-range enemy fire, took his own course of action:

There were occasions when enemy personnel were observed several hundred metres away and [were] not successfully engaged by our grunts with their M-16s.[284]

He tried desperately to obtain an old M-14 for sniping and using a rifle captured back from the VC he had an armourer fit it with a Weaver 6× scope and mount that his father shipped out to him. Unfortunately, the appalling weather conditions (in summer often 100°F and 100% humidity) and rough handling quickly showed up the problems of using a commercial scope:

After a few weeks in the field my Weaver scope had begun to fall apart ... the lenses were fogged up most of the time, and the mount would not hold zero. I reluctantly had an M-16 sent out and abandoned the M-14.[285]

Clearly the military authorities needed to get their house in order, and the following year the Department of the Army at last published a chapter on advanced marksmanship.[286] HQ US Army Vietnam instructed that Army commanders should 'determine the organisational, doctrinal and material requirements for sniper operations by US Army units in the Republic of Vietnam'.[287] In a sniping role the main requirement was for a tough, battle-proven rifle with 1,000 yard capability and a telescopic sight rugged enough to withstand prolonged use in a hostile environment: the M-14 was the logical choice. Finding a scope for it might have proven problematical, particularly in view of the trouble the Army had in selecting anything suitable during the Second World War, but fortuitously the Redfield Company had introduced a variable power 3 × 9 hunting scope in 1962, with an in-built rangefinding capability. Around the same time, a young officer named Jim Leatherwood, stationed at Fort Benning, Georgia, had been applying himself to the problem of developing a method of eliminating the guesswork from range estimation and consequent bullet drop to a target, always the sniper's *bête noir*. Leatherwood, Franklin Owen and Vincent Oddi came up with a modified design that utilised a ranging cam actuated by a ring positioned just in front of the ocular lens on the Redfield which, when turned in conjunction with the power ring, automatically compensated for bullet drop for the standard M118 ball ammunition. Fitted to specially handbuilt or 'accurised' M-14s the Leatherwood scope was to see service for the first time in mid-1968 when around 50 were sent to the 9th Division Sniper School, where rifle and scope combination were given the designation XM-21 and it was officially sanctioned by the Army on St Valentine's day, 1969. That this new scope, the ART (Auto Ranging Telescope), was effective is beyond doubt, for between January and July of that year the 9th Infantry accounted for 1,139 of the enemy. Despite some practical criticisms, and a distinct unwillingness on the part of the US Marine Corps to adopt it, the new rifle was to prove an effective weapon in the hands of Army snipers. James Gibbore was issued his shortly after qualifying as a sniper:

> The XM-21 was incredible! All you had to do was turn your scope cam ring
> until your target's picture was dead centre ... you couldn't miss. At three

hundred yards we were putting two out of three bullets into a hole the size of a dime. The weapon was so easy to shoot that it built up our confidence, thinking no target was too far away.[288]

The Army still needed to establish a training programme so, under the guidance of Major Willis L. Powell, the 9th Infantry Division set up a programme. Initially it comprised a mere 46 hours of instruction, less time than was devoted to training the driver of a half-track. By 1969 this had been much extended to 18 days and students rarely failed, partly because most selected were already classified as expert marksmen but also because of the skill and dedication of their Gunnery Sergeant Instructors. The gunnies formed the backbone of sniper training in both the Army and Marines and many were experienced competitive shooters and had themselves been combat snipers in the Second World War or Korea. The training followed the normal pattern laid down by the Allies in the First World War: range and wind estimation, target identification, rifle and sight maintenance, fieldcraft and camouflage and, above all else, marksmanship training. Most of the neophyte snipers had served some time in-country and a few were already combat veterans who understood jungle warfare and its inherent dangers. Few, however, had any skill in using optically sighted rifles in jungle environments, so range time was maximised. As there existed no purpose-built ranges, suitable areas were selected and cleared of brush by the recruits and 105 mm artillery shell cases were then secured. By a happy coincidence these were available in great numbers and their size roughly equated with the body mass of a small man. Slipped over wooden stakes driven into the ground they were easy to spot and gave out a satisfying 'clang' when hit, but over time the ranges became more organised and silhouette targets were adopted.

The snipers also had the task of converting mentally from yards to metres, as the Army worked in the metric system while almost all shooters had learned to work in imperial units. As part of their duties as observers, snipers would call in air and artillery strikes, so computing distances in the incorrect units could prove at best embarrassing and at worst catastrophic. The training was arduous, Joseph Ward recalling that in a six-day week he fired 720 rounds and spent an equal amount of range time spotting for his partner. It paid off though, for as he commented, 'we became "stoned to the scope". I eventually found it harder to hit a target at five hundred yards than at a thousand.'[289]

Silence and Night Vision

The science of silencing had been considerably improved since Hiram Maxim had fitted a suppressor to Springfield rifles earlier in the century. It should be understood that noise suppression is not silencing; the former reduces the sound of discharge, making it difficult to determine where a shot is coming from, whereas the latter actually masks almost entirely the sound of the shot. The limiting factor being that suppression enables full power ammunition to be used out to near maximum range, whereas silencing requires sub-sonic ammunition of reduced power, adequate in a full-bore rifle to reach perhaps 200 yards. In Vietnam, the leader in noise suppression was Sionics Inc. who produced a wide range of suppressors, of which two, the MAW-A1 for the M16A1 and the M-14SS for the M-14/XM-21. found particular use within the sniping community. In night operations, suppressors were of considerable use, as the flash of discharge was almost invisible and in the jungle the sound of the shot was soon swallowed up by the dense vegetation. On one night operation, James Gibbore used his suppressed, Starlight equipped, XM-21 to shoot 14 NVA sentries one after the other:

> Squeezing the trigger – Thud! A round went out. I saw the VC I was aiming at get hit and go flying. No one saw a thing. I went down their perimeter line. As they moved to their furthest position away from each other, I hit each one, one after the other like ducks in a shooting gallery. It was almost a joke it was so easy.[290]

The snipers were materially helped by another item of equipment that had been more or less perfected since the Second World War, a night-sight capable of producing recognisable images that would enable the sniper to see in the dark. The light-gathering ability of the telescopic sight in poor light was good, but in situations where there was no natural light at all, even the finest scopes were rendered useless. After the Army's early attempts in 1943 to produce an infra-red night scope, work had quietly continued and a new generation began to make an appearance. Two, the Smith & Wesson Star-Tron and the AN/PVS-1 Starlight were available initially but it was the more powerful AN/PVS-2 that saw the most use. An image intensifier that magnified available light by 75,000 times, it was so effective that the manual contained dire warnings about not switching it on in daylight or unusually bright night conditions as it would burn the screen out. This unit suffered from two problems, its huge expense, about $3,000 each at 1970 prices, and its size and weight, for mounted on an M-16 it almost dwarfed the rifle and it made for a very heavy combination when fitted to the M-21. It had focussing control and adjustment for elevation and windage. While most snipers trained with it out to 1,000 yards, in practice most night combat took place at ranges of under 400 yards.

Paradoxically, the US Army were not the only ones using night-imaging technology, for some NVA units were equipped with the Second World War vintage American made M1 or M2 Sniperscopes, supplied to them via the Soviet Union who were using up stockpiles of obsolete weapons left over from the Second World War. Private Gibbore found this out during a novel piece of counter-sniping. Using his own Starlight equipped XM-21 he spotted a bright red light emanating from the tree line ahead of him:

> It looked like he was sitting in a tree with a big red flashlight on. I could see him plain as day. I took my eye off the scope and could see nothing but pitch dark. The light from Charley's scope was so bright I thought I would have to put my light filter on the scope. I took dead aim. He turned his scope and rifle slowly to look around ... the red light shined into my crosshairs dead centre. Thud. Goodrich picked up the old Second World War army M-1 sniper rifle Charley used. It had a big old ultra-violet [more probably infra-red] scope mounted on it. It was in good shape except for a smashed lens from me putting a round right down through the centre and into Charley's eye.[291]

The Marines' Way

Geographically, the Army snipers were more fortunate than their Marine counterparts, for the majority of Army operations took place in the south of Vietnam, where the land was wetter, flatter and more heavily farmed.

This provided the snipers with better observation and gave them the ability to shoot at longer ranges than in the thickly forested north, where most Marine operations were undertaken. If the Army were more or less happy with their adoption of the XM-21, the Marine Corps were not satisfied with the concept of a semi-automatic rifle for their snipers.

The lack of a weapon was just one problem, for they, like the Army, had no trained sniper teams to field at the start of the conflict anyway, so the unenviable task of putting this right was given to Captain Robert E. Russell, 3rd Marine Division, who was already a veteran of three previous wars. He selected five experienced gunnies, all Distinguished Marksmen, Sergeants Hurt, Lange, Bowen, Barker and Goller and set up a Scout-Sniper Training School at Phu Bai in late summer 1965. For months Russell begged supplies and equipment while he and his team worked tirelessly on preparing, practising and evaluating their training programme and shooting skills. He had a number of minor problems to contend with, such as the lack of material for targets or anywhere to actually shoot. A 1,000 yards range was bulldozed out and 105 mm shell cases, old mess tins and empty gasoline drums acquired as targets. He could only use the strip three days a week as it was in use by the rest of the time by the ARVN. Rifles were the other problem. At the start of the war in Vietnam the USMC had a small collection of Second World War era sniping rifles, mostly .30 calibre Winchester Model 70s with 8× Unertls or Lymans, some M1903 Springfields and M-1C and D Garands, but there was no standard issue rifle available to snipers in any quantity.

Russell was not the only marine tasked with forming a Divisional Sniping School. The new commander of the Marines, 1st Division, Major-General Herman Nickerson Jr., also needed snipers who didn't currently exist. He selected Captain Jim Land to form a sniper school. It was an inspired choice for, as well as having been the captain of the Marines Pacific Shooting Team, Land had already been assisting Russell in finding men and rifles for the 3rd Division School and, usefully, he held a list of all of the Marine Corps' most proficient serving shooters, which he trawled through to find instructors. He gathered skilled men such as Sergeants Wilson, Reinke, and Roberts as well as a young Sergeant called Carlos Hathcock with whom he had shot at Camp Perry matches and, between them, what they didn't know about shooting wasn't worth knowing. The problem was that only Hathcock had done any actual sniping, and with that curious logic that often affects the military mind, he had been posted as a military policeman in Chu Lai, nowhere near the combat lines. Land quickly located him and, working on the principle that you cannot teach what you haven't experienced, he and his instructors went into the Marines' lines at Hill 55 to embark on a rapid self-taught course in combat sniping. Land and his men had to re-learn many of the lessons that previous generations of snipers had learned. Allowing for the abilities of improved rifles, ammunition and scopes, Land came up with a new method of zeroing rifles for he was dissatisfied with the traditional range of 300 yards:

> You sight your rifle in at 450 yards and then use a centre hold for 100 yards to 450 yards. The only time you need to readjust your sight is for shots longer than 600 yards.[292]

Some idea of their effectiveness during this period was that in the area around Hill 55, enemy sniping dropped from over 30 incidents per day, to one or two per week. Their training schedule was almost identical to that of Russell's school, with a rapid assessment of abilities and a swift weeding out of candidates who lacked the required mental tenacity or physical skills. Around 25% were returned to their units as unsuitable and Land constantly pushed one idea into his snipers' minds – one shot, one kill. The lessons they learned proved to be invaluable, but they needed the tools for the job.

With the sniper training underway, the Marines' next task was to obtain supplies of a suitable rifle and telescopic sights with which to equip their newly trained snipers. The first Winchester Model 70s to arrive had been the very ones that the Marine shooting teams had been using for competitive shooting back home. Winchesters were sourced from anywhere they could be found, but this situation clearly couldn't continue, particularly as the .30 calibre cartridge was being phased out and a new rifle had to be found that chambered the 7.62 mm NATO round. The Marine Corps specifications were straightforward enough:

1. The rifle must be of 7.62 calibre.
2. The telescope must be adjustable up to and including ranges of 1,000 yards.

June 1952. Staff Sergeant John Boitnott loads his Garand M1-D for the benefit of the camera. He famously shot nine Korean soldiers with nine rounds at 900 yards (823 metres), proving that there were not really any limitations in terms of range for the M1 sniper rifle. (US Marine Corps)

Vietnam. Here a three man Marine sniper team comprising A. Miranda and D. Birdwell with Lieutenant A. Bodenwiser spot for Vietcong soldiers. Miranda holds a Remington M700 with Redfield 3x9 scope. (Courtesy of David Douglas Duncan)

One of the most successful (and notoriously shy) Army snipers to serve in Vietnam was Adelbert
Waldron III. Working in the 9th Division his official kills totalled 109, the highest in the US forces.
Here he poses for the camera with his preferred XM21 sniping rifle. (US Army)

Two young snipers of the 25th Division pose with Sionics suppressed XM21 rifles fitted with AN/PVS (Army, Navy Passive Viewing System) night sights. Their bulk and weight made them impractical for daytime patrols, but they excelled at night. (US Army)

Chuck Mawhinney, the US Marines highest scoring sniper, holds his Remington M40-A1 rifle (now in the National Museum of the Marine Corps) and wears a typical combat belt with Colt M1911 pistol, grenades and ammunition pouches. (Courtesy of Chuck Mawhinney)

Early night-vision equipment was not compact. This photo shows a Vietnam-era Starlight scope mounted on a British L1A1 SLR rifle of the type used in the Falklands. Although effective, its weight and sheer bulk made it awkward to carry.

Modern sniping rifles are no longer limited to the use of military ball ammunition. This image shows .223 inch, .338 Lapua, .50 BMG and 20mm Vulcan rounds. (Anzio Ironworks)

Armourers are a vital component for a sniping unit. Here Staff Sergeant J.Quiram of the 2nd Marine Logistics works on an M40-A3 rifle at Camp Lejeune. (US Marine Corps)

A Bosnian irregular holds a carefully camouflaged SVD, or Eastern-Bloc variant. Men such as this posed a serious problem to UN Peacekeepers, often being impossible to identify as friend or foe.

A US soldier in Iraq looks through a third generation AN/PVS10 8.5 x weapons sight. This provides the standard features of a day scope, but with the added ability of providing the sniper with effective night vision. (US Marine Corps)

An American Marine holds a captured Iraqi sniping rifle. Although partly obscured, it appears to be a Lee-Enfield of First World War vintage, with a Russian PSO scope and enormous home-made silencer. It's effectiveness is unknown but it shows that a lack of modern weaponry is no deterrent. (US Marine Corps)

This photograph of an insurgent underlines the problems faced by Coalition forces in Iraq. He wears no uniform and he will mix freely with civilians. Having fired then hidden his weapon, he will merge with the crowd. Identifying and eliminating such an enemy is vital, yet fraught with difficulties.

A scout-sniper looks through the scope of his 7.62 mm M110SASS rifle. These semi-automatic Designated Marksmen's rifles provide accurate firepower out to around 985 yards (900 metres) with the advantage of semi-automatic firepower. (US Army)

Russia has continued to improve the SVD family of sniping rifles. Here a sniper poses with the latest incarnation, an SVD with synthetic furniture and an upgraded PSO-3 3-9x24 rangefinder scope. Interestingly, bolt-action sniping rifles have also recently been adopted by Russian Special Forces.

The Mk14 Model 0 Enhanced Battle Rifle, an upgraded M-14 produced by Rock Island Arsenal. Designed to bridge the gap between the bolt-action rifles and the now obsolete M21's, approximately 5,000 have been produced to date and are issued in Afghanistan on the basis of two per infantry squad. (US Army)

A Barrett M107 being test fired. Some idea of the size of the gun and the energy generated on firing can be gleaned as the back-blast lifts the sand from the bench. The ejected cartridge is visible just above the right sandbag. (US Marine Corps)

The immense 20 mm Anzio Ironworks rifle. With an effective 5,000 yard (4,615 metre) range, take-down ability, low recoil and light weight (well, relatively speaking) of between 59 and 130 lbs depending on model, it has distinct possibilities for a future sniping role. (Anzio Ironworks)

3. The rifle/scope combination must be capable of shooting within two minutes of angle.

4. The rifle/scope combination must be simple, sturdy and explainable with the minimum amount of instruction.

5. The rifle/scope must be capable of use in conditions of high humidity, requiring a well-sealed scope.[293]

In late 1965 some commercial rifles were tested to find a suitable replacement for the M70 and these included Remington Models 600, 700 ADL and BDL, and 700-40X, Harrington & Richardson Ultra-rifle and Winchester Model 70, as well as seven different scopes. It was the Remington Model 40X that was to emerge the favourite and an initial order was placed for 700 of them with shipment to begin in June 1966. The specification called for a heavy target barrel, 24 inches long, with a magazine capacity of 5 rounds and green parkerised barrel and receiver. It had an American walnut stock with a Monte-Carlo cheek-piece and it was to be equipped with the Redfield Accu-Range 3 × 9 scope which exhibited the best moisture resistant qualities as well as having a built-in ranging scale out to 600 yards (548 metres).

It was not only their rifles that the Marines were concerned with, for ammunition was also important. However, snipers in Vietnam did have a source of supply of high-grade match ammunition in the form of M72 and M118 National Match cartridges manufactured by Lake City and Frankford Arsenals, in .30 and 7.62 calibres respectively, but even the quality of this match ammunition could vary depending on the lots supplied, and every box was stamped with its lot number. Once his rifle was zeroed for a particular lot, the sniper would do his damnedest to ensure that he kept a ready supply available. Although the ideal combination would be to use heavier bullet weights for longer ranges (the Sierra 180 grain Match-King was a very good long-range bullet) in the field it was impractical and the Sierra 168 grain boat-tail was employed by all snipers, both army and marine. It says much for the quality of these rifles that the Remington Model 700 was given a service life expectancy of ten years, with an active combat life of no more than five years but it is still in use, in slightly modified form, in the 21st century.

Fighting Charlie

The Marine snipers were soon in the field, and learned quickly that the NVA and VC snipers were not to be underestimated. Mostly they were equipped with Second World War vintage Soviet Mosin-Nagant 91/30 rifles, with PU or PEM scopes, and some Czech built Vz57 rifles, based on the Mosin. Tokarev M40 semi automatics also appeared and on occasion a Winchester, M-14 or Remington M700 (later known as the M40-A1) that had been captured would be turned on its former owners. Many American soldiers believed that the NVA and VC snipers were barely trained conscripts but evidence shows that they were well trained, with a 12-week course, and that they were employed as three, ten-man squads within their regiments, each squad, because of its importance, being guarded by a combat platoon of Vietcong soldiers. Their limiting factor appeared to be a shortage of suitable ammunition:

> They spend eight hours a day snapping in. However they were allowed to fire only three rounds of live ammunition every five days. Their prime targets are NCOs, officers and radiomen. These kills were made at ranges of between 600 and 700 metres. Their rifle is considered extremely accurate at these ranges.[294]

While there is little doubt that the US Army and Marines training was superior, the VC snipers did pose a serious threat and counter-sniping was often an exasperating business as the jungle effectively hid everything and everybody, the Americans often having to resort to tactics of calling in mortar, artillery or even air strikes to try and destroy the sniper's position. Jim Land recalled how he tried to plot the position of a particularly troublesome sniper by even checking the bullet wounds in the GIs and mapping the trajectory. It was the sharp eyes of his Sergeant, Reinke, who spotted that the birds habitually avoided a certain area at the edge of the forest. A small patrol soon established that there was a network of trails and tunnels through the brush to and from a hide, and Land decided on an unconventional approach to dealing with the sniper. He met with the platoon leader in the Marines outpost:

> 'Boresight a 106 directly on that spot.' The marine swivelled the long 106 mm recoilless antitank weapon and deflected the barrel until it pointed directly at

the sniper's hide. The gunner slammed in an HE round and locked the breech. All he had to do was slap the push-button trigger. Late in the afternoon … a shot rang out from the field. While grunts either dropped where they were or leaped into the nearest bunker, the 106 gunner dashed for his weapon. He made a headlong dive for the gun's sandbagged emplacement and hit the push button. The muzzle belched a stream of flame at the field; the rocketlike backblast exploded in a cloud of dust. It was a dead centre hit.[295]

Effective counter-sniping meant that the NVA soon became much warier and the American snipers found it increasingly difficult to find targets, so a new US policy of search and destroy was adopted, where sniper teams, usually with a squad of infantry for backup, would be inserted into enemy territory with instructions to shoot anything that could be proven to be enemy. The problem, as American and Allied troops had found out in the jungles of Burma and the Pacific, was that in close quarter fighting a bolt-action rifle was not the best thing to be armed with. Marine sniper Ed Kugler found this out and he took to carrying an M-14 as well as his sniping rifle, which was no easy task in the heat of the jungle:

It was tough trying to walk through the jungle with a big barrel sticking up to catch onto everything. On the other hand, it was also pretty fruitless to carry a weapon that could shoot for over a thousand yards in jungle where I couldn't see twenty feet.[296]

Many snipers also carried a second weapon. Carlos Hathcock always carried a Colt .45 automatic pistol, a potent sidearm for close-range firefights. Gradually, the number of American snipers working in Vietnam began to increase to the point where they could rightfully claim the jungle as theirs during the day, although few would argue that the VC owned it at night. In addition, snipers had adopted the sensible policy of using the M49, a 20× spotting scope, which was not only compact and powerful but also produced far better images than binoculars.

Some Marine armourers were themselves experienced target shooters, and on occasion the temptation to see how their handiwork performed proved too much to resist. Gunnery Sergeant Bill Meredith had repaired an

M700 and was asked to return it to the unit snipers, who were currently guarding a hard-contested hill. He took the rifle in its transit case to the sniper's post, placed in a compound with an expansive view ahead. After the sniper had checked out the rifle Bill asked to fire a couple of shots to ensure the zero was spot on. Sighting on a white boulder in a very distant clearing, he estimated 1,200 yards and fired, the bullet hitting low. With maximum elevation he was able to place further shots on the rock. As he let the barrel cool, the observer called 'Look'. A puzzled VC soldier, an AK47 slung over his shoulder, had emerged from the woods, examined the rock, then looked up into the air. Gunny Meredith slid another cartridge into the chamber and took steady aim, then fired. The Vietcong dropped like a stone. As the snipers sat looking wordlessly at each other, the observer hissed 'Look' again. Bill thought to himself 'this can't be happening', as a second VC walked out into the clearing towards the rock. Once more the gunny took aim and the second man dropped within a few feet of the first. He had made what were arguably two of the longest shots in the history of sniping, in excess of 1,500 yards, using a rifle he wasn't supposed to shoot, from a place he wasn't supposed to be in and he couldn't tell a soul. Swearing the other snipers to secrecy he returned quietly to his armourer's bench.[297]

Most of the snipers who rotated through Vietnam did a one year tour of duty, and it was enough, for even the youngest and fittest were worn down by the stress of combat and the oppressive climate. 'It was either hot or wet or both but just occasionally we would get some respite. Then it would be cold and wet.' There were however, some important lessons learned from the conflict with regard to American tactical doctrine and its use of riflemen and snipers. Teaching soldiers to shoot accurately was a vital skill, and the correct use of snipers, in offensive or defensive roles could make a considerable difference to the outcome of operations. By the time the war eventually wound to its ill-starred conclusion the NVA had put a bounty on the head of any American sniper killed (in the case of Hathcock, an astonishing $30,000). Post-war, the US began to reassess its priorities, and sniping began to be taken seriously.

12

INTO A NEW MILLENNIUM

The Bolt-Action Rifle

There have been many technological developments since 1945 that have paradoxically conspired to make the life of the combat sniper at once easier and yet far more dangerous. He is now more mobile than ever before and sniper teams can be inserted anywhere using radar-shielded helicopters and HALO[298] parachuting techniques. With GPS systems, high frequency radios and tracking devices as well as four-wheel drive vehicles and motorcycles, they are highly mobile, although this can lead them into trouble, as a British SAS team found out to their cost during the first Gulf War, when bad planning and a communications failure led to their having to try to walk through Iraqi-occupied territory to safety.[299] However, during *Desert Storm*, Afghanistan and the 2003 Gulf conflict the employment of such teams proved of the utmost importance to the Coalition forces and the value of snipers inflicting damage on materiel rather than human targets was enormous. Since the 1970s, countries that have been involved in limited war conflicts around the world have developed a far more realistic understanding of not only what a highly trained specialist such as a sniper can achieve on the modern battlefield, but also how this ability is inextricably linked to improvements in both firearms and optical technology. As countries have now benefited from decades of development work in manufacturing technology, that means that the choice for modern armies is a very broad one indeed. The bolt action continues to provide the basis for the majority of sniping rifles in service, although this is constantly under review in Europe and the United States, as improvements make the semi-automatic a steadily more attractive proposition.

The adoption by the US Marine Corps of the Remington M700/M40 as a sniper standard in 1966 was something of a landmark, for it underlined their fundamental opposition to using a modified service rifle for sniping, and it was a choice that has served them well. In 1977 the Marines went a step further by doing away with the traditional wooden stock and replacing it with a fibre glass one, produced commercially by Gale McMillan and impregnated with camouflage colours. This is impervious to heat, moisture and splitting and the new rifle, the M40-A1, had a 24 inch, free-floating barrel which, allied to the use of a new Unertl 10× telescopic sight, offers greater magnification, a much improved field of view and improved weather sealing. It gives snipers an effective 1,000 yard capability with a guaranteed first-shot hit at 656 yards (600 metres).

The US Army also realised that its sniper weapons system, based on the old Garand design, was outmoded, as was much of its approach to sniping. A new sniper training school was set up at Fort Benning, Georgia, and the Army looked to replacing the M-21 that had served it so well through the Vietnam War. In 1977 they began testing at Aberdeen Proving Ground, looking at a number of existing weapons, including the Marines' M40-A1, the Winchester M70, the Parker Hale 1200TX, and the French FR-F1. The Army liked the Remington 700 and its ease of maintenance, but its short action meant that it was only capable of chambering the 7.62 mm cartridge, and there were some sound arguments in favour of adopting a bigger calibre as sniper standard. The US Government's Armament Research Development and Engineering Centre in New Jersey quickly recognised the futility of attempting to purpose-design a new weapons system from scratch, and they recommended the adoption of a suitable existing long action commercial rifle. In view of Remington's experience in producing the highly successful Model 40X, and its Marine use, it was the proposal for a Remington Sniper Weapons System (SWS) that was eventually given approval in July 1988. Remington went to extraordinary lengths to ensure the highest possible build quality for these new rifles, called the M24:

> We spent far more money up front than we originally anticipated. Just to give
> an example, when we were conducting our trigger pull tests, we found that

the equipment that is generally accepted today was not adequate. To accurately measure trigger pull and trigger pull retention, we had to design and build a special machine at a cost of $35,000. We now have one of the most sophisticated machines available ... and accurately measure trigger pull within 1/10th of an ounce.[300]

Improvements in steel manufacture and barrel construction mean that the M24 shows no appreciable fall-off in accuracy after 10,000 rounds, which is a considerable improvement over the expected 500 round life of the British SMLE of the First World War. For a company that had never before officially produced a production sniping rifle, this was a considerable achievement. The cost of the first batch of 100 rifles, delivered on 20 December 1988, was $4,995 each, the next 500 costing $3,900,[301] an extremely competitive price for a purpose-built sniping rifle. The long action, whilst a little more awkward for the shooter to use, also gave the rifle the capability of being re-chambered for a larger cartridge, such as the .300 Winchester Magnum, a precaution that was to prove sensible in the wake of later experience.

Of course, the Americans were not alone in appreciating that modified service rifles did not meet the criteria for long-range military sniping, for European armed forces had been toying with commercially-based rifles since the Second World War. The introduction in Britain of the Parker Hale M82 rifle in 1982 was a brave attempt by a commercial manufacturer with a long tradition to break into the potentially lucrative military market. The M82 was a 7.62 mm rifle using the reliable and strong Mauser bolt system into which was fitted a fully floating, heavyweight hammered barrel. This was bedded into the wooden stock with epoxy resin to give the best possible fit, and the butt thickness was adjustable for the shooter by the use of spacers. For military use, the safety was silent operating and worked on trigger, bolt and sear simultaneously so accidental discharge was almost impossible. It was adopted by Canada as the C3A1 and in New Zealand and Australia as the Rifle, 7.62 mm Sniper System, but not by Britain. In service it was generally equipped with a Kahles Helia ZF60 6 × 42 scope graduated to 875 yards (800 metres) and it was another nail in the coffin of the military use of adapted service rifles.

In general, the tide had turned in favour of properly developed custom-manufactured rifles and in Britain, since the mid-1980s, there had been widespread agreement within the armed forces that the L42A1 had reached the end of its service life, both in terms of development and of spares availability. The Ministry of Defence, in a restricted report produced in January 1982, stated that if the L42 were not replaced 'best evidence suggests that from 1985 onwards the [supply] situation will become critical'.[302] What could not be agreed on was the type of rifle that should be adopted in its place. The draft proposal published by the MOD outlined the requirements for a new standard rifle to be adopted by all of Britain's armed forces:

> The requirement is for a simple, highly accurate, reliable and robust rifle for use by snipers in the Army, RM [Royal Marines] and RAF Regiment in Limited and General War. Additionally there is a recognised sniper role in counter-insurgency and Internal Security operations. It would of course be possible to develop a custom tailored sniper rifle to meet Service specifications, but this would take time and be an expensive option. There are however, several commercially produced target shooting rifles, which could be easily and inexpensively modified to meet the Services' more stringent operational requirements. Equally a wide range of telescopic sights are also now available from commercial sources.[303]

Selected rifles were acquired and tested at the Army School of Weapons at Warminster in Wiltshire and the winner was the Accuracy International PM sniper rifle system produced by a company based in Portsmouth, Hampshire. The PM was designed by the late Malcolm Cooper, a highly skilled competitive shooter, and it was his vision of what the perfect target rifle should be. To eliminate structural weaknesses, the receiver is machined from a solid piece of forged steel and forms a stressed part of the action. It was offered in two action lengths, short for standard rifle calibres, and long to chamber magnum cartridges such as the .338 inch Lapua Magnum. The action cocks on opening and the bolt has a short lift of 60° which ensures the shooter is able to eject and re-chamber a fresh cartridge with minimum effort and without moving his head off the cheek rest. Even the cartridge headspacing can be reset by means of a removable steel locking ring pinned inside the front bridge of the action. It has a 24-inch free-floating heavy stainless steel barrel, built onto an anodized aluminium chassis. It is normally equipped with a specially designed Schmidt and Bender 6 × 42 scope called almost inevitably, the L1A1, and thus equipped it is capable of first shot hit, hot, cold or with a fouled barrel, at 656 yards (600 metres). Tests with 168 grain ammunition at 100 yards (91 metres) provided ten-shot groups of under half an MoA (half an inch) and it is supplied as a complete package, comprising rifle, scope, bipod, five magazines, sling, cleaning kit and tool roll, encased in a fitted transport case. Adopted into service as the L96A1, the Accuracy proved a very suitable rifle indeed, and has seen considerable use in Afghanistan as well as in both Gulf wars. There is no doubt that it is able to perform remarkable feats of accuracy in the right hands.

During the 2003 Iraqi conflict, a Royal Marine sniper and his partner were tasked with eliminating two troublesome Iraqi riflemen. Corporal Matt Hughes had some technical problems to overcome, the first being the range, which initially was beyond that from which a definite shot could be made, and the second the wind, as it was blowing a fierce gale:

> I knew I only had one shot and had to get the angle exactly right. It was hot and the wind was blowing strongly and steadily from left to right as we crept up to a vantage point about 860 metres from the target. I saw I had a clear shot at my man – he was in what he thought was a secure position but his head and chest were exposed. My training then took over and I got ... into the perfect sniping position. I was concentrating so hard that I didn't have time to think about him as a person or the fact I was just about to kill him. He was just a distant shape magnified ten times in the telescopic lens. He was a target, the enemy.[304]

Both men fired and hit their respective targets, having had to allow for some 56 feet of drop and 38 feet of drift in their calculations. It has been argued that it is unlikely that the current range of bolt-action rifles can be developed much more, and some designers and engineers argue that they have reached the zenith of their efficiency. However, many were predicting that by the 21st century battles would be fought by robots. As yet, this hasn't happened either.

Current Rifle Development

Despite the general adoption of the bolt-action as a sniping standard rifle, the semi-automatic sniping rifle is a very viable proposition, and has been for many years. In the mid-1980s Walther manufactured the radical WA2000 sniping rifle chambered for the .300 Winchester Magnum. It was a very compact, gas-operated semi-automatic, fully adjustable in every conceivable dimension and accurate to 1,100 yards (1,000 metres) and it was light years ahead of the nearest competition. It was also five times the price of its nearest rival and production was soon stopped.

The initial trend to move away from the use of modified service rifles towards the adoption of purpose designed, or very heavily modified, commercial rifles is now being balanced out by the use in many countries, such as Israel and Germany, of specially modified semi-automatic service rifles in the sniping role, such as the Galil and MSG-90, which are both equipped with the best optics and use very high quality ammunition. Because of construction and design improvements in the 21st century it may well be that such rifles will re-emerge to challenge the dominance of the bolt-action. There is no doubt that the firepower of such weapons can be vital in certain circumstances, as the US found in Vietnam and the Gulf and as Russia experienced in Afghanistan and Chechnya. Indeed, the US Marine Corps has adopted a 7.62 mm DMR (Designated Marksman Rifle) for use by observers in place of the current M-16 based on the much tried and tested M-14 design, with a carefully bedded Kreiger barrel and McMillan M2 stock. To ensure optimum efficiency the barrel and gas take-off are welded together, all parts are blueprinted and the DMR comes with a Leupold Mk. 3, 10× scope, which can be changed to accept any other optical equipment. A Marine sniper who has test-fired one commented that 'it is a real comfortable weapon, light [11 lbs, 5 kg] and though it won't carry much beyond 600 metres it's way more accurate than the M-21'.[305]

The Russian Army has also been continuing its sniper development programme, and it has been materially aided by the conflicts in which it has been engaged in the late 20th century, predominantly in Afghanistan and

Chechnya. In the wake of the invasion of Afghanistan in 1980, it became very clear that there would be no traditional fighting but a conflict consisting of lightning raids and guerrilla warfare. The Soviet forces were slowly drained of willpower and manpower by their inability to do what every other invading army had also failed to do, subdue the Afghan rebels, who waged an effective campaign around their extraordinary shooting skills. For the most part, the Soviet soldiers never saw their enemies:

> Our carrier [armoured personnel carrier] struck a mine, and we opened the rear doors to jump out, but every one of my comrades who tried, was shot before he had run two paces. Although it was burning, it was safer in the vehicle for us, and we stayed there until more tanks arrived. No-one ever saw who was shooting at us but the nearest cover on the mountains was over 500 metres away.[306]

Russian sniper training is thorough and longer than in any other country, involving a year of infantry and specialist training. The Soviet experiences of fighting in Afghanistan underlined the limitations of employing their unwieldy SVDs as the sole counter-sniping weapon in their arsenal, and development work was begun on adopting a more compact version, the SVDS, which uses a folding tubular butt and shorter barrel. By 1990 the basic design of the SVD was becoming old, so work was begun on a new rifle, the bolt-action SV-98.[307] As with the American M-40 and British L96, this was a military variant of a successful commercial design, the Record-1 target rifle, designed by Vladimir Stronsky. Chambered for 7.62 × 54R Russian, it is also available in 7.62 mm NATO and .338 Lapua, demonstrating an interesting new awareness on the part of the Russians toward the possibilities of export sales. As with most precision rifles, the SV-98 has a cold-forged steel barrel which can be chrome lined to order, and a fully adjustable trigger. Test firing indicates it is easily capable of ten-shot sub-MoA (half-inch) groups at 110 yards (100 metres). In view of experience gained in hot climates, the rifle comes with an anti-mirage strap. This device was devised as a result of the heat waves given off by the long, hot SVD barrel in the scorching Afghan summer, a problem that made accurate shooting extremely difficult. It consists of a simple broad black webbing strap that clips underneath the forward scope mount, and runs along the barrel to the foresight. It not only protects the barrel from the direct rays of the sun, but also helps disperse the heat haze that radiates from the barrel. It has been adopted by NATO forces in the wake of their own experiences in the Middle East.

The other formative experience for the Russian armed forces has been the First and Second Chechen Wars, the second still ongoing at the time of writing. Russia has been involved in the war against Chechen separatists for some years, and the invasion of Grozny between 25 December 2000 and 6 February 2001 unexpectedly gave the Russian Army an opportunity to engage in urban sniping on a scale unseen since Stalingrad. The Russians had forgotten much of what their fathers' generation had learned, for the Chechens used the huge underground drain system to infiltrate Russian lines and inflict damage. Russian Sniper 'Zegei', a 30 year old veteran of the war, found that his squad were continually taking heavy casualties from the rear, so drain clearance became a major part of the operations for his squad. Even in supposedly safe areas, concealed Chechen snipers, using their SVD rifles, still posed a serious threat:

> We had secured the area and General Malofeyev came forward, under armed guard to examine the entrance to the drains, it was then that a Chechen sniper opened fire, and he dropped dead with a bullet through the neck.[308]

Still, if it can be said that any civil war has a silver lining, once Grozny had been cleared the Russian Army found that they had an entire city in which to learn sniping tactics with live ammunition and try out new weapons. This gave them an unprecedented opportunity to teach the most up-to-date tactics as well as testing their latest weapons. Indeed, so highly regarded are Russian ex-military snipers that many who leave at the end of their service are offered lucrative employment elsewhere as 'irregular' snipers, and many with Jewish backgrounds have moved to Israel to help train, and fight with the Israeli Army.

If France had been lacking in sniping equipment up to 1945, it soon began to make up for it, incorporating in each infantry platoon a sniping squad that worked closely with it, and it proved a very effective system.

France was finding that in the wake of world change after 1945 its dominant colonial position in North Africa and Indo-China made the requirement for a good sniping rifle imperative and the FR-F1 was adopted in the early 1960s. This was based on a modified receiver taken from the obsolete Mas36 rifle and chambered for the 7.62 mm NATO cartridge. It had a practical ten round box magazine and fixed bipod as well as the excellent Modèle 53bis 4× scope. This proved to be a good, reliable and very accurate combination and was to remain in service until gradually replaced by the uprated FR-F2 which entered service in 1983. Of the several little-known innovations on the FR-F2 series was the use of a black plastic sleeve around the barrel. This provided several useful benefits by reducing its thermal image, making detection by infra-red equipment harder and cutting the likelihood of the barrel becoming overly hot in tropical or desert climates, where daytime temperatures are often 100°F and barrel warp is an ever-present factor. It also lessened the heat haze that clings to barrels, a problem addressed on most other rifles by the use of a mirage strip.

Large Calibre, Anti-Materiel Sniping Rifles

Germany had taken a small but important step forwards in early 1918 with the introduction of a 13 mm anti-tank rifle, the T-Gewehr M1918. This Mauser-manufactured single-shot rifle resembled a Gew. 98 after an intensive body-building course, for it was a truly monumental weapon, 66 inches (1.68 metres) in length, with a 38.6 inch (983 mm) barrel and weighing an impressive 39 lbs (17.7 kg) empty. Although the recoil was fearsome, being capable of breaking the collarbone if the weapon was fired from the prone position, there was little that the armour-piercing bullet could not penetrate, including double steel sniper plates and not only the armoured side of a British tank, but also the engine block as well. It did not take a genius to appreciate the potential that a cartridge of this type had for long-range sniping and post-1918 the USA took a great interest in it, eventually developing the .50 calibre Browning round from it. Certainly some German M1918 rifles appear to have been factory-converted to sniping use, and at least two examples exist with Oigee scopes mounted on substantial bases fitted to the breech and receiver. The scopes are marked

'8/400' and calibrated from 220 to 1,100 yards (200 to 1,000 metres). There is little doubt these rifles had tremendous potential but, perhaps fortunately for the Allies, the war ended before they had a chance to prove themselves in widespread use. The occasional use of anti-tank rifles for sniping in the Second World War can't justifiably be referred to as developmental work, but in Korea and Vietnam the ability of long-range rifles sparked considerable interest among the sniping fraternity.

Use of such large calibre rifles against humans was generally wasteful, but a comparatively new tactic has gradually evolved. Accurate long-range shooting using calibres such as .338 inch Lapua Magnum, .50 calibre Browning or even 20 mm cannon can be made against enemy installations such as static aircraft, missile launchers, command and communication posts, and lightly armoured vehicles, and this is termed anti-materiel sniping. With a £2.50 ($4.80) cartridge a sniper can disable a £15 million ($27 million) fighter aircraft from ranges well in excess of 1,000 yards, and this has provided an entirely new role for snipers, although some argue that use of such rifles is not sniping in its pure sense, although those that have done it will disagree.

In its earliest form the Barrett M82A1 'Light Fifty', introduced in 1983, met the requirements for a long-range sniping weapon perfectly. With its semi-automatic recoil operation, it was, if not exactly pleasant to shoot, certainly nowhere near as punishing as something like a Boys rifle of the Second World War, a fact the author can attest to, and its effective design of muzzle brake reduces the felt recoil by 65%. Using the versatile .50 calibre cartridge, it is capable of making between 1 and 1.5 MoA hits at 1,640 yards (1,500 metres). This usefully equates to about the size of a human torso, the radiator of a vehicle, or the turbine intake of a jet engine. Some .50 calibre rifles were used by US Marines during the Beirut conflict and in the invasion of Panama in 1989, but these large calibre rifles really came into their own during Operation *Desert Storm* in 1991. Used by Special Forces to neutralise aircraft, radio and radar equipment and even AFVs, in the hands of a good shot these rifles proved a fearsome battlefield tool as Sergeant Kenneth Terry, 3rd/1st US Marines proved. Firing his Barrett at a range in excess of 1,200 yards (1,100 metres) he stopped two Iraqi YW531 armoured personnel carriers, quite literally in their tracks, by firing two rounds of armour-piercing/incendiary ammunition. If this doesn't seem very remarkable, consider that in desert conditions heat haze, unpredictable vortexes caused by hot air and strong winds, can make even close-range shots hard to calculate and even more difficult to achieve.

The fact that the .50 bullet can penetrate 1 inch (25 mm) of armour plate at 400 yards (369 metres) and still have sufficient energy at 1,750 yards (1,615 metres) to penetrate ½ inch (13 mm) of armour is testimony to its usefulness as an ultra-long range sniping rifle. Many believed that a weapon that weighed 28.4 lbs (12.9 kg) and was almost five feet in length was impractical as a hand carried rifle and it is difficult to argue its practicality as a portable weapon for a war of movement. Nevertheless, these rifles have become a valuable addition to the sniper's arsenal, and more are being developed. McMillan in the USA also produced a bolt-action .50 calibre rifle in 1987 and revised it in 1993 as the M93 and it is in use with Canadian forces. It has the useful provision of a hinged butt that makes for a more compact load when folded and during the late 1990s a number were purchased by European armies.

The world record for long-range shooting currently belongs to a McMillan, used by a Canadian sniper working in conjunction with US forces in Afghanistan during March 2002. Sporadic fighting had been continuing throughout the country as small groups of Taliban and al-Qaeda fighters led forays against the local populace and Allied patrols, and US infantry from 2nd Battalion, 3rd Brigade, 101st Airborne Division, 1st Battalion, 2nd Brigade and 10th Mountain Division were dropped by helicopter into the Shah-i-Kot Valley as part of Operation *Anaconda*. They were accompanied by two detachments of Canadian snipers comprising six men, from Princess Patricia's Light Infantry. The group split, one working with the 101st Airborne who also had three Special Forces snipers with them, armed with M-24 Remingtons. The Canadians were equipped with C31A1 rifles as well as a McMillan .50 in. Tactical Anti-Materiel Sniper Rifle System. Only introduced to two Canadian Battalions in spring 2002, they were fitted with Leupold 16× scopes and fired AMAX Match .50 calibre ammunition. As the US 101st tried to advance against a 10,000 foot ridge on the west side of the valley they came under sustained fire from the well dug-in al-Qaeda fighters. A long-range firefight developed as the snipers tried to concentrate on the enemy machine-gun and mortar positions. One sniper commented 'as soon as we got rid of one guy, another would come up, and another'. The Canadians kept up steady shooting with the McMillan to enable the American infantry to advance:

> We helped them [US forces] by taking out certain positions so they could carry on with the primary task. Our engagement distances that day were from 777 metres to 1,500 metres.[309]

Although a Canadian military spokesman proved coy about stating the number of kills achieved by the sniper teams, it was believed to have been in the region of 20. However, he also neglected to mention that during this action, one Princess Pat's sniper managed to break Carlos Hathcock's long-standing Vietnam record of 2,400 yards (2,215 metres). Shooting at a machine-gunner, the corporal from Newfoundland first made a chest shot with his McMillan at 1,841 yards (1,700 metres) then followed it up by killing an enemy rifleman at the extraordinary range of 2,700 yards (2,430 metres). His thoughts while shooting were entirely visceral. 'Firing it feels like someone slashing you over the back of your hockey helmet with a hockey stick.'[310]

The .50 calibre rifles have not been the only large calibre rifles developed. In Britain, Accuracy International were not confining themselves solely to looking at service calibres, their AWM rifle was being developed expressly to use .338 inch Lapua Magnum or .300 inch Winchester Magnum ammunition, and they were also developing a new model capable of firing the .50 calibre Browning cartridge. The .338 has recently been adopted by Britain's Royal Marine snipers, and it gives the shooter first-shot hit capability at 1,000+ yards. It has proved a very competent rifle indeed in conflicts in the former Yugoslavia and the Gulf. PGM Precision, a Swiss/French conglomerate, have developed the PGM Model UR Hecate, chambered for .50 calibre with a two-stage trigger. The Hungarians have gone a stage further, having manufactured the Gepard M1, which soon progressed to M2 and then M3 models. The M3 is a semi-automatic long-recoil rifle chambered for no less a calibre than the Russian 14.5 × 115 mm cartridge, a monumental round developed for the heavy KPV machine-gun and widely used as an anti-tank round during the Second World War. The M3 is a strengthened M2 with a similar long-recoil system employing a hydraulic buffer, spring recuperator and large muzzle brake. The 988 grain bullet reaches an impressive 3,280 feet/sec (1,000 metres/sec) and can penetrate 1 inch (25 mm) of armour at 656 yards (600 metres). South African forces are also experimenting with a 20 mm anti-materiel rifle and, whilst frightening to watch, it is reportedly actually more pleasant to shoot than some .50 calibre rifles, although pleasant must be a relative term here.

Ammunition

There is little point in continually reiterating the old adage that a rifle is only as good as its ammunition, and some idea of the practical difference high quality ammunition can make was illustrated to the author recently when firing a Russian SVD rifle on the range. Using Russian service ammunition of 1990s manufacture the rifle proved impractical for accurate shooting at any ranges beyond 546 yards (500 metres). The bullet could certainly reach further, but point of impact fluctuated widely, with some flyers whose destination could possibly have been outer space. When this ammunition was replaced by hand-loaded cartridges, the rifle became exceptionally accurate, capable of consistent shooting out to 800 yards, scotching the oft heard comment that 'it is a good sharpshooters' rifle, but not a real snipers' weapon.' Strangely, for decades the Soviet Union did not appear to consider the issue of special ammunition a priority, their snipers continuing to use ordinary heavy ball or AP cartridges, but in recent years they have produced an improved 7.62 × 54 R sniper ammunition manufactured to far higher tolerances and using a more powerful powder charge. They use the traditional copper-washed steel cartridge case, but the bullet is a 158 grain metal-jacketed boat-tail that incorporates a hardened steel core to give better penetration and is known as the 7N14. It is based on the Russian 'Extra' target match ammunition.

In Britain, in the 1970s the Royal Ordnance plant began the production of 'Green Spot' 7.62 mm match quality ammunition but because of the unsuitability of the new .223 inch (5.56 mm) bullet for long-range shooting, there has been no attempt by the many armies who use .223 inch to develop it as long-range round, although this is quite feasible. However, considerable research work has been undertaken over the last few years in developing a new calibre that would provide the infantryman with a cartridge that had greater range and stopping power than the .223 inch (5.56 mm) as well as being a useful calibre for medium range sniping, without the penalty of having to use a large cartridge case. To this end Remington Firearms have developed a 6.8 mm cartridge that provides an **effective** range of about 656 yards (600 metres)and combines moderate recoil with a bullet that is heavy enough (120 grain) to penetrate most types of foliage or light cover. There have also been developments with the standard 7.62 mm round, with heavier bullets being offered. The German Army have tested a 180 grain, solid machined copper bullet, harking back to the French use of all-copper bullets in their 8 mm service rifles during the First World War. Tungsten-cored bullets are not new, having been used for AP ammunition since then as well, but Winchester/Olin Industries have manufactured a .22 calibre sabot that sits inside a standard 7.62 mm bullet, which has very great penetrative qualities and is able to defeat light armour such as flak jackets at moderate ranges. Subsonic ammunition is also being improved, and there are now a number of companies producing a 7.62 mm round that can be successfully used in a silenced (as opposed to suppressed) rifle out to 328 yards (300 metres).

Optical Advances

It is not simply rifle technology and good training that makes modern rifles so potentially accurate, but also the ability of the sniper to see his target through the telescopic sight. Post-1945, it was realised that it was not only new weapons that snipers needed, but much improved optical systems. Telescopic sights have subsequently become increasingly powerful, with 10× rapidly becoming the military standard and lens designs giving a far wider field of view than before. When they adopted the M-24 rifle, the US Army also turned to a new 10× Leupold-Stevens M-3A scope with turret mounted focus and windage adjustment now available in half minute clicks. The 42mm objective lens is multi-coated and the scope graduated from 100 to 1,000 yards. In recent years there has been a gradual trend toward manufacturing larger objective lenses, with 38–40 mm being quite commonly used. Snipers wanted better vision in low-light conditions and to enable that to happen, optical companies such as Leupold began developing 50 mm lenses – and 56 mm are also becoming available. There is however, a practical limitation to the development of these large objective lenses, which is their physical size, for the lens diameter dictates impracticably high mounts to enable the scope to be mounted clear the barrel of the rifle. There is a point, and 56 mm has probably reached it, where the line of sight simply becomes too high for the shooter to obtain a comfortable shooting position on the stock.

Russia, too, has been progressing with its optical development. Having always had a strong industry for the production of high quality glass, as well as considerable experience in the field of manufacturing telescopic sights, the Russians had stuck, somewhat rigidly, to the use of the PSO-1 and improved PSO-1M2 4× scopes on the SVD. The increasing range of rifles such as the SV-98 called for a more powerful scope and they have developed a whole new range of 1PN scopes in powers from 3× to 6.5×. The 1PN93-4 for example, has a 3.7× magnification, a 10° field of view and image intensifier and will function from +50°C down to –50°C.

Previously, the higher the lens magnification the narrower the field of view became, but it is now possible to design and manufacture lenses that are capable of high magnification as well as providing relatively wide fields of view. In fact, the transformation of the lens-manufacturing industry as a result of computer-integrated design and manufacture is largely unappreciated outside the industry itself, yet it has revolutionised the production of all forms of lenses. A cheap £50 ($85) telescopic sight manufactured in China today has better resolution, magnification and light gathering properties than the very best optical scopes of 50 years ago, and in all probability it is not even using glass for its lenses, but optical grade plastic.

The speed with which lenses can now be designed and manufactured is also something that would have been incomprehensible to a skilled lens-grinder of even 25 years ago. No longer does a specialist company have to manufacture the optical glass, and a skilled man have to sit and grind the lenses to specification, although this process can still be found in use for the very finest optical glass. In essence, lenses for telescopic sights may now be produced by machine more quickly, more cheaply and more cost-effectively than ever before. Where variable-power scopes are concerned, the better quality ones now also have their graticules mounted in the second image plane instead of the first, as was previously the custom. In use, this means that as the variable magnification power of the scope is increased, the reticle remains the same size instead of enlarging and obscuring the target at longer ranges. One small but extremely important innovation has been the adoption by the US Marines of the Mil Dot reticle system, which uses a series of equally spaced dots along the crosshairs. Early telescopic sights used various methods of comparative measurement to assist the sniper in determining distance, but the Mil Dot system enables the shooter to calculate range extremely accurately. By determining the amount of space his target occupies along the dots and then referring to a ballistic reference chart he will be able to work out any given range.[311] The Mil Dot system is more finely adjustable than minutes of angle, although attempting to convert from one system to the other on the range without the use of a calculator is an almost certain guarantee of still having pristine targets at the end of the day. The British Army found this to its cost when Mil Dot scopes were first issued without any method of converting their measuring system from imperial measurement to metric.

Lasers and Night Vision

Optical technology has had wider benefits than solely in the field of telescopic sights, for a new breed of highly accurate hand-held laser rangefinders, manufactured by optical companies normally better known for their cameras, such as Leica, Pentax and Nikon, have been developed and these are commonly accurate to within +/- 1 metre at 1,000 metres. Miniaturization means that it will be a matter of time before rangefinders are small enough to be built into a scope. The Russian 1PN83 × 3 night sight incorporates a laser target marker for designating targets in poor light and works in conjunction with a second generation image converter, all of which are powered by tiny on-board batteries. In total darkness it is capable of detecting a human at 328 yards (300 metres). Yet this science is a double-edged sword, for it also creates a far more dangerous environment for the future sniper. One development to illustrate this is the thermal imaging device. These have been around for some years, and large units have been employed in aircraft, helicopters and AFVs. For ground use, their bulk made them awkward for infantry and impossible for snipers to drag around the battlefield, but at the close of the 20th century, science has enabled thermal imagers the size of small video cameras to be fitted to rifles. Thermal imaging has now proved to be a problem for snipers, for even the most efficient camouflage cannot conceal the radiant heat from the human body. In a properly constructed hide this can be disguised to a certain extent, but for mobile snipers working on the battlefield it is a serious problem, for clothing has changed very little from the ghillie suits of the 1914–18 war. Now even dense woodland is no hiding place from thermal detection.

Sometimes, though, unexpected results can happen as a spin-off from totally unrelated research. An American company, Spectro Dynamic Systems, based in North Carolina, were conducting experiments into the possible uses of waste coal dust when it was discovered by chance that a formula they had devised provided excellent protection against infra-red imaging. Clothing treated with this substance, allied to the use of special face paint, gave almost complete immunity from detection and, despite initial scepticism from the US Department of Defense, intensive testing is being undertaken.[312] The day of the Stealth Sniper may yet be upon us. Also the subject of much development has been the image intensifier, or night vision scope. Since the first generation Starlights, the AN/PVS series have gradually become smaller, lighter and more efficient. Indeed, the latest AN/PVS-10, that the US Army is at the time of writing preparing to purchase, is barely recognisable in comparative size or weight when placed next to an original PVS-2 of the Vietnam era. Other optical devices such as the Simrad KN200 and 250 use a different principle, with the unit being attached to the scope of the rifle. This removes one of the biggest drawbacks in the use of dedicated night vision equipment – loss of vision and target picture in bright light – and this is particularly important when sniping in urban areas. Aside from infra-red and thermal imaging, new forms of sound wave detectors have been developed that are capable of tracking the path of a bullet and plotting it on a map in a matter of milliseconds. When carried on tanks or other weapon-equipped armoured vehicles, this information can be relayed instantly to an on-board gunlaying computer for the vehicle's own weapons system to send out accurate returning fire and it can even be forwarded to artillery units for saturation fire. This system can also be monitored by counter-sniper teams, who would no longer need to search fruitlessly to find an enemy sniper.

The list of modern technology available to the 21st century sniper would, quite literally, fill a book of its own. Development will continue in every sphere, and training methods will constantly be improved and refined, although there seems little chance that for the foreseeable future sniper training will become any easier. It seems unlikely, though, that the role of the combat sniper will ever be supplanted by pure technology. As one serving sniper put it, 'until they design a machine that works for peanuts, is totally silent, can move invisibly and get close enough to guarantee a first round kill, then my job is safe'.

13

21ST CENTURY SNIPING

The dawn of the new millennium witnessed some dramatic changes, not least of which was the steady rise in incidents of extremist terrorism, the 2001 attack on New York (leaving 2,976 dead) currently being the apogee of a string of atrocities. Much of this new wave of violence is perpetrated by suicide bombers who have no regard for their own lives and who are proving exceedingly difficult to combat. As a result of the New York bombings a Global War on Terrorism (GWOT) was announced by the US, backed by a UN mandate. In reality, this had been ongoing since the last decades of the 20th century and the First Gulf War (August 1990–February 1991), but it escalated in the wake of 9/11 and US-led operations in Iraq and Afghanistan. Initially, sniping as a means of combating terrorist actions was barely considered, indeed through the entire duration of Operation *Desert Storm* it is believed no more than 70 insurgents were killed by the coalition snipers.

However, after the invasion of Iraq (March–May 2003), the war in Afghanistan that had originally begun in October 2001 escalated. It soon became apparent that the enemy the coalition faced were largely unidentifiable. Insurgents, be they Taliban, Al-Qaeda or localised factions wore no uniforms, carried concealed weapons and normally operated from urban bases. This made their identification and subsequent elimination almost impossible for regular ground forces. Pitched battles were rare, as assaults on coalition forces were usually by means of rockets or mortar fire, sniping or improvised explosive devices (IEDs), all of which were launched or triggered from distances that made any form of rapid response impossible. Afterwards, insurgents simply hid their weapons and merged back into the local populace. Some front-line coalition commanders began to appreciate that it was the forward observation units of scouts and snipers that were the only troops to report contact with the enemy. This was because the enemy did not appreciate that they were under observation, or within direct line of fire from sniper units. So permission was increasingly being granted to snipers to engage the enemy because they were the sole combat units able to observe and pre-empt the possibility of terrorist attacks. Other ground forces could only react to what was happening as it happened, but snipers could often prevent a lethal situation from occurring.

> Almost immediately I spotted motion in a third story window about two hundred yards away. Two men were setting up an RPK light machine-gun. I knew the Marine in the turret of the headquarters Amtrac [was] unaware that an enemy machine gunner was about to open up on him, but if I yelled a warning, the Iraqis would start firing. I had to act. I did a quick laser range check... Boom! My bullet went in two inches below his heart and the soldier's knees buckled and he slumped over dead. Shit. Wrong guy. I could see the other soldier was the real gunner and was about ready to open fire. But instead of shooting or jumping aside ... he compounded his mistake by turning his attention away from the [Amtrack] to look for me. That gave me a small pause ... time enough to manipulate the bolt of my rifle. I again squeezed the trigger. It slammed the soldier completely around, a sure kill shot, and his machine gun toppled back inside the room.[313]

The realization by those in higher command of the tactical importance of scout/snipers grew swiftly, for they had quite literally become the eyes and ears of the coalition forces. For perhaps the first time in the history of sniping, the sniper's unique abilities were appreciated by those who had previously regarded snipers as nothing more than an irritating and expensive adjunct to the infantry. It was not long before conflicts in both Iraq and Afghanistan had become known as 'sniper's wars'. Suddenly, equipping the sniper was a prerequisite and items of kit that had previously been begged borrowed or otherwise liberated when no one was looking became freely available. For the US snipers, supply was not an issue as they were the best equipped of all of the coalition forces, but for the British, dryly referred to by the Americans as 'the Borrowers' it was long overdue. For years British snipers had been buying their own laser rangefinders, binoculars, clothing and other specialized items, because the standard issue items were either inadequate or unavailable. 'We used to get all sorts of kit sent to us from home and we were forever blagging stuff from the Americans. I think at the start [of the Afghanistan war] half of my stuff was US supplied, the only thing we would never had traded with them was our rifles.'[314] After 9/11 things began to improve quickly and in the wake of the avowed GWOT it suddenly seemed that nothing was too good for the snipers.

Re-Arming and Upgrading

Aside from actually determining who the enemy were, there were two analogous problems facing the snipers working in Iraq and Afghanistan. The first was shooting at relatively close ranges in heavily built-up areas, the second was the total extreme – shooting at very long ranges in desert or mountain conditions. One of the major drawbacks with bolt-action rifles when fighting in built-up areas was their slow rate of fire. The Soviet Army had appreciated this limitation in the fighting for Stalingrad, and their snipers were normally secondarily armed with sub-machine guns for close protection. The same problem beset the US forces in Vietnam, where jungle fighting imposed tactical limitations on the use of bolt-action rifles. The solution of carrying two weapons was not satisfactory; snipers needed to move quickly and were already over-burdened with the normal issue equipment and ammunition, without having to carry another weapon that often required cartridges of a different calibre. In addition, the European-based wars that snipers had been trained for in the late 20th century were not the wars that they found themselves fighting during the 21st. Snipers required rifles that were easily portable (there has been a regrettable tendency for sniping rifles to become heavier) and powerful (many insurgents worked from behind cover) while still providing sufficient weight of fire to be useful in a fire-fight. Clearly such a broad remit was not possible for the current range of bolt-action NATO sniping rifles. The solution seemed to be one that had already been tried, not altogether successfully, by the US in Korea and Vietnam, which was the more widespread adoption of a semi-automatic sniper rifle. In the wake of past experience, it had only been Russia and its Eastern Bloc satellites that had remained faithful to its post-war decision to equip its snipers with the SVD rifle, which provided a competent sniping rifle for ranges of up to 975 yards (900 metres), but also the firepower of a semi-automatic when required. Many of the old problems besetting the use of such rifles such as high build-cost, complexity and indifferent long-range performance had been overcome by the late 20th century, and while Russia has also adopted bolt-action rifles such as the SVU, SVU-A and silenced VSS for specific sniping roles, the SVD is still the mainstay of their sniper forces.

The US Army had successfully issued re-worked M21's, based on the pre-Vietnam M14 rifle, and these have seen considerable service in the Middle East, issued as Designated Marksman's Rifles (DMR). These soldiers do not undergo full sniper training, but are competent to shoot out to the maximum service range of their weapons. This concept allowed for sharpshooters trained to work at greater distances than infantry M16-A3 rifles could be used, and who could bridge the gap between the ordinary rifleman and sniper. But supplies of the 40,000 or so rifles held in store since the late 1970s have now been used up and American forces had begun casting around for a suitable alternative. A part solution has been the limited scale issue to troops serving in Afghanistan of the Mk14 Model O Enhanced Battle Rifle, a DMR based on the M14 but using a telescoping light alloy stock, match barrel machined for a suppressor, and inevitable Picatinny rail. At 11 lbs (5 kg) it is light, had low recoil and with optics fitted can shoot accurately out to 875+ yards (800 metres). The same problem beset the British Army, whose L85 series rifles were adequate as an infantry combat rifle but whose 5.56 mm cartridge lacked both penetration and range. Traditionally, Britain had never embraced the concept of semi-automatic rifles for sniping, always preferring a bolt-action, but tactical demands were putting pressure on them to review this. One issue not faced before was the widespread use of vehicles for use in suicide bombings. A 5.56 mm bullet cannot normally do serious damage to an engine block; indeed it will often fail to penetrate bodywork or even an angled windscreen, whereas the 7.62 mm NATO round could.

We saw the truck coming fast towards the checkpoint, and it was clear it wasn't stopping for anyone. We opened up with the L85's, there must have been five Toms shooting at him, then the snipers on the roof fired. I think they put five or six rounds into the cab and it swerved off the road then rolled. When we got to it, the driver had taken three hits from the rifles, all fatal, but of the 40 or so [5.56 mm] rounds that hit, none had penetrated the cab. The back was packed with explosive and would have totally fucked us if it had detonated.[315]

For some time the US Special Operations Command [SOC] had been using a commercial 7.62 mm semi-automatic rifle, the Knight Mk. II manufactured by Knight Armaments of Titusville, Florida which was based on the original Stoner AR-10 design, and from which the M16 was derived. The Mk. 11 rifle was much improved though, employing a revised gas system using a direct port in the barrel, thus cutting down on parts, weight and reliability problems. It further used a free-floating match barrel capable of being fitted with a silencer, two-stage trigger and the option of ten or 20 round magazines. The Picatinny rail fitted will take any accessory and the rifles were fitted with Leupold 3.5-10 x 30 scopes. Although quite heavy at 16 lbs (7.3 kg) it has proven reliable and accurate and is capable, with match ammunition of achieving ½ moa groups, producing 3 inch (7.6 cm) groups at 656 yards (600 metres). For a semi-automatic weapon, this is an impressive performance, so it was no surprise that the US Military adopted it in 2007 as the M110SASS (Semi-Automatic Sniping System). It will eventually supersede the old M21 rifles as they wear out. The US Marines have followed suit, calling their variant the Squad Advanced Marksman's Rifle (SAM-R) and these reached the operational front line in May 2007. Encouraged by the success of the design, Britain followed suit, although their rifle, the L129A1 is a variant supplied by Law Enforcement International of London and manufactured by the Lewis Machine and Tool Company of Illinois. Of similar specification, the rifles have been classified as Sharpshooters Rifles and have been issued to riflemen trained to engage out to the 975 yards (900 metres) service maximum of the weapons. In the UK the adoption of this rifle means it will replace the old 7.62 mm AW/L118 series rifles but by no means does this spell the end of the traditional bolt-action snipers weapons.

Large Calibre Rifles

The difficulty of engaging targets at extreme ranges (over 975 yards / 900 metres) has meant that the .50 calibre rifles have evolved as counter-sniping weapons, rather than being solely used for their original anti-materiel role. This has led to considerable political and legal debate about the legality of using .50 calibre ammunition against human targets to the extent that the US were forced to issue a statement clarifying that their use was not against NATO rules. There was no doubt that the .50 Browning cartridge is the king of long-range shooting, until 2009 holding the record for the longest range kill, at 2,400 yards (2,215 metres). Its massive cartridge produces 14,000 feet/lbs (18,970 joules) of energy compared to the 2,648 feet/lbs (3,588 joules) of the NATO 7.62 mm cartridge, but such power comes at a price and there are drawbacks to using such large rifles. Aside from the ammunition being bulky and heavy to carry, the most obvious problem is the weight and size penalty, for Barrett's, TAC-50's, Hecate and other .50 calibre/12.7 mm variants weigh in at anything between 28 and 35 lbs (12 and 15 kg) and are the length of a pair of skis. Once set-up, these rifles are not easily moved and to carry one on a long foot patrol is impossible. Despite efficient muzzle-brake designs and internal recoil springs which can reduce felt-recoil by 85%, they are still unpleasant to shoot for any length of time. It seemed that what was required was a compromise calibre of somewhere between 7.62 mm and .50 calibre, with good long-range capability, a relatively flat trajectory, strong penetrative power and moderate recoil. In fact, the cartridge already existed and had been used for some time in limited numbers by Great Britain in the guise of Accuracy International's AWM rifle. This was chambered for the .338 inch Lapua Magnum cartridge, a Finnish manufactured hunting round that propelled a 300 grain hollow-point bullet at a velocity of 2,710 feet/sec (826 metres/sec). Although not generating anything like the power of the big .50 calibre, it still produced an impressive 4,892 feet/lb (6,632 joules) of energy enabling it to defeat NATO issue body armour out to 1,083 yards (1,000 metres) whilst being relatively docile to shoot. The bullet has a very low drag-coefficient and is also available as Armour Piercing and Armour Piercing Incendiary. Of secondary consideration was the fact that the cartridge could be used in almost any long-action rifle, and so the new rifle, adopted by Britain as the

L115A3, while bearing a close similarity to the original L118 differs in several respects. It has been improved with a folding stock, adjustable recoil pad and cheek piece, butt spike for added stability, adjustable bipod, suppressor and a Schmidt and Bender 5-25 x 56 scope and the 27 inch stainless barrel has unusual 1:11 twist rifling to make the most efficient use of the bullet weight. In America, the Barrett Company have also produced a version capable of chambering either the .338 inch or .300 inch Win-Mag cartridges.

That it has proven capable since its introduction in Afghanistan in May 2008 is unquestionable, for it currently wears the laurels for achieving the longest recorded kill, outperforming even the venerable .50 calibre. In November 2009, Corporal Craig Harrison, a sniper of the Household Cavalry was working in Musa Qala, within Helmand Province. He observed two Taliban machine-gunners who had opened fire on a command vehicle, but they were beyond the advisory tactical range of 1,640 yards (1,513 metres) for his rifle. Despite calculating the range at 2,706 yards (2,475 metres) he still fired. 'Conditions were perfect, no wind, mild weather, clear visibility. The first round hit a machine gunner in the stomach ... the second insurgent grabbed the weapon and my second shot hit him in the side.'[316] To prove beyond doubt that this was not a fluke, he followed with a third shot that disabled the machine-gun. Despite the simplicity of his account, the practical difficulties of making such a shot are quite extraordinary. As Musa Qala is 1,113 yards (1,043 metres) above sea level Corporal Harrison had to allow for the air density being far lower as well as calculating the very extreme range exactly. In addition he had to allow for the possibility of winds that he could not feel (at such a range there could be localized pockets of turbulence unknown to the shooter). Furthermore the flight time of the bullet was a little in excess of three seconds, enough time for the target to move. Such a shot was only possible using the 25x power of the Schmidt and Bender scope, for at such a distance a human being would not be clearly visible to the naked eye.

By no means are the .50 calibre/12.7 mm rifles the largest currently being developed, for 20 mm examples have been taken into service by some countries; the RT20 by Croatia and RK20 in Finland, both of which chamber the Hispano-Suiza 20 mm cartridge and the South African Denel-

Mecham NTW20 that utilizes the Russian 13.7 mm round. They do suffer from being extremely heavy of course, the NTW weighing in at a colossal 57.2 lbs (26 kgs). However, even here moves are being made to produce super-large calibre weapons that are more portable, and the Anzio Iron Works of St. Petersburg, Florida now manufacture a 20 mm sniping version that weighs a near feather light 39 lbs (17.7 kgs), has an effective range in excess of 3,062 yards (2,800 metres) and they have projectile combinations of armour piercing, high explosive, HE incendiary and observation. In these cost-conscious times, the fact that the single shot variant costs a relatively modest $7,000 is very attractive. Although coalition forces have not, as yet, adopted such monster rifles, it is surely a matter of time before some are brought onto strength for very specialist tasks.

Optics and Electronics

It is extraordinary that in little more than the space of 100 years optical science has advanced from 2x non-adjustable telescopes to 25x instruments with focus adjustment, built-in inclinometers to determine what allowances must be made for shooting up or downhill, bullet drop compensators, parallax adjustment, ballistic turrets and mildot stadia, which was first used on the Western front in 1915 by artillery units. A mil-dot is a milliradian, shown as a series of dots on the vertical and horizontal crosshairs. Each subtends 1 yard of a 1,000 yard radius, or 1 metre of 1,000 metre radius. The formula for calculating the distance is:

Width or height of target/number of mildots covered x 1000 = the distance.

Thus an object 1 metre tall or wide is exactly 1 milradian tall or wide at 1,000 metres, so a man of average 6 feet (1.8 metres) height who covers three mildots is 600 metres away (1.8/3 x 1,000 = 600). The latest generation mildot scopes such as the M8541 Schmidt and Bender 3-12 x 50, used on the US Marines M40A3 rifles have a mark in between each mildot to give even more precise ranging. Of course, if the target is of unknown height, then the use of a ballistic chart is required but these are now routinely downloaded as an application onto a soldier's mobile phone or palm computer. Increasingly, snipers use laser rangefinders which are accurate up to 1 yard at under 866 yards (1 metre at 800 metres) or +/- 5% in excess of 1,083 yards (1,000 metres). It should be stressed that, at the moment, such aids are regarded as an adjunct to the sniper's own estimating skills rather than a replacement for his skill but miniaturization of electronics is already leading to laser rangefinders being incorporated into optical sights by makers such as Burris and Swarovski. As yet these have not been accepted for military use, but it is surely a matter of time before this happens. The general adoption among NATO forces of the Mil-STD-M1913 Picatinny mounting rail on sniper weapons has meant that a wide range of additional equipment can now be used. This includes the new third generation of night vision sights such as the image intensifying AN/PVS-22. This is not much bigger than a large torch and running on two AA batteries provides up to 40 hours of field life. Mounted in front of the scope, its major advantage is that it can be quickly removed without disturbing the zero on the weapon. Using night vision devices like this in conjunction with non-visible wave-length laser illuminators such as a 100 miliwatt laser, which is about the size of bar of chocolate, greatly enhances the efficiency of night vision equipment and can enable a human being to be illuminated at distances of up to a mile. Thermal imaging units such as the Raytheon/Zeiss TWS (Thermal Weapons Sight) AN/PAS-13 are even more sophisticated, working in zero light conditions and with the capability to recognize a human at 1,625 yards (1.5 kms, almost a mile) in total darkness. Although made of carbon fibre, they are still relatively heavy at a little over 4.4 lbs (2 kgs) but there is no doubt that they will be scaled down as technology marches inexorably forwards.

The Future

Some mention must also be made of the training of the modern sniper, which in most NATO countries is the most expensive to run and most difficult of any specialist courses to pass, with the exception of Special Forces. Today's six-week course would mostly be familiar to a soldier of the Second World War, covering aptitude, basic rangefinding, weapons handling and shooting, then moving on to target recognition and recording, observation and communication, particularly with mortar and artillery units, and then a week of practical testing. Candidates must pass everything and the drop-out rate is high, around 60% in the UK. As in the US Military there are different sniper courses for Army and Marines, there are moves to try and combine the training to cut costs and speed up the number of available personnel. In the UK the possibility has been mooted of cutting the course to four weeks, but understandably, this has met with some stiff opposition. Advances in materials technology have enabled the parameters of the sniper to be increased dramatically. Whereas in the 1980s snipers were taught to achieve a first round hit at 656 yards (600 metres), by the late 1990s this had increased to 875 yards (800 metres). Today, a new method of training for long-range sniping has been devised that makes a first round hit with a 7.62 mm bullet at 1,083 yards (1,000 metres) possible, and 1,300 yards (1,200 metres) with the .338 Lapua round. That hits are being regularly recorded now at ranges well in excess of 1,083 yards (1,000 metres) is testament to the increased efficiency of both the weapons systems and the training of snipers; no rifle, however accurate, is of any use in the hands of a poorly trained soldier. No longer is a sniping rifle simply a modified service rifle, but a high-precision tool in its own right, that must unfailingly achieve the accuracy of the very best long-range target rifles, with the robustness of a general service weapon. No wonder that they are expensive, the current price of the L115A3 rifle and accessories being a hefty £23,000 ($35,000).

Certainly, with the current speed that weapons science and technology are advancing, the adoption of new generation optics incorporating laser rangefinding and night vision is very real. Neither is ballistic science sitting still (no pun intended), as new calibres are tested and the military look more closely at cartridges that have already been successfully developed for long-range target and hunting use (the .338/.300 Magnums being a prime example), rather than simply relying on military specification ammunition. Large calibre rifles have proven very useful particularly in situations where a sniper is fighting in built up areas and for extreme range shooting, but I suspect that intermediate calibres that have similar performance without all the drawbacks will always be more numerous. Exactly how the sniper will be employed in the next few years is of course impossible to predict with any accuracy, but currently he is one of the busiest soldiers on the battlefield. For the first time since the First World

War the British Army has sniper sections with their full complements of men, evidence of their invaluable use in a war that has no visible enemy. The danger is that sniper training will continue to concentrate on the lessons of the Middle-Eastern conflict and ignore the very real possibility of further European wars. There is always a tendency to rely on what had already been learned, and not look to the future, difficult as it may be to predict. In the light of current developments though, doubtless this chapter will once again need to be reviewed before very long, for the story does not stop here.

GLOSSARY

Ammunition:

AP:	Armour piercing. A hardened steel core, inside a jacketed bullet, capable of penetrating light armour.
Ball:	The term for standard military bullets, normally of pointed, jacketed lead type.
Tracer:	A bullet filled with a burning compound that illuminates it during its flight. Useful for target spotting and indication.
Explosive:	The bullet contains a small explosive charge ignited by impact. Designed for air use to ignite fuel tanks.

ANZAC: The Australian and New Zealand Army Corps.

Bases: The mounting points on the body of the rifle onto which a telescopic sight and its fittings lock. These are normally of steel and comprise front and rear pads, although sometimes a single base may be used and this is often mounted offset, to the left of the rifle.

Bullet drop: As soon as a bullet leaves the barrel of a rifle, gravity starts to pull it towards the earth. Using the elevation adjustment this can be compensated for by raising, or lowering, the muzzle of the rifle. See also Trajectory and Elevation.

Cartridge: This comprises a brass case, primer, propellant and bullet. Upon firing the empty brass case is ejected from the rifle.

Cheek rest: A raised portion of the stock, enabling the shooter to rest his cheek firmly onto it to obtain correct eye relief and sight picture when a telescopic sight is used. It also assists in steadying the aim. A cheek rest may be an integral part of the stock, or simply an attachment such as a leather pad.

Collimate: Ensuring the telescopic sight is perfectly aligned with the bore of the rifle.

Compensator: Used on larger calibre rifles, this is the process of porting the muzzle or adding an attachment, which deflects the emerging gas away from the firer, as well as reducing the felt recoil by counteracting the tendency of the muzzle to rise on firing. Particularly useful on semi-automatic rifles. See also Muzzle brake.

Crosshairs: Intersecting vertical and horizontal lines visible through a telescopic sight. They provide the point of aim for the shooter. Also referred to as graticules or reticles.

Deflection: The art of calculating the speed of a moving target, and aiming sufficiently in front to ensure that the bullet and target meet at a predetermined point. A difficult skill to master.

Elevation: Raising the barrel of the rifle to compensate for bullet drop. The further the distance, the greater the muzzle angle will have to be.

Elevation drum: An adjuster drum, normally on the top of the scope body, that can be turned to raise or lower the horizontal crosshairs of the sight.

Eye relief: The distance between the eye of the shooter and the rear (ocular) lens of the telescopic sight. The average is normally 3 inches [75 mm].

Field of view: The extent of the image seen through an optical sight. Generally, the higher the magnification the narrower the field of view, although advances in optical technology are gradually improving this.

Foresight blade: The vertical blade on the muzzle of a rifle that, in conjunction with the rearsight, provides the shooter with a (theoretical) impact point for the bullet.

Flyer: A bullet that has missed its target by a very wide margin.

Globe sights: A popular target sight comprising a small spherical foresight and aperture rearsight.

Graticules: See crosshairs and reticles.

Lenses: Modern telescopic sights have multiple lenses contained within their bodies. The only visible lenses from the point of view of the shooter are the ocular lens, at the rear of the scope and the objective lens, at the front.

Line of sight: The view that a shooter has along the barrel of his rifle onto his target. The straighter and less interrupted it is, the more efficiently he can operate.

Mean point of impact:	Used for zeroing. It requires firing a group of shots to determine the amount of sight adjustment required to obtain an exact point of aim. See also zeroing.
Minute of angle:	1 minute of angle almost exactly equals 1" at 100 yards, 2" at 200 yards, etc. A ½ MOA is therefore a ½" group at 100 yards. Scope adjustments are now in ¼" MOA, so it takes four clicks on the adjuster drum to alter the point of impact 1" at 100 yards.
Mirage:	Heated air causing thermal disturbance that affects the sight picture. This phenomenon is exacerbated by use of optical sights.
Mount:	The means of attaching a telescopic sight to the rifle. Usually these take the form of a pair of rings fitted on the body of the scope with projecting lugs which fit into the bases mounted on the rifle. A spring-catch enabling quick-release is often used.
Muzzle brake:	An attachment fitted to the muzzle of a large calibre rifle, normally of over .50 calibre, that deflects the emerging propellant gas to the side and slightly rearwards. An effective design incorporates both of these elements and can reduce the recoil by up to 85%. Similar in operation to a compensator.
Offset scope:	A telescopic sight mounted to the left side of a rifle, to enable loading by means of a clip of cartridges. It is not the most efficient means of mounting a scope and can make it difficult for the shooter to obtain a good sight picture.
Overbore scope:	The mounting of an optical sight directly above the barrel, so it is in a direct line with the shooter's sight and the bore of the rifle.
Patchbox:	A hole on the right side of a musket's stock in which is kept patches, flint, percussion caps or any small item useful to the shooter. Usually closed with a brass or wood cover.
Rangefinder:	An optical device that computes distance mechanically or electronically.
Recoil:	The physical reaction caused by the energy generated by a bullet leaving the muzzle of a firearm. The larger the calibre, the greater the recoil force. This can be compensated for by increasing the weight of the firearm, which helps to absorb it. Some very large rifles of 14.7 mm or 20 mm use hydraulic dampers to enable them to be shoulder-fired without injury. Often referred to as 'felt recoil'.

Reticles:	This term is predominantly used in the United States and refers to crosshairs or graticules.
Screw-Pillar:	An early form of breech loader. The trigger guard is attached to a threaded breech-block (pillar) which unscrews as the guard is rotated. This exposes the breech for loading.
Set trigger:	A mechanism normally only found on target and sniping rifles, comprising a second trigger, mounted behind the first. This 'sets' the firing trigger and allows for an extremely sensitive mechanism, as well as providing a very light trigger pull.
Sight picture:	The view of the target provided to the shooter through the optical sight.
Silencer:	A muzzle attachment, or an outer casing inside which is the barrel, that uses a series of discs or baffles to greatly reduce the sound of the discharge. To work efficiently it can only be used in conjunction with sub-sonic ammunition.
Suppressor:	An attachment similar to a silencer, fitted to the muzzle of a rifle to muffle the sound of the gunshot. This helps prevent locating the position of the shooter from the sound of the report. Ordinary high-velocity ammunition may be used with a suppressor.
Sub-sonic:	Ammunition that travels below the speed of sound, thus eliminating the supersonic 'crack' of the bullet passing overhead. Some sniping ammunition is specially manufactured to ensure it is sub-sonic.
Trajectory:	The path of a bullet in flight. The distance to the target and the wind strength must be known if the trajectory of the bullet is to be compensated for by elevation and/or windage adjustment.
Trigger pull:	The strength of resistance of the trigger spring required to release the firing pin and discharge the firearm. Most modern sniping rifles have fully adjustable triggers and between 1½ and 2½ lbs of pull is regarded as acceptable.
Velocity:	The speed of a bullet in flight. Normally quoted at the moment it leave the muzzle [Muzzle velocity] it drops quite rapidly as air resistance acts upon it.
Windage:	The effect on a bullet of lateral forces, such as wind, that will push it to the left or right while in flight. Also, the gap between the bullet and bore on a musket.

Windage drum: Normally mounted on the right side of the telescopic sight, it moves the vertical crosshair to the left or right.

Zeroing: Ensuring that the place at which the iron sights or crosshairs intersect is also the exact point at which the bullet will strike. This is always checked at a pre-determined distance. Once known, it enables the shooter to calculate for longer or shorter ranges as well as assessing windage. Also known as 'point of impact' or 'point of aim'.

NOTES

1. Hay, Gen. J. H. Jr. *Tactical and Material Innovation*, Vietnam Studies, Department of the Army, 1974.

CHAPTER 1

2. Sharples, Niall M., *Maiden Castle*, Batsford Press, Dorset, 1991.
3. Cellini, Benvenuto, *Autobiography*, translated by G. Bull, London 1956.
4. Information courtesy of Rocky Chandler, Iron Brigade Armoury, North Carolina.
5. Personal interview with 'Russ'.
6. *The New York Times*, 16 August 1861.
7. Mitchell, George, Pte., Australian War Memorial, Papers PRO5047.
8. Lukowiak, Ken, *A Soldier's Song*, Secker and Warburg, London, 1993.
9. Shingleton, Lt. S. F., *Reminiscences of the War 1914–1919*, typescript, London 1923.
10. Personal interview.
11. Bradley, Gen. Omar, recounted in the diary of Capt. D. Hastings, US Army Military Historical Society, Carlisle Barracks, Virginia.
12. Kramer, Franz, *Im Auge des Jägers*, edited by Albrecht Wacker, Herne, Germany, 2002.
13. Sleath, Lt. F., *Sniper Jackson*, Herbert Jenkins, London, 1919.
14. Personal interview.
15. Mrs J. Bates, interview with the author.
16. Notes provided by Harry Furness.
17. Fulcher, John, quoted in Sasser, Charles W., & Roberts, Craig, *One Shot, One Kill*, Pocket Books, New York, 1990.
18. Provided by Andrew Evans-Hendrick.
19. Interview, *Yorkshire Post*, circa September 1944.

20. George, Lt. Col. John G., *Shots fired in Anger*, NRA Publishing, Washington, 1981.

21. Cass, Daniel Webster Jr., quoted in Sasser, Charles W., & Roberts, Craig, op. cit.

22. Personal interview.

23. Sasser, Charles W., & Roberts, Craig, op. cit.

24. Gibbore, James, *Soldier*, Brundage Publishing, New York, 2001.

25. Interview with the author.

26. Personal interview with 'Russ'.

27. Gibbore, James, op. cit.

CHAPTER 2

28. The barrel of this gun is still in the care of the Dyott family, who reside in Lichfield.

29. Information from Swiss sources kindly provided by Gerry Embleton.

30. Robins, Benjamin, *New Principles in Gunnery*, London, 1742.

31. Lowell, J., *The Hessians and other German Auxiliaries of Great Britain in the Revolutionary War*, London, 1884.

32. *The Moneypenny Orderly Book of the 42nd Royal Highlanders*, Reids Co., 1758, facsimile dated 1969.

33. *Civil War Smallarms, Reprints 1948–1960*, The National Rifle Association, Washington.

34. Hanger, G., *The Life, Adventures and Opinions of Col. G. Hanger by Himself*, J. Debrett, London, 1801.

35. Huddlestone, J. D., *Colonial Riflemen in the American Revolution*, Pennsylvania, 1978.

36. *The Pennyslvania Packet*, August 1775.

37. Hanger, G., op. cit.

38. Gilchrist, M. M., *Patrick Ferguson*, National Museum of Scotland, Edinburgh, 2003.

39. Dann, John C., *The Revolution Remembered, Eyewitness Accounts of the War for Independence*, University of Chicago Press, Chicago, 1980.

40. Surtees, William, *Twenty Five Years with the Rifles*, London, 1819.

41. Harris, Benjamin, *The Recollections of Rifleman Harris*, ed. C. Hibbert, Windrush Press, Gloucester, 1977.

42. Papers of Field Marshal Soult, quoted in Lanning, Michael Lee, *Inside the Crosshairs: Snipers in Vietnam*, Ivy Books, New York, 1998.

43. *The Army and Navy Journal*, September 1852.

44. Hanger, G., op. cit.

45. Russell, W. H., *The Noise of Drums And Trumpets, Reports from the Crimea*, reprint 1972.

46. Gorbunov, Naum, unattributed, translation provided by Alexi Vassilipov.

47. 'Lieutenant-Colonel Davidson's Patent Telescopic Rifle Sight', *The Army and Navy Journal*, August 1864.

48. From a letter written by Henry Green, quoted in Lambrick, H. T., *Jacob of Jacobabad*, Cassel & Co, London, 1940.

49. Frere, Right Hon. Sir Henry Bartle, Bart., *A Letter to Colonel Durand on the reorganisation of the Indian Army*, 25 November 1857, privately printed, British Library Cat. 8831.g.20.

CHAPTER 3

50. *Scientific American*, October 1893.

51. The Layard lens is held in the collection of the British Museum, London.

52. 'Lieutenant-Colonel Davidson's Patent Telescopic Rifle Sight', *The Army and Navy Journal*, August 1864.

53. Ibid.

54. Ibid.

55. Ibid.

56. Ibid.

57. Chapman, John R., *The Improved American Rifle*, 1844, reprint, New York, 1926.

58. Gould. A. C., *Modern American Rifles*, 1892, reprint, Plantersville S. C., 1946

59. *The New York Times*, 16 August 1861.

60. Berdan, H., quoted in Katcher, Philip, *Sharpshooters of the American Civil War*, Warrior 60, Osprey, Oxford, 2002.

61. Ibid.

62. Dunlop, Maj. W. S., *Lee's Sharpshooters or The Forefront of Battle*, reprint, Morningside, Ohio, 1988.

63. Ibid.

64. Morrow, J. A., *The Confederate Whitworth Sharpshooters*, Georgia, 1999.

65. Marcot, Roy, *Civil War Chief of Sharpshooters, Hiram Berdan*, Northwood Heritage Press, Tucson, 1989.

66. Morrow, J. A., op. cit.

67. Green, Jonathon, *Famous Last Words*, Chancellor Press, London, 1993.

68. Ripley, Lt. Col. William, *Vermont Riflemen in the War for the Union, Co. F. United States Sharpshooters, 1861 to 1865*, Rutland, Vermont, 1883.

69. Crum, Maj. F. M., *Memoirs of a Rifleman Scout, Part 1*, private publication, Stirling, 1950.

70. Ibid.

71. Ibid.

72. *General Annual Return of the British Army for 1902 and 1903*, MOD Pattern Room Library, Leeds.

CHAPTER 4

73. Lucy, J. F., *There's a Devil in the Drum*, reprint, Naval and Military Press, London, 1992.

74. Skipp, Cpl. William, quoted in Arthur, Max, *Forgotten Voices of the Great War*, Ebury Press, London, 2002.

75. Crum, Maj. F. M., op. cit.

76. Shingleton, Lt. S. F., *Reminiscences of the War 1914–1919*, typescript, London 1923.

77. Hesketh-Prichard, Maj. H., *Sniping in France*, Hutchinson & Co, London, 1920.

78. Extract from Gossen's diary, 1914–1917, privately owned, translated by D. Richter.

79. Sleath, Lt. F., op. cit.

80. Hesketh-Prichard, Maj. H., op. cit.

81. Crum, Maj. F. M., op. cit.

82. Cloete, Stuart, *A Victorian Son*, Hutchinson, London, 1984.

83. Penberthy, Maj. E., 'British Snipers [part ii]' in *The English Review*, London, 1920.

84. Hesketh-Prichard, Maj. H., op. cit.

85. Gossen, M., op. cit.

86. Freemantle, Maj. T. F., *Notes of Lectures and Practices in Sniping*, privately printed, Leicester, 1916.

87. Forbes, Sgt. J. K., *Student and Sniper Sergeant*, Hodder and Stoughton, London, 1916.

88. Crum, Maj. F. M., *Memoirs of a Rifleman Scout, Part 2*, privately published, Stirling, 1950.

89. *The War Office, Contract records for 1915–1916*, PRO WO935.

90. Freemantle, Maj T. F. op. cit.

91. *The War Office Contracts 1914–1918*, PRO WO936–9.

92. MOD Pattern Room collection, Leeds, Rifle R6, Record No. 717.

93. McBride, Herbert, W., *A Rifleman Went to War*, Lancer Militaria, Arkansas, 1987.

94. Skennerton, Ian, *The British Sniper*, Skennerton Publishing, Margate, Australia, 1983.

95. *Army specification SA.390*, 4 May 1915, Public Records Office, Ordnance Board proceedings, Copy held in MOD Pattern Room Library, Leeds.

96. Ibid.

97. Hesketh-Prichard, Maj. H., op. cit.

98. Freemantle, Maj. T. F., op. cit.

99. A term that originated in India where products of the Dum-Dum Arsenal were often modified by snipping off the bullet tip, or cutting a cross into it to increase the severity of the wound.

100. National Archives of Canada, extract from lecture notes for Sniping NCOs at the School of Instruction, 2nd Army, 4 April 1917, HQ General Staff Folder 107, file 2.

101. Sleath, Lt. F., op. cit.

102. Ibid.

103. Hesketh-Prichard, Maj. H., op. cit.

104. McBride, Herbert W., op. cit.

105. Herbert, A. P., *The Secret Battle*, Chatto and Windus, London, 1970.

106. Brent, Pte. Frank quoted in Arthur, Max, op. cit.

107. Gilbert, Cpl. G., quoted in Macdonald, Lyn, *1915: The death of innocence*, Headline, London, 1993.

CHAPTER 5

108. Hesketh-Prichard, Maj. H., op. cit.

109. Crum, Maj. F. M., op. cit.

110. Penberthy, Maj. E., 'British Snipers [part i]' in *The English Review*, London 1920.

111. Pre-war, Gray had won the Kings Prize, Scottish Open Championship and the Caledonian Shield.

112. Penberthy, Maj. E., op. cit.

113. Personal interview with ex-Pte. Jack Rogers, 2/7th Sherwood Foresters Regiment.

114. *Notes of Lectures & Practices in Sniping*, 1916, MOD Pattern Room Library.

115. Sassoon, S. L., *Sherston's Progress*, Faber, London, 1936.

116. Hills, Pte. James, quoted in Arthur, Max, op. cit.

117. Hesketh-Prichard, Maj. H., op. cit.

118. Crum, Maj. F. M., op. cit.

119. Cloete, Stuart, op. cit.

120. Ghillie. A term derived from the Gaelic *gille*, meaning a servant. The Oxford English Dictionary states the earliest known use being 1596. By the 19th century its use had altered, referring to 'one who attends sportsmen in the Scottish Highlands'.

121. Crum, Maj. F. M., *With Riflemen Scouts and Snipers*, privately printed, Oxford, 1921.

122. Freemantle, Maj. T. F., op. cit.

123. Taylor, F. A. J., *The Bottom of The Barrel*, Regency Press, London, 1978.

124. Idriess, Ion, *The Australian Guerilla, Book 2, Sniping*, Sydney, 1942.

125. Rogers, Jack, op. cit.

126. Hancox, Pte. G. quoted in Arthur, Max, op. cit.

127. National Archives of Canada, RG9 III Folder 8, file 1, 13 June 1917.

128. McBride, Herbert, op. cit.

129. Ibid.

130. National Archives of Canada, RG9 III C3/4057/35/3, 15 May 1916.

131. McBride, Herbert W., op. cit.

132. Methven, N. W., published in *The Journal of the Military Medal Society of South Africa*, December 1984.

133. *Annual Report of the US Board of Ordnance, 1913*, Library of Springfield Armory Museum, Springfield, Mass.

134. Penberthy, Maj. E., op. cit.

135. *Report to the Chief of Ordnance, by the US Army School of Musketry, 18 December 1915*, Library of Springfield Armory, Springfield, Mass.

136. Cowan, Sam K., *Sergeant York and His People*, New York, 1920.

137. Preserved in the Musée de l'Armée, Paris.

138. Translation from *The History of Infantry Regiment No. 70* provided by Serge Cormerais.

139. Penberthy, Maj. E., op. cit.

140. Ibid.

141. Rogers, Jack, op. cit.

142. Penberthy, Maj. E., op. cit.

143. Bloem, Hptn. W., 12th Brandenburg Grenadier Regiment, quoted in Macdonald, Lyn, 1918, *The Last Act*, London, 1998.

144. National Archives of Canada, MG30, Vol 1, Armstrong Papers, Scouts, Sniping, Belgium, 1916.

145. Account by Yeoman Warder A. H. Cook DCM MM, former Warder at the Tower of London.

146. Army Inspection Department, Catalogue of Arms June 1927, MOD Pattern Room Library, Leeds.

CHAPTER 6

147. Lukin, B., *The Sniper in Modern Warfare*, Moscow, 1938, courtesy of Paul Tamony.

148. Ibid.

149. Ibid.

150. Cooper, J., *Guns & Ammo* magazine, January 2001.

151. Busyatskiy, Col. A. A., & Palkevich, Maj. D. A., *The Soviet Sniper's Handbook*, Moscow 1942, translated by J. F. Gebhardt and Paul Tamony.

152. Ibid.

153. Zaitsev, Vasily, *There Is No Land For Us Beyond The Volga*, Moscow 1944, translation by US Department of Defense, MOD Pattern Room Library.

154. Ibid.

155. Ibid.

156. Sakaida, H., *Heroines of the Soviet Union*, Elite 90, Osprey, Oxford, 2003.

157. Vysokoostrovskiy, L., battalion commander, 'Snipers', in *Krasnaya Zvezda* No 7, 9 January 1942.

158. Busyatskiy, Col. A. A., & Palkevich, Maj. D. A., op. cit.

159. Shore, Capt. C., *With British Snipers to the Reich*, Paladin Press, Colorado, 1988.

CHAPTER 7

160. *A History of the 465 Infantry Regiment 1939–1945*, translation supplied by Otto Meyer.

161. Kramer, Franz, op. cit.

162. Blackstone, G., *Interview with a German Sniper*, Karabiner Collectors Network, November 1994.

163. Senich, Peter, *The German Sniper*, Paladin Press, Colorado, 1982.

164. Law, Richard D., *Sniper Variations of the K98k rifle*, p.139, Ontario, 1996.

165. Shore, Capt. C., op. cit.

166. 345 confirmed kills between June 1943 and May 1945.

167. Ibid.

168. Letter to Gen d. Infanterie Chef General St.d.h. dated 21 July 1944, quoted in Senich, Peter, op. cit.

169. Senich, Peter, op. cit.

170. Law, Richard D., op. cit.

171. Zaitsev, Vasily, op. cit.

172. Memo to Gen d. Infanterie Chef. General St.d.h. Nr. 2263/45 dated 13 March 1944, quoted in Senich, Peter, op. cit.

173. Interview published in *Truppendeinst* magazine, Vienna, October 1967, ed Capt. H. Widhofner.

174. Kramer, Franz, op. cit.

175. Kern, Erich, *Dance of Death*, translated by Paul Findlay, London, 1951.

176. *Truppendeinst* magazine, op. cit.

177. Ibid.

178. Ibid.

179. Kramer, Franz, op. cit.

180. On 6 December 1941 the recorded daytime temperature was –50° F.

181. Senich, Peter, op. cit.

182. Kramer, Franz, op. cit.

183. 257 confirmed kills between December 1942 and May 1945.

184. Kramer, Franz op. cit.

CHAPTER 8

185. *The Annual Report of the US Chief of Ordnance, 1900*, Library of Springfield Armory, Springfield, Mass.

186. *Report of the US School of Musketry, Fort Sill 18th December 1915*, National Archives, Washington.

187. Report to the Director, Plans and Policies, USMC, dated 8 April 1941, National Archives, Washington.

188. Van Orden, George O., & Lloyd, Calvin A., *Equipment for the American Sniper*, report to the Marine Corps, Washington, 1940.

189. Cass, Daniel Webster Jr., quoted in Sasser, Charles W. & Roberts, Craig, *One Shot, One Kill*, Pocket Books, New York, 1990.

190. George, Lt. Col. John, *Shots Fired in Anger*, The National Rifle Association, Washington, 1981.

191. Ibid.

192. Report dated 29 July 1942 from USMC Depot to HQ Quartermaster, quoted in Senich, Peter, *US Marine Corps Scout Sniper*, Paladin Press, Colorado, 1993.

193. Recommendation of the US Marine Equipment Board, dated December 1941.

194. USMC report dated February 1944, US Marine Corps Historical Centre, Quantico.

195. Smith, Col. J. C., letter dated 22 October 1940, Marine Corps Historical Centre, Quantico.

196. George, Lt. Col. John, op. cit.

197. Tregaskis, Richard, *Guadalcanal Diary*, New York, 1944.

198. *US Marine Corps Gazette*, January 1945.

199. Translation from private diary provided by T. Sashiro.

200. George, Lt. Col. John, op. cit.

201. US Marine Intelligence Report, November 1942, US Marine Corps Historical Centre, Quantico.

202. Cass, Daniel Webster Jr., op. cit.

203. Idriess, Ion, op. cit.

204. Wright, Leslie, interview published in Guns Australia, October/December 2003.

205. Braddon, R., *The Naked Island*, London, 1953.

206. Cooper, Lt. K. W., *A History of the Border Regiment 1939–1945*, London 1948.

CHAPTER 9

207. Personal interview with the author, 1998.

208. MOD Pattern Room collection, Leeds, England.

209. Shore, Capt. C., op. cit.

210. Ibid.

211. Ibid.

212. Furness, Harry, personal correspondence with the author.

213. Law, C. M., *Without Warning*, Report of the Canadian Inspection Board on the manufacture of SAL No4 [T] rifles, Service Publications, Ontario, 2004.

214. Cooke Troughton & Simms, Houghton Butcher Manufacturing Co, Kershaw Ltd [later A. Kershaw & Son], Taylor Hobson & Co, William Watson & Son, Vickers Instruments Ltd.

215. Senich, Peter, *The Pictorial History of US Sniping*, Paladin Press, Colorado 1980.

216. Jones, William E., op cit

217. Letter to the Commandant, Springfield Armory, from the Office of the Chief of Ordnance, May 1945, Library of Springfield Armory Museum, Springfield, Mass.

218. Pte. Luther Ericsson, conversation with the author.

219. Karl Krauss, letters to the author.

220. Fulcher, John, quoted in Sasser, Charles W., & Roberts, Craig, op. cit.

221. Jones, William E., quoted in Sasser, Charles W., & Roberts, Craig, op. cit.

222. Karl Krauss, op. cit.

223. Jones, William E. quoted in Sasser, Charles W., & Roberts, Craig, op. cit.

224. Furness, Harry, op. cit.

225. Ibid.

226. Furness, Harry, unpublished notes.

227. Ibid.

228. Shore, Capt. C., *With British Snipers to the Reich*, Lancer Militaria, Arkansas, 1988.

229. Furness, Harry, op. cit.

230. Young, Brig. Peter, DSO, MC and two bars, *Storm From The Sea*, W. Kimber, London, 1958.

231. Shore, Capt. C., op. cit.

232. Furness, Harry, op. cit.

233. Wynne, Barry, *The Sniper*, Macdonald, London 1968.

234. Carr, Fg. Off. Ronald, personal interview.

235. Furness, Harry, letter to the author.

236. Williams, C. 'Wally', *The Rain, The Mud, the Blood, The 6th Royal Welsh Fusiliers 1939–1945*.

237. Pieter Gottlieb, interview with the author.

238. Furness, Harry, op. cit.

239. Ibid.

240. Correspondence with the author.

241. Jones, William E., quoted in Sasser, Charles W., & Roberts, Craig, op. cit.

242. Ibid.

243. Cartledge, Rick & Carl H., 'Johnson's Boys', in *The Small Arms Review*, Vol. 3 No 5, February 2000.

244. Jones, William E., quoted in Sasser, Charles W., & Roberts, Craig, op. cit.

245. Furness, Harry, op. cit.

246. Jones, William E., op. cit.

247. Wynne, Barry, op. cit.

248. Furness, Harry, unpublished notes.

249. Scott, D. W., *Polar Bears from Sheffield, The Hallamshire Battalion of the York and Lancaster Regiment in World War Two*, Sheffield, 2001.

250. Harry Furness, op. cit.

251. Scott, ex-Lt. Bill, conversation with the author.

252. Interview with Pte. F. Miller kindly provided by Pauline Richardson.

253. Furness, Harry, op. cit.

CHAPTER 10

254. Wynne, Barry, op. cit.

255. George Santayana, 1863–1952.

256. Dunlap, Roy, *Ordnance Went up Front*, Small Arms Technical Publishing Co, Plantersville, 1948.

257. *Project 757, Study of Snipers Rifles, Telescopes and Mounts*, Marine Corps Equipment Board, Quantico, Virginia, 1951.

258. Canfield, Bruce N., *The M1 Garand Sniper Rifles*, A. Mowbray, Rhode Island, 1999.

259. *Project 757, Study of Snipers Rifles, Telescopes and Mounts*, op. cit.

260. Senich, Peter, *Limited War Sniping*, Paladin Press, Colorado, 1977.

261. Hicks, Maj. N. W., 'Team Shots Can Kill', in *Marine Corps Gazette*, December 1963.

262. Ibid.

263. Ibid.

264. Hamilton, Cpl. Chet, quoted in Sasser, Charles W., & Roberts, Craig, op. cit.

265. Cotterill, Daniel, interview with Ian Robertson in *Guns Australia*, April/June 2003.

266. Ordnance Report dated March 1944, MOD Pattern Room Library.

267. Personal interview with the author.

268. Ibid.

269. Ibid.

270. Van Orden, George O. and Lloyd, Calvin A., op. cit.

271. *Project 757, Study of Sniper Rifles, Telescopes and Mounts*, op. cit.

272. Chandler, Col. Norman A. and Roy F., *Death from Afar*, Vol I, Iron Brigade Armory, Maryland, 1992.

273. Personal conversation with the author.

274. Lukowiak, Ken, *A Soldier's Song*, Secker and Warburg, London, 1993.

275. Bramley, Vincent, *Two Sides of Hell*, Bloomsbury Press, London, 2002

276. Ibid.

277. Personal interview with the author.

278. Ibid.

279. Lukowiak, Ken, op. cit.

CHAPTER 11

280. *Infantry School Quarterly*, April 1954.

281. *The Army* magazine, February 1957.

282. Wagner, Col. Lones, Jr, quoted in Sasser, Charles W., & Roberts, Craig, op. cit.

283. *American Rifleman* magazine, September 1969.

284. Sotherland, James W., quoted in Lanning, Michael Lee, *Inside the Crosshairs: Snipers in Vietnam*, Ivy Books, New York, 1998.

285. Ibid.

286. *Manual No. FM 23-7*, December 1966.

287. Letter of Intent, Headquarters, US Army in Vietnam, [USARV] 23 February 1967, National archives, Washington.

288. Gibbore, James, *Soldier*, Brundage Publishing, New York, 2001.

289. Ward, Joseph T., *Dear Mom*, Ivy Books, New York, 1991.

290. Gibbore, James, op. cit.

291. Ibid.

292. Land, J., quoted in Sasser, Charles W., & Roberts, Craig, op. cit.

293. Report to the Commandant, Marine Corps from OiC MTU, Quantico, Virginia, 9 February 1966, US Marine Corps Library, Quantico.

294. Childs, Gunnery Sgt J., USMC *Sea Tiger* magazine, 19 July 1966.

295. Land J., quoted in Sasser, Charles W., & Roberts, Craig, op. cit.

296. Kugler, E., quoted in Sasser, Charles W., & Roberts, Craig, op. cit.

297. First hand account from Bill Meredith via Mark Humphreville.

CHAPTER 12

298. High Altitude, Low Opening.

299. McNab, A., *Bravo Two Zero*, Pan, London, 2000.

300. 1988 Report by John Rogers, Senior Marketing specialist for Remington Arms Company Inc, reproduced in the *Remington Society Journal*, 1st Quarter 2000.

301. *The Ilion Evening Times*, November 8th 1988.

302. Delegated Naval, General and Air Staff Requirement, D/GS(OR)2/1/82, dated 2 January 1982, MOD Pattern Room Library, Leeds, England.

303. Ibid.

304. *The Times*, Saturday 5 April 2003.

305. Interview with the author.

306. Anonymous Russian soldier, interview translation provided by Alexi Shellin.

307. *Snaiperskaya Vintovka*, Mod. 1998.

308. Furness, Harry, unpublished notes.

309. *The Edmonton Sun*, Wednesday 10 July 2002

310. Ibid.

311. The US Marine Corps developed Mil Dot reticle system uses a series of evenly spaced dots along the crosshairs. Each one equates to 1/17th of a degree, which translates to 3.6 inches at 100 yards, or 3 feet at 1000 yards.

312. *Bulletin of the US Defense Advanced Research Projects Agency* [DARPA], undated.

CHAPTER 13

313. Coughlin, J., Kuhlman, C. and Davis, D., *Shooter*, St Martin's Press, New York, 2005.

314. Personal conversation with the author.

315. Ibid.

316. Quote by Cpl. Harrison, taken from British Army press release, November 2009.

SELECT BIBLIOGRAPHY

The following books should all be currently available. Some older titles have been reprinted.

Chandler N. A. and Chandler R. F., *Carlos Hathcock, White Feather*, Iron Brigade Armory, N.C., 1997.

Chandler N. A. and Chandler R. F., *Death from Afar*, Vols. 1–5, Iron Brigade Armory, N.C., 1992–98.

Chandler N. A. and Chandler R. F., *The One Shot Brotherhood*, Iron Brigade Armory, N.C., 2002.

Coughlin, J., Kuhlman, C. and Davis, D., *Shooter*, St Martin's Press, New York, 2005.

Gibbore, James, *Soldier*, Brundage Publishing, New York, 2001.

Gilbert, Adrian, *Sniper one-to-one*, Sidgwick and Jackson, London, 1994.

Gilbert, Adrian, *Stalk and Kill*, Sidgwick and Jackson, London, 1997.

Hesketh-Prichard, H. V., *Sniping in France*, Leo Cooper, London, 1994.

Hogg, Ian V., *The World's Sniping Rifles*, Greenhill Books, London, 1998.

Kramer, Franz, *Im Auge Des Jägers*, edited by Albrecht Wacker, V. S. Books, Herne, Germany, 2002.

Kugler, Ed, *Dead Centre*, Ivy Books, New York, 1999.

Laidler, Peter, *An Armourer's Perspective: .303 No.4 (T) Sniper Rifle*, Greenhill Books, London, 1993.

Law, Richard, *Sniper Variations of the K98k Rifle*, Collector Grade Publications, Ontario, 1996.

Lanning, Michael Lee, *Inside the Crosshairs: Snipers in Vietnam*, Ivy Books, New York, 1998.

Lukowiak, Ken, *A Soldier's Song*, Secker & Warburg, London, 1993.

McBride, H. W., *A Rifleman Went To War*, Lancer Militaria, Arkansas, 1987.

Mills, Sgt. D., *Sniper One*, Penguin, London, 2007.

Pegler, M., *Sniping in the Great War*, Pen and Sword, Barnsley, 2008.

Pegler, M., *Sniper Rifles*, Osprey Publishing, Oxford, 2010.

Plasterer, Maj. J. L., *The History of Sniping and Sharpshooting*, Paladin Press, Colorado, 2008.

Sasser, Charles W. and Roberts, Craig, *One Shot, One Kill*, Pocket Books, New York, 1990.

Senich, Peter R., *The German Sniper*, Paladin Press, Colorado, 1996.

Senich, Peter R., *The Long-Range War*, Paladin Press, Colorado, 1996.

Senich, Peter R., *The One Round War*, Paladin Press, Colorado, 1996.

Shore, Captain C., *With British Snipers To the Reich*, Greenhill Books, London, 1997.

Skennerton, Ian, *The British Sniper*, Skennerton Publishing, Margate, Australia, 1983.

Spicer, Mark, *Sniper*, Salamander Books, London, 2001.

Ward, Joseph T., *Dear Mom*, Ivy Books, New York, 1991.

INDEX

About the Author

Martin Pegler has a BA Hons in Medieval and Modern History and an MA in Museum Studies, both from University College, London, and was for many years the Senior Curator of Firearms at the Royal Armouries Museum, Leeds. He now lives in the Somme, France, where he and his wife run a small bed and breakfast, which is situated on top of the old German front line! Martin has established The Somme Historical Centre (www.martinpegler.com), where visitors can see the technology used in the 1914–18 trench warfare. Martin enjoys shooting historic firearms, and has participated in many shooting competitions. He is currently an author and firearms consultant and he also lectures at local Great War museums. In his spare time Martin runs motorcycle tours of the battlefield. He is the author of a number of books including *The Military Sniper since 1914* (Osprey, 2001) and *Firearms in the American West 1700–1900* (The Crowood Press, 2002), and he has also contributed to a number of magazines. In the 1980s he had the privilege of interviewing many World War I veterans about their wartime experiences, and the recordings are now part of the sound archives of the Imperial War Museum, London.